NAVIGATING
THE
NONPROFIT
RAPIDS

Strategies & Tactics
for Running
a Nonprofit Company

TED EDLICH

Georgia

Navigating the Nonprofit Rapids
Strategies and Tactics for Running a Nonprofit Company
© 2016 Ted Edlich. All rights reserved.

Published in the United States by WriteLife Publishing
(An imprint of Boutique of Quality Books Publishing Company)
www.writelife.com

Printed in the United States of America

978-1-60808-143-1 (p)
978-1-60808-144-8 (e)

Library of Congress Control Number: 2015947311

Book design by Robin Krauss, www.bookformatters.com
Cover design by Ellis Dixon, ellisdixon.com

PRAISE FOR NAVIGATING THE NONPROFIT RAPIDS

Ted Edlich was an incredible trailblazer for 40 years as the CEO of TAP. Now he shares the ingredients of his success to help others elevate their work to higher levels.

~ Kenneth Ackerman, VirtualCAP.org

Wow! I love it! I could not put it down. Having served on nonprofit boards for 35 plus years it is dead on. I find this book to be an outstanding roadmap for anyone serving in the nonprofit world. Edlich tells many wonderful real life stories that he and his staff experienced while serving at Total Action for Progress (TAP). This book is also a great history read. It reveals the evolution of a very successful community action agency in its mission to fight poverty. He follows each chapter with compelling questions that all organizations should consider. Chapter 11 is one of my favorites - it discusses the importance of networks, partnerships, collaborations and collective actions. Strong partnerships and collaboration, with more than 100 public and private supporters allowed TAP to implement and sustain over 30 successful programs. Edlich gives first hand examples of why it is necessary in today's world to obtain serious funding from outside sources.

~ Michael Wise, retired CFO of Corvesta, Inc.
and Delta Dental of VA

What kind of world do you want this to be? For those seeking a more just world, with increased opportunities for the most vulnerable in our society, Ted Edlich offers *Navigating the Nonprofit Rapids*, an excellent handbook on leading nonprofit organizations. Edlich's book offers clear guides to action—principles of nonprofit leadership and management—and brings the principles to life with many, lively examples drawn from his forty-year career as a nonprofit executive. Nonprofit managers and board members—and those who aspire to these positions—will all benefit from this thoughtful, easy-to-read, practical guide to nonprofit management. I know I will encourage my nonprofit management students to learn and borrow from the advice and many success stories that Edlich provides. There is much wisdom in this volume.

~ Professor Alan Abramson, George Mason University

In my opinion, *Navigating the Nonprofit Rapids: Strategies and Tactics for Running a Nonprofit Company,* should be required reading for leaders, directors, and managers of nonprofits. Other key persons in other corporations would benefit from this book, especially Chapter 9: The Right Who, Chapter 10: Organizational Culture, and Chapter 14: Keeping it Together: Managing Stress. Ted Edlich's book is a compilation of 40 years of experience that combines the science of nonprofit management with the art of nonprofit management, which is unique, beneficial, and interesting. Mr. Edlich's research is thorough and well documented throughout his book. The take-away questions at the end of each chapter apply to any organization and are worth the read; in addition, the questions are compiled and listed in the Appendix. I recommend *Navigating the Nonprofit Rapids: Strategies and Tactics for Running a Nonprofit Company* to current and prospective leaders in all types of organizations. Furthermore, this book should be required reading in business schools.

~ Professor Thomas Lachowicz, Departments of Marketing and Management, School of Business, Radford University

Ted led TAP for many years and is a pioneer in leadership and nonprofit innovation. Well, he has finally written a book, and it is an excellent one. I have tremendous respect for his work ethic, leadership, dedication, and wisdom. We need more people out there like him.Ted Edlich brings a private sector attitude to the world of non-profits. It is one of the keys to his success. Be aggressive, make things happen, and run a non-profit like you would a private business. He is truly a pioneer. Ted's book serves as a model for all sectors — private, non-profit, and public service as well. Ted's passion for results makes those around him better. He is a visionary, and I am proud to consider him a friend.

~ Fred Helm,Vice President & Counsel, Kemper Consulting

This is a must read! The nonprofit sector is an expanding and important part of our economy, producing jobs and meeting community needs often overlooked by others. Ted Edlich's new book is a highly readable text touching on core leadership issues applicable to anyone who is involved in the nonprofit world, as well as anyone interested in business and management generally. I have personally known the extraordinary people whose contributions are used to illustrate the fundamental business principles. Congratulations to Ted for 40 years of phenomenal nonprofit leadership. Everyone should read this book as Ted does an amazing job of eloquently communicating the many lessons he learned over those four decades of service.

~ Senator Mark Warner, Senior Senator from
the Commonwealth of Virginia

Ted Edlich is the master of navigating the non-profit world. With this book, he shares his experience and skills from 40 years of leadership for a non-profit dedicated to helping those in need.

~ Congressman Bob Goodlatte, United States House
of Representatives

This book is surely a must read for executives and leaders in any sector, be it nonprofit, business, education, or government. But it is much, much more. It is a lesson in how to embrace the most important challenges we face as a society, how to overcome persistent obstacles, and grow a community of change makers who create lasting value. Ted Edlich epitomizes what most people only talk about; how to actually make a difference. For those who are tired of all the noise, and are ready to step up and choose to be relevant, this book will show you how. If it was on the must read list for students entering college, many would chart a different path, and the world would be a much better place.

~ Bob Halsch, CEO, Greater Bergen County
Community Action Agency, former Board Member,
National Community Action Foundation.

Navigating the Rapids is the perfect title for this roadmap of leadership success. Today's nonprofit environment requires nimbleness to adjust to changing conditions and confidence to head directly into the rough waters. Community Action has been the training ground for many nonprofit executives and Ted gives us the practical lessons we need based on a lifetime of dedication and achievement. A must read for nonprofit leaders who want to effect change and make a difference in today's challenging environment.

~ Denise L. Harlow, MSW, CCAP, Chief Executive Officer,
Community Action Partnership

For
The people of Total Action for Progress
and
the National Community Action Network

I have one life, and one chance to make it count for something . . . My faith demands that I do whatever I can, wherever I am, whenever I can, as long as I can, with whatever I have to make a difference.

~ President Jimmy Carter[1]

---

1 "Quotes About Giving, Generosity, and Making a Difference," *Celebrations of Life*, https://celebrationsoflife.net/making-a-difference/making-a-difference-quotes/ (accessed May 10, 2015).

FOREWORD

I first met Ted Edlich in 1986 when he was trying to sell me on the need for assisting his not-for-profit company during the very difficult years of the great recession. However, it was years later after I had left the chairman's role, during a week of day hiking with Ted in the deserts of Southern Utah combined with beer drinking at night in the pubs of Moab, that I realized Ted needed to write this book. The man has 47 years of experience running programs to fight poverty combined with the memory of an elephant. The stories he shared in the desert heat and later over a cold brew convinced me that he had a lot to say about how to help the poor, how to motivate smart people, and how to run effective organizations, during both good and bad times. More importantly, I was convinced he needed to share that knowledge with others aspiring to be leaders in improving the lives of those less fortunate.

This book is a pouring forth of Ted's knowledge, wisdom, and passion. It is in part a history of the war on poverty that started in the 1960s and continues to be waged today. It is in part a treatise on how the not-for-profit community action agency Total Action for Progress (TAP) was built and evolved over the last fifty years with compelling examples of phenomenal successes as well as a few failures. But it is mostly a guided tour, coupled with real world examples, through the principles and practices of developing and managing an effective, efficient, and accountable not-for-profit organization. I have been in the organization leadership business in one form or another for thirty-four years (still nearly twenty less than Ted), and I really wish

I had known at the start what I know now and what Ted has astutely laid out and explored in this book.

Ted brings meaning and insight to management and motivational concepts in current literature such as: getting the right people on the bus; creating a learning organization; remembering who you work for; be the change you work toward; no more organization than necessary; shared leadership; collaborative networks; the importance of social capital; and many others. While explaining the organization development, growth, and changes taking place at TAP, he trolls through the management concepts that he has developed himself and borrowed from key management and motivational books published over the last twenty years. Among these are Jim Collin's *Good to Great*, Grant and Crutchfield's *Forces for Good*, Morino's *Leap of Reason*, Bell, Jeanne, Masaoka, and Zimmerman's. *Nonprofit Sustainability: Making Strategic Decisions for Financial Viability* Hunter's *Working Hard — and Working Well: A Practical Guide to Performance Management for Leaders Serving Children, Adults, and Families*, Sagawa and Jospin's *The Charismatic Organization: Eight Ways to Grow a Nonprofit*, Goleman's *Emotional Intelligence* and many more. He also draws from classics like Blake and Mouton's *The Managerial Grid: Key Orientations for Achieving Production Through People* and Herzberg's *The Motivation to Work*. If you have read these books, then Ted's discussion of their key points and how he has applied them will help you draw genuine meaning from their insights. If you have not read them, no matter, because Ted provides an introduction to many of their main points from the perspective of running an effective not-for-profit organization This summary collection and review of a generation of published organizational and management tools and insights into one document, is alone reason enough to read Ted's book.

Ted's organization of the book into bite size chapters on key areas of leadership, management practices, and corporate governance makes for easy reading. You can review and digest a chapter a day, a week, or a month and then come back to it over and over as a future reference as the world around you and your organization changes.

As it most surely will. The inclusion of "Profiles in Excellence" about key people in the life of Ted and TAP provides real world examples of successful inspirational leaders, some of who came from poverty or very difficult circumstances to rise to prominence while working on the effort to eradicate poverty and improve the lives of their fellow human beings. It is Ted's way of both recognizing people who have helped make TAP successful, and reminding us all that organizations really are the sum of their people and that great leaders and successful people come from very varied backgrounds. I had the great privilege of knowing a few of these people and am delighted to read Ted's acknowledgement of their exceptionalism.

Ted may be at his philosophical best in *Chapter 10: The Organizational Culture.* It embodies Ted's beliefs, insights, and passion for service and how he, with the help of many others, built a people focused and service driven organization. Ted was an early and continuous advocate for improved race relations and he has no sympathy for any form of discrimination or class stratification. It is evident throughout the book, but shines in his review of building a lasting and highly functioning organizational culture. Ted grew up a son of privilege in Manhattan, but gave up that lifestyle to come south and fight poverty and discrimination. The community action agency mission and the Commonwealth of Virginia, at the least, and perhaps the anti-poverty effort nationwide are better for it. He has "made a difference" and this book is his effort to help others do the same. I take a tiny bit of credit for getting him to think about the value of making such an effort. I am thankful to Providence that he did. After reading *Navigating the Nonprofit Rapids* I think you will be too.

I believe the timing of this book is fortuitous. Now more than ever, we need our not-for-profit organizations to be effective and efficient. Partly because there are now so many such organizations with the number increasing daily, but mostly because of the steadily growing limitations of government programs, for reasons ranging from budget constraints to partisanship, among others, that we could all debate infinitum. Regardless, current government programs and public education seem unable to stem the increasing trend of inequality. The rising cost of higher education and the displacement of many middle class jobs by technology and off shoring portends a return to societal stratification into distinct economic classes that we thought was no longer a component of modern society. The desired bell curve of income distribution in the United States is again starting to look more like the dumb bell distribution shape of the nineteenth century. Our inner cities appear as if they are being lost in chaos and the American dream seems to be slipping away. As a former corporate CEO, capitalist, elected official, father, and sometimes soldier in the war on poverty, I am becoming more and more concerned with the growing economic stratification and ethnic divisions of our society. We talk about race issues, and of course discrimination based on race still exits, but I believe the big issues to be solved in the next generation are tied to income disparity driven by the growing opportunity disparity.

The impact of technology and job loss for those not in the right hand side of the income and computer competence distribution will continue to worsen. I have no answers, only questions and concerns. Further, I doubt answers will be found in academia or government. That leaves the ranks of future business leaders, social entrepreneurs and other out of the box thinkers. I sincerely hope Ted's effort in developing this book, and other authors like him, will help future leaders of not-for-profit organizations and the community and business leaders that constitute their governing boards be more competent in dealing with our growing societal problems. A great deal is riding on it.

~ John Williamson

John Williamson is Chairman of RGC Resources, Inc. He served for sixteen years as its CEO. He is a corporate director for Optical Cable Corporation, Corning Natural Gas Holdings Corporation, Luna Innovations Incorporate, Bank of Botetourt, and Friendship

Retirement Community. He is the former Chairman of the Board Directors of the Taubman Museum of Art, Total Action for Progress, Virginia Western Community College Education Foundation, Roanoke Regional Chamber of Commerce, Roanoke Business Council, Roanoke Valley Economic Development Partnership, and the Small Company Council of the American Gas Association. He served as County Administrator for two Virginia localities and was elected to the Board of Supervisors in Botetourt County, Virginia. He earned a degree in business administration from Virginia Commonwealth University and an MBA from the College of William and Mary.

TABLE OF CONTENTS

Foreword   ix

Chapter 1:
A Calling in a Growing Industry   1

Chapter 2:
The Quest to Make A Difference: Launching a Project   13
Profile in Excellence: Jayne Thomas   34

Chapter 3:
Making a Larger Difference: Scaling Up and Collective Action   37
Profile in Excellence: Wilma Gene Casey Warren   54

Chapter 4:
Creating a Vision   57
Profile in Excellence: Jeri Rogers   69

Chapter 5:
Executive Leadership   73
Profile in Excellence: Annette Lewis   93

Chapter 6:
Boards of Directors   95
Profile in Excellence: Alvin Nash   112

Chapter 7:
Managing for Results   115
Profile in Excellence: Cleo Sims   144

Chapter 8:
Economic Engine and Economic Accountability   147
Profile in Excellence: Owen Schultz   163

Chapter 9:
The "Right Who"   165
Profile in Excellence: Rick Sheets   180

Chapter 10:
The Organizational Culture   183
Profile in Excellence: Angela Penn   205

Chapter 11:
Networks, Partnerships, Collaborations, and Collective Action   207
Profile in Excellence: Lin Atkins   218

Chapter 12:
Marketing: Getting the Story Out   221
Profile in Excellence: Joe Jones   235

Chapter 13:
Social Capital: It Is Who You Know   239
Profile in Excellence: Curtis Thompson   246

Chapter 14:
Keeping it Together: Managing Stress   249

Chapter 15:
Conclusion   267

Afterword   275
About the Author   277
Appendix: Take-Away Compilation   287
Bibliography   297
Permissions   301

ACKNOWLEDGMENTS

I am one of the most fortunate people in the world. At the age of thirty-eight, I was given the opportunity of a lifetime: to serve at the helm of Total Action for Progress and spend my life working to create opportunity for those most in need in this great country. I have learned from incredible mentors and extremely talented colleagues. I have been inspired by participants in our projects who have endured multiple hardships, demonstrated heroic persistence, and changed the future for themselves and their communities. I have participated in one of the great periods of American history in which we declared a war on poverty and envisioned an America of real opportunity for all—a dream that will have to be fully realized if we are to remain a world leader. In spite of the challenges and significant difficulties, there has never been a day that I have dreaded going to work or wished for some other occupation.

I am indebted to Cabell Brand, Founder of TAP, and my mentor, Bristow Hardin, Jr., for their encouragement. I am grateful to the members of the TAP's Board of Directors, numbering in the hundreds, for their faith in me and for their support over the last forty years as we worked together.

The content and stories in this book would not have happened without the work of the thousands of staff members and volunteers for Total Action for Progress and its affiliates. Nor would it have happened without the involvement of the many thousands of individuals and families who collaborated with TAP to create brighter futures for themselves and their communities.

In May 2013, my friend and former TAP Board Chairman John

Williamson and I were hiking in the Moab area of Southeast Utah. In the course of our week together, I began telling "Bristow stories" inspired by my experience with the first executive director of TAP. John planted the seed for this manuscript by saying, "You ought to write a book." After my initial resistance, I retained a life coach, Ken Redick, to help me create a plan for the next twelve months that included this book. I am pretty good at planning for the organization I serve, but not terribly good at planning my own future. Ken created the supportive accountability structure to keep me on task. I am grateful for my friends and colleagues who read various renditions of the manuscript and have helped to improve the final product, including Ken Ackerman, Rob Goldsmith, Bob Halsch, Annette Lewis, Jeff Sturgeon, Don Wilson, Alan Abramson, Owen Schultz, John Williamson, Anna Lawson, Gilian Corral, David Bradley, Cabell Brand and Stanley Zimmerman.

I am grateful to my family. My wife, Liz, and five children, Connie, T.J., Sutton, Maria, and Eva, are a continual source of joy and inspiration. So too are my grandchildren, Jessica, Diana, Eliza, and Pierce. My brother, Dr. Richard French Edlich, has inspired me with his incredible life achievements. He was a distinguished leader in innovative health care as Professor of Plastic Surgery at the University of Virginia Medical Center, in spite of crippling MS.

As I began writing this manuscript, I had the good fortune to work with grant writer Emily Pielocik, also Housing Planner for TAP, with whom I had earlier collaborated on an op-ed column for *The Roanoke Times*. She is such a great writer, and our collaboration was so effortless that I immediately asked her assistance, working on her own time, with this book. While the content is mine, her editorial work and active red pen have contributed incredibly to the form. I also owe a great deal of appreciation to Kristen Moses, Vice President of Planning and Resource Development at TAP, who read the last draft and served as my accomplished editor prior to the manuscript's acceptance by my publisher. Amy Hatheway, who serves as co-vice president with Kristen, was helpful as well. A very special debt of appreciation goes to my WriteLife editor, Ty Mall; project manager, Ellis Dixon; and to Terri Leidich, President and Publisher of WriteLife Publishing, for their exacting and experienced hands in greatly improving the original manuscript and preparing it for publication. Of course, any of the shortcomings or errors in the manuscript are mine alone. It's my sincere hope that this book will attract more people of talent and vision to the nonprofit sector and inspire those in nonprofit leadership positions to be more effective in their quest to make a difference.

Ted Edlich

Chapter 1

A Calling in a Growing Industry

You are not here merely to make a living. You are here in order to enable the world to live more amply, with greater vision, with a finer spirit of hope and achievement. You are here to enrich the world, and you impoverish yourself if you forget the errand.

~ Woodrow Wilson[2]

Your profession is not what brings home your weekly paycheck, your profession is what you're put here on earth to do, with such passion and such intensity that it becomes spiritual in calling.

~ Vincent Van Gogh[3]

This book is written for leaders of nonprofit organizations, whether they serve as CEOs, members of the organization's board of directors, or are significant contributors to the organization's work. It is also

2 Woodrow Wilson, "Address of President Woodrow Wilson" (delivered at Swarthmore College, Swarthmore, PA, October 25, 1913), https://archive.org/stream/addressofpreside07wilsonw/addressofpreside07wilsonw_djvu.txt (accessed May 10, 2015).

3 Sarah Phillips, "More Than a Paycheck," *The Washington Institute For Faith, Vocation, and Culture*, (blog), June 17, 2013, http://www.washingtoninst.org/5134/more-than-a-paycheck/ (accessed May 8, 2015).

written to those who aspire to leadership in such organizations, including students who might one day choose leadership in a nonprofit organization as their career path.

For the last four decades, I have been privileged to serve as President and CEO of Total Action for Progress, which has had statewide and national impact as a private, nonprofit corporation based in five cities and six counties of Southwest Virginia. TAP is one of more than a thousand community action agencies (CAAs), the large majority of which are private nonprofit corporations, established as a result of the passage of the Economic Opportunity Act of 1964 and the ensuing War on Poverty.

At the start, I'd like to clear up any confusion that may result when people hear the word "nonprofit." What makes a nonprofit organization different from a for-profit corporation? There are some significant differences. A nonprofit is exempt from state and federal corporate income taxes. A nonprofit organization is not owned by investors, stockholders, or private individuals. Most nonprofits are governed by volunteer boards of directors whose members are not paid for their service. The value of a nonprofit is not measured by the profits it makes but by the outcomes it produces that impact the individuals, families, and communities it serves. Nonprofits depend on a wide variety of resources that include contributions such as grants, donations, volunteer labor, and tax credits, rather than the proceeds from sales of a product or service. Nonprofits can engage in for-profit endeavors that are related to their mission, as long as the proceeds are directed back into the work of the organization. Aside from these differences, there are many similarities that will be addressed in this book.

It should be noted that the word "nonprofit" is a bit of a misnomer. The word denotes what these organizations are *not*, giving little suggestion of their worth or what they do. "The industry is alternatively called civil society, the citizen sector, the social sector . . .or the third sector."[4] I personally like the term a colleague developed, *public service corporations*, that denotes both their intent and their private, corporate nature.

This book is a compilation of the most important lessons I have learned about nonprofit leadership. These lessons are essential for great leadership because they constitute more than the story of a single great nonprofit organization. They also represent the collective wisdom of those across the country who have led and studied great nonprofits. Here are five reasons why nonprofit leadership is worth consideration:

1. The nonprofit community is a growing industry, particularly in the United States.
2. Nonprofit leadership is both an art and a science.
3. Nonprofit leadership success is greatly determined by how it addresses key areas.
4. Nonprofit leadership is more than a job: it is a sacred trust.
5. Nonprofit leadership is an adventure—not unlike running the rapids.

Nonprofits: A Growing Industry

When I came to the Roanoke Valley in 1965, aside from hospitals, churches, and traditional organizations like the Girl Scouts, Boy Scouts, and Red Cross, there were comparatively few nonprofit organizations. Today, there are nearly seven hundred nonprofits in the city of Roanoke, Virginia, alone. In fact, I would list the growth of the nonprofit industry as one of the chief institutional changes across America in the last fifty years.

The phenomenal growth of the nonprofit sector is confirmed by The Urban Institute, an authority on nonprofits: "The nonprofit sector has been growing steadily, both in size and financial impact for more than a decade. Between 2001 and 2011, the number of nonprofits has

---

4 Crutchfield, Leslie R., and Heather McLeod Grant. *Forces for Good: The Six Practices of High-Impact Nonprofits.* (San Francisco, CA: Jossey-Bass, 2008), p. 2.

increased 25 percent, from 1,259,764 to 1,574,674 today. The growth rate of the nonprofit sector has surpassed the rate of both the business and government sectors."[5]

At the same time, there is a crisis in the number of jobs replaced by technology in the for-profit and government sectors. Jeremy Rifkin is President of the Foundation of Economic Trends, linking scientific and technological changes to the economy, and author of twenty books. In *The End of Work: The Decline of the Global Labor Force and the Dawn of the Post-Market Era*, Rifkin predicted that with the development of technology and automation there would be a decrease in the number of jobs requiring people to perform them.[6] This trend is confirmed daily in news and magazine articles. A September 18, 2004, article in *The Roanoke Times*, "A Crossroad in Technology," by Lois Caliri indicated that unmanned trains were already being directed in rail yards by remote control technology with fewer accidents than those directed by onboard personnel. "Norfolk Southern hailed robot trains as a high-tech way to enhance safety, increase efficiency, and save money."[7]

On December 26, 2014, *The Roanoke Times* carried an *Associated Press* article noting that after WWII, far shorter trains than today's demanded seven crew members, which was "reduced to five people in the 1970s and two in 1991." The story went on to say that railway executives were proposing to reduce that count to one person, indicating that "a new automated braking system" further minimized risk of accidents. The article concluded: "If railroads can successfully implement the braking system and stop trains remotely, the advances might open the door to one day operating trains entirely by remote control or with robots."[8]

5 Urban Institute, "Research Area: Nonprofit Sector," http://www.urban.org/nonprofits/more. cfm (accessed March 26, 2015).

6 Rifkin, Jeremy. "Life Beyond the Marketplace," in *The End of Work: The Decline of the Global Labor Force and the Dawn of the Post-Market Era* (New York: G.P. Putnam's Sons, 1995), p. 239–248.

7 Lois Caliri, "A Crossroad in Technology," *The Roanoke Times*, September 18, 2004, http://www.roanoke.com/webmin/business/a-crossroad-in-technology/article_8362a782-a582-5868-82ff-8581a2a594ca.html (accessed March 26, 2015).

8 Josh Funk and Jeff Sturgeon, "Railroads want only one person at helm of trains." Roanoke

Assistant Managing Editor of *TIME Magazine* and economics columnist Rana Foroohar noted in a column titled "Hard Math in the New Economy" that "44 percent of U.S. firms since 2008 reduced their head counts in part because of automation" and "47 percent of U.S. jobs are at high risk of becoming automated in the next twenty years, according to Oxford University research."[9] In a previous column she had quoted the McKinsey Global Institute prediction "that new technologies will put up to 140 million service jobs at risk in the next decade."[10]

Rifkin also suggested that there were many functions important to our society that would not be taken care of by the normal market forces of supply and demand. Rifkin wrote that it would be the nonprofit community sector that would fill the void, address these issues, and produce employment opportunities.[11]

In fact, the nonprofit community today has an increasing economic impact in terms of jobs produced and dollars that turn over in the community marketplace, each adding substantially to the economic vitality of the community.

In 2007, the Council of Community Services of the Roanoke Valley published a study titled "The Economic Impact of Nonprofits in the Roanoke Virginia Region." Of the 650 nonprofits sent the survey, 120 responded. The study summarized the data from those 120 organizations. The following data reported in the Executive Summary constituted just 18 percent of the nonprofits in the region:

> The non-profit respondents employ 2,563 staff members full-time and another 1,759 workers part-time. In addition, non-profits and those they serve benefit from the involvement of over 32,000 volunteers, the equivalent of another 984 full-time employees. If

---

Times, December 26, 2014.

9 Foroohar, Rana. "Hard Math in the New Economy." TIME Magazine, March 16, 2015, http://time.com/3733113/hard-math-in-the-new-economy/ (accessed April 22, 2015).

10 Foroohar, Rana. "The 3% Economy, Yes, it's better than 2%. But for most Americans, it's actually more worrisome," *TIME Magazine*, September 25, 2014, http://time.com/3429656/the-3-economy/ (accessed March 29, 2015).

11 Rifkin, *The End of Work*, p. 239–248.

all of these employees worked for a single non-profit, it would be the fourth largest employer in the community.

Non-profits must have money to support their mission. Annually, this group of 120 survey participants raises and spends over $220 million. The United Way of the Roanoke Valley, by comparison, raises and distributes approximately $6 million a year.

Significantly, 50 percent of the money that funds the missions of non-profits in the region comes from outside of the community. This is the equivalent of a $110 million grant every year. The Regional Commission calculates that this $110 million creates an economic impact in the community of $183 million each year—a significant impact indeed.[12]

The economic impact of nonprofits is a national phenomenon. *Forces for Good* in 2008 reported that: "In the United States alone, 1.5 million nonprofits now account for more than $1 trillion in revenues annually of the nation's economy. During the past fifteen years, nonprofits grew faster than the overall economy, with thirty thousand new organizations created each year. In fact, nonprofits are now the third-largest industry in the United States, behind retail and wholesale trade, but ahead of construction, banking, and telecommunications."[13] That share of the market also represents an increase in employment opportunities and jobs produced.

The Urban Institute estimates support these conclusions: "In 2010, nonprofits contributed products and services that added $779 billion to the nation's gross national product, 5.4 percent of the GDP. Nonprofits are also a major employer, accounting for 9 percent of the economy's wages, and over 10 percent of the jobs in 2009."[14]

The growing importance of the nonprofit sector is further

---

12 Nonprofit Resource Center of Western Virginia, "The Economic Impact of Nonprofits in the Roanoke Virginia Region," http://www.councilofcommunityservices.com/wp-content/uploads/2010/12/The-Economic-Impact-of-Nonprofits-in-the-Roanoke-Virginia-Region1.pdf (accessed March 4, 2015).

13 Crutchfield and Grant, *Forces for Good*, p. 2.

14 Urban Institute, "Nonprofit Sector."

highlighted by the fact that nonprofits can also play a significant role in addressing issues that reduce the need for public expenditures in many areas. In 2013, TAP distributed an economic impact statement that highlighted the following points: TAP's $17.9 million funding stream translated into an economic impact of $29 million, a savings in remedial education of $1.3 million, a $2.8 million savings in Supplementary Nutrition Assistance Program (SNAP), unemployment and Temporary Assistance to Needy Families (TANF) benefits through training and employment programs, and a $13 million savings in incarceration costs through programs designed to reduce the number of repeat offenders.[15]

Finally, with growth and importance comes the spotlight of accountability. The urgency of issues to be addressed, exacerbated by cutbacks in government services, increases the need and opportunity for the nonprofit sector to fill the void. As the nonprofit role expands, so too does the need for accountability. Since the nonprofit sector is an expanding percentage of the overall economy, there is more intense scrutiny of all that we do. As a result, nonprofit leadership is required to develop best practices in its management processes and its organizational outcomes.

Nonprofit Leadership: Art and Science

The playing of chess is frequently referred to as both an art and a science. The personality of the player creates distinctive elements that move the game beyond sheer calculation. The explosive combination play of a Bobby Fischer or Gary Kasparov is very different from Anatoly Karpov who, like a python, squeezes the life out of his opponent by accumulating one small advantage after another until checkmate. However, like science, chess has certain rules. There are strategies for openings, middle, and end games that are ignored at the player's peril.

---

15   Total Action for Progress, "2013 Economic Impact Statement," http://www.tapintohope. org/downloads/EIS_Jan_2014_FINAL_12914.pdf (accessed March 19, 2015).

Nonprofit leadership is also both an art and a science. The distinct personality of the leader connecting with a particular organization in a particular place and time creates an organization that differs from others, even in the same business. Yet there is a growing body of information that constitutes a "science" of what a nonprofit leader must do to promote organizational success.

The intent of this book is to address issues important to any nonprofit organization. In addition to the many inspirational and talented people I have worked with over the last four decades, I am indebted to thinkers who have contributed greatly to my understanding of how to run an effective organization. Chief among them have been the following: Jim Collins, *Good to Great: Why Some Companies Make the Leap . . . and Others Don't* and *Good to Great and the Social Sectors*; Mario Morino, *Leap of Reason: Managing to Outcomes in an Era of Scarcity*; David E. K. Hunter, *Working Hard - Working Well*; Leslie R. Crutchfield and Heather McLeod Grant, *Forces for Good*; Shirley Sagawa and Deborah Jospin, *The Charismatic Organization*; and Tony Hsieh, *Delivering Happiness*.

Themes that recur in all of these works are:

- The importance of the right leadership and the right people.
- Management in terms of outcomes rather than outputs.
- The use of data to evaluate the effectiveness of outcomes.
- The necessity of continued evaluation of mission, goals, benchmarks, and outcomes.
- The need at all times to face the brutal facts of the situation at hand.
- The requirement for continued innovation to improve performance and adapt to an ever-changing environment.
- A strong preference for teamwork and shared leadership.
- A priority for building a culture that combines trust, respect, and a "can-do" mentality.
- The power of building external relationships with partners, networks, and outside leadership.

Most nonprofits are local organizations. However, nonprofits that frequently get the most attention in print are those at the national level. While the principles of organizational development outlined in this book relate to nonprofits anywhere, the illustrations come from a local nonprofit serving five cities and six counties in Southwest Virginia. Though TAP has had statewide and national impact through its innovative programming, it has experienced most of the difficulties and limitations of other local nonprofit organizations. In that regard it is highly relevant to the concerns most nonprofit leaders face.

Each chapter in this book addresses issues important to any nonprofit organization, from the essentials of visionary leadership to the importance of having a strong board of directors, from innovative program development to finding ways to reduce stress and burnout.

There is no one way to order these chapters other than my conviction that organizational history is the result of leadership. Yet an organization's values, culture, and processes also determine the type of persons that are drawn to the organization and the behavior of those who work for it. This is true of any organization but particularly nonprofits since the size of the paycheck is often not the greatest attraction. The connection between people and processes is organic, and their constant interaction determines the organization's character and destiny.

Readers will find that while this is not a comprehensive textbook, there are practical suggestions on most pages. The reader may find it helpful to read the chapters as presented in sequence or to pick the chapters that seem most relevant as a place to start. At the end of each chapter is a list of "take-away" questions designed to highlight the important issues of nonprofit leadership. In addition, the book is filled with stories of delightful, real people of character who have done incredible things. I have concluded chapters with "profiles in excellence" that tell their stories.

A Sacred Trust

Few of us in the nonprofit leadership community will make a lot of money. Many people think it sufficient if they are able to provide a good life and college education for their children and, perhaps, a modest retirement for themselves. The real payoff is the opportunity to earn a living by doing something meaningful: improving the quality of life for a community and forming the bridge of opportunity for those with the least resources. There are a great many jobs in the for-profit community that contribute significantly to others. My appreciation for the nonprofit sector in no way diminishes those contributions. Yet, we all know many people who labor day after day with no sense of mission other than earning the week's paycheck and a possible retirement pension. There is truth in the adage: if you love what you do, you will never have to work a day in your life. Giving meaning to life is central to the nonprofit community and those of us who work in that sector. Furthermore, nonprofit service is a matter of keeping faith with others, whether the most vulnerable in our society, the well-being of a fragile planet, or simply the quality of life in one's community. It is a matter of keeping faith with donors, be they private contributors or taxpayers who fund government initiatives. In all of these categories, working in the nonprofit sector is more than a job. It is nothing less than a sacred calling.

An Adventure

Finally, a word about the title of this book. Participating in nonprofit leadership is very much like running the rapids of a fast-moving, swollen body of water with unforeseen obstacles and unexpected twists and turns, separated by short periods of calm water and punctuated with the growing roar of new rapids up ahead. It is always an adventure and not for the faint of heart. A successful river run is greatly enhanced when the parties have the right equipment, receive the right training, think ahead, prepare for emergencies, and work together as a team. Every run is well served by a guide who has done the trip successfully. For those in the business or seeking to get in the business of nonprofit leadership, this is just such a guide. Here's wishing you Godspeed in an exciting adventure.

Chapter 2

THE QUEST TO MAKE A DIFFERENCE: LAUNCHING A PROJECT

Few will have the greatness to bend history itself; but each of us can work to change a small portion of events, and in the total of all those acts will be written the history of this generation.

~ *Robert Kennedy*[16]

What all nonprofit organizations have in common is the goal to make something happen to improve the lives of others. The mission of Total Action for Progress (where I served as CEO) was broad. Our intent was to improve the lives of low-income individuals, families, and communities by creating the "opportunity for education and training, the opportunity to work, and the opportunity to live in decency and dignity."[17] That wonderful phrase, "to live in decency and dignity," was broad. In our experience with low-income families, the notion of living in decency and dignity included health care, housing, and transportation, at least. These things are vital to what Christian ethicist Paul Lehmann refers to as "to make and to keep

16 Robert Kennedy, "Day of Affirmation" (speech, University of Cape Town, South Africa, June 6th, 1966), http://www.rfksafilm.org/html/speeches/unicape.php (accessed May 10, 2015).

17 Economic Opportunity Act of 1964, Pub. L. No. 88-452, 78 Stat. 508 (1964).

human life human."[18] It also included helping people who had made mistakes get a second, or even a third, chance to succeed.

- In retrospect, fifty years later, the results are impressive:
- TAP's Head Start and Early Head Start programs have served more than forty thousand low-income children since 1965, with a proven record of success.
- TAP's workforce training and placement programs under the banners of New Careers, Neighborhood Youth Employment Program, Mainstream, the Center for Employment Training, and This Valley Works have increased the education and employment of tens of thousands, enhancing their earning ability. The clientele have included high school dropouts, homeless veterans, ex-offenders, and those seeking refuge from domestic violence.
- More than fifteen thousand individuals' housing has been vastly improved through weatherization, emergency home repair, full renovations, single-family home construction, indoor plumbing renovations, a transitional living center, and a complete renovation of a 187-unit apartment complex.
- TAP's Financial Services programs that include small business development, a free tax clinic, and matched savings Individual Development Accounts have served roughly 1,000 individuals each year since 1994.
- TAP developed the Demonstration Water Project affecting more than a thousand area residents—a program that grew into the Southeast Rural Community Assistance Project, a network that has brought potable water and wastewater to millions of Americans.
- Virginia Community Action Re-entry System (Virginia CARES), a network launched by TAP in 1980, has reduced the crime-relapse rate of more than 30,000 Virginia ex-offenders returning to the community.

18 Lehmann, Paul L. *Ethics in a Christian Context.* (New York and Evanston: Harper & Row, 1963), p. 99.

- TAP was instrumental in the development of the Child Health Investment Program (CHIP), a statewide Virginia network of health care delivery that has served thousands of children age seven and younger who previously only received health care sporadically from hospital emergency departments.
- TAP's Project Discovery program evolved into a statewide network of college access programs that, since 1992, have assisted 10,000 low-income students who were the first in their family to attend and graduate from college.
- TAP, in partnership with the New River Community Action Program, developed a unique cars-to-work program, Responsible Rides, in partnership with Freedom First Credit Union and Enterprise Auto Rental, helping low-income families access affordable, reliable transportation.
- TAP's community and economic development projects transformed the first African American high school, the Harrison School, from a vacant, vandalized shell into a mixed-use building that houses the Harrison Museum of African American Culture on the first floor and twenty-eight apartments for the elderly and handicapped on the upper floors, helping to strengthen the adjacent community and support residential housing values. TAP also transformed the vacant Dumas Hotel in the heart of Henry Street, the center of African American life before the Civil Rights Act, into a $4.1 million theater that led to the renewal of the historic buildings across the street and the creation of a memorial to the late civil rights champion, Dr. Martin Luther King, Jr.
- TAP's assistance has been vital to the development of the Legal Aid Society of the Roanoke Valley, the Southwest Virginia Development Fund, Planned Parenthood in the Roanoke Valley, Feeding America Southwest Virginia (formerly Second Harvest Food Bank), Roanoke Area Dial-A-Ride (RADAR), Habitat for Humanity in the Roanoke Valley, and the League of Older Americans (LOA).

All of these outcomes are a result of separate initiatives that were launched from particular starting points. The purpose of this chapter is to examine some of those starting points and to illustrate them by real-life examples. These points include:

1. Starting from scratch
2. Surfing for change
3. Replicate and enhance
4. One success triggers another

Starting from Scratch

One of the most rewarding places for a nonprofit to start is with an identified but unaddressed need that does not have an immediate solution. This is what I refer to as starting from scratch. There are other steps between starting with an identified need, implementing a solution, and evaluating and refining that solution. These are:

1. Identifying a community need and determining who needs it.
2. Constructing a solution to that need.
3. Creating a leadership team to move the project forward.
4. Packaging the solution in a way that solicits support for its implementation.
5. Securing institutional commitments to address that need and support the proposed solution.
6. Implementing the solution.
7. Evaluating and refining the solution.
8. Adapting to a changing environment.

What follows is an illustration of those steps in two TAP projects: The Harrison Museum for African American Culture and the Dropout Recovery Program.

The Harrison Museum of African American Culture

Since the late 1960s, TAP has been involved in a large number of projects that began with organizing residents of both urban and rural low-income communities. Organizing began by visiting residents and asking about their present concerns and their vision for the future. Through these visits, early needs were identified including the lack of swimming pools serving African American children, the refusal of *The Roanoke Times'* publisher to put the pictures of African American brides on their Society page, and the need for an African American pride youth group. To combat these issues, TAP found resources to build six small neighborhood pools in African American neighborhoods. A one-day picket by young people angered by the refusal of *The Roanoke Times* to print the pictures of African American brides on the Society page resulted in a media policy change. Now Us, an organization of young African Americans, was formed prior to the death of Dr. Martin Luther King, Jr. Now Us chose to lead a community march to the blood bank rather than shed blood in a riot on the anniversary of his assassination.

In 1977, TAP applied for and received a grant to organize six neighborhoods in the predominantly African American northwestern section of the city of Roanoke. The grant called for the development of a written neighborhood plan based on the identified needs of the residents and their vision for the future of that community. Each neighborhood had a community organizer to help facilitate meetings and a planner to write the prospectus for the future.

The Northwest Improvement Council was formed in a neighborhood located around the Harrison School, the first African American high school in the city of Roanoke. The senior citizen group—led by Mrs. Hazel Thompson, Mr. Edwards, Mrs. Muse, and Mrs. Dorothy Mendenhall—was encouraged by TAP organizers to develop a vision for their community. Their dream was to transform the then-vacant school, which had been subjected to vandalism, into a museum for African American culture so that the history of African American courage and achievement would not be lost on the new generation. Prior to the building of Harrison, there had been no high school opportunities for African American children. The Harrison school was a historical icon in the struggle for civil rights.

The organization was formed, meetings held, and a plan developed based on the Northwest Improvement Council's vision for their community. However, the initial grant did not provide enough resources for project implementation. The project plan could easily have languished on an office shelf were it not for TAP's commitment to provide support and do whatever it took to make their dream come true.

The Need: Transform an important relic of the past into an asset for the future of that neighborhood and the larger African American community.

The Solution: Turn the vacant Harrison School into the Harrison Museum of African American Culture.

The Leadership Team: One-half of the team was in place. Mrs. Hazel Thompson, a teacher for forty-seven years in Roanoke City Public Schools and known by her students as "Butch Thompson," was a larger-than-life personality. She combined the disarming behavior of a kind old lady, the tenacity of a prizefighter, and a poet's eloquence. Hazel Thompson would later receive a standing ovation from the entire gathering at a Congressional House Subcommittee Hearing when she testified on behalf of TAP, closing her remarks with a recitation from the Declaration of Independence from memory.

To complete the team, I called on TAP's Director of Special Projects, Jayne Thomas. Jayne was an experienced project developer who could connect with elected officials, the business community, and leaders in the larger community. Overnight, she had already created a million dollars' worth of youth projects for TAP. Hazel and Jayne were individually impressive; together they were a powerful force.

Packaging the Solution and Institutional Commitments: For more than a year, Mrs. Thompson would face down objections by those in the City of Roanoke who had slated the school for demolition with her inspiring lectures on African American history. The visioning project provided the outline for Jayne's packaging the project to the Department of Housing and Urban Development (HUD), the Southwest Savings and Loan Bank, and Congressman Caldwell Butler, who, in order to make the project affordable, secured the last twenty-eight Section 8 Rehabilitation vouchers in the United States. Developers Fralin and Waldron were then engaged to renovate the school into twenty-eight apartments for the elderly and handicapped and provide a fifteen-year, rent-free, ground-floor lease for the Harrison Museum of African American Culture.

The Implementation: The building was completed by the developer and a separate nonprofit was formed to operate the museum rent-free for fifteen years. Melody Stovall, a very talented TAP leader, was elected by the new board to head it.

The Evaluation: For three decades, the Harrison Museum has highlighted the accomplishments of African American leaders in the Roanoke Valley and been a venue for displaying the works of African American artists. As an outgrowth of the project, the Harrison Museum annually sponsors the Henry Street Festival in Roanoke's Elmwood Park, in the heart of the city. The festival is a family day of music, dance, food and art vendors, and a celebration of African American heritage.

The Adaptation: Today, the Harrison Museum shares an important space in downtown Roanoke's Center in the Square, which houses a planetarium, science museum, history museum, and is a block away from the prestigious $65 million Taubman Art Museum. The Harrison School project ultimately harnessed the vision and energy of a small group of seniors, who no one had previously taken seriously, and transformed a part of the city of Roanoke for years to come.

The Harrison Museum has found a permanent place in the Roanoke Valley community and provided the African American community with greater public visibility and prominence.

The Dropout Recovery Program

The Need: In 1994, *The Roanoke Times* ran an article indicating that every year, five hundred Roanoke City Public Schools' high school students were dropping out and not graduating. The graduation rate hovered around an appalling 58 percent. Further, most of those dropping out were African American males who were from low-income families.

The Solution: The immediate solution was to reconnect with the young people who had dropped out and see if we could get them back in school or at least enroll them in a GED program—ours or another that was available. It made sense for a third party to make the contact since it was likely students might feel jaded by a contact from the place where they had too often failed. The long-term solution was for Roanoke City Public Schools to make adjustments to improve the graduation rate.

The Leadership Team: Anna Lawson, Chair of the Board of Visitors for Hollins University, was also Chair of the TAP Education Task Force, which comprised community leaders commissioned by the TAP Board to discern future roles for TAP in improving opportunities for education and employment for low-income residents. When news of the dropout crisis became public, we made appointments to meet with all of the public school superintendents in our area to ask if we might be of help. We were well received by all, with the exception of the superintendent of Roanoke City Public Schools. He told us in no uncertain terms that the school system was doing all that could possibly be done, and that there was nothing that we could do to help.

Sherman P. Lea was Regional Director of Community Corrections in Southwest Virginia. He had more than two decades with the Department of Corrections and was all too aware of the fact that the majority of male inmates in correctional institutions are African

American.[19] He knew what happens to young men, particularly African Americans, when they drop out of school. Unemployed, they look for ways to support themselves. Far too often they are recruited by the criminal element, break the law, and end up in prison. Sherman Lea happened to be both the vice-chair of the TAP Board and the vice-chair of the board of Roanoke City Public Schools. Sherman met with the superintendent and encouraged him to cooperate with TAP.

After that meeting, I met with the superintendent. He indicated that although he still didn't think that TAP could be of help, he was willing but his hands were tied. He could not give us the list of those who had dropped out of school because the names of former students and their contact information were privileged and confidential. For the school to provide that information would be breaking the law. Furthermore, even if he could provide the information, the school had no money to pay for the project of reconnecting with the young people.

Institutional Commitments: Will Dibling, Roanoke City Attorney, also acted as the attorney for Roanoke City Public Schools. Will was a conservative city attorney but a concerned citizen and a practical person. I presented the problem to Will, expressing TAP's position that losing five hundred students a year to the streets represented a dismal future of such magnitude that there had to be a solution. It took Will all of thirty seconds to reply. All RCPS had to do was enter into a no-money contract with TAP to connect with those who had dropped out and seek to get them back into school. TAP then became an agent of the public school system, and RCPS was legally authorized to give the names and contact information of students to TAP. Will also agreed to draft the contract. At the next meeting of the school board, supported by the vice-chair, I made the proposal for a dropout recovery initiative that the board endorsed.

The Implementation: TAP entered into a partnership with the Radford University School of Social Work and utilized the services of

---

19 "Incarceration Rates by Race and Ethnicity, 2010," Prisonpolicy.org, http://www. prisonpolicy.org/graphs/raceinc.html (accessed March 31, 2015).

student interns studying toward master's degrees to reach out to the students on the list provided by RCPS. These "education outreach workers" contacted the students and developed a relationship. They helped them reenter school, enroll in TAP's remedial/alternative education GED program, enter a job-related learning situation, or find a job (sometimes a combination of these). In March of 2000, TAP hired a full-time education specialist to assist the recovery effort. In 2001, TAP hired a student psychology intern from Roanoke College to reach even more students who had dropped out.

To support the dropout retrieval project, TAP reached out to local funding sources. The Carilion Foundation, United Way of Roanoke Valley, and Wachovia Bank contributed financial support. To further support the initiative and bring heightened visibility to the dropout issue, Sherman Lea—supported by Annette Lewis, TAP's Senior Vice President of Programs and Director of This Valley Works—organized the first Western Virginia Education Classic in the city of Roanoke that brought together football teams from two of Virginia's historic African American colleges. Over a period of thirteen years, the annual WVEC raised more than $250,000 for the project and increased public awareness of the dropout issue. In addition, the student athletes visited school classrooms as ambassadors, encouraging students to stay in school and prepare for a college education.

The Evaluation and Adaptation: The Project Recovery program has retrieved more than one thousand students who have dropped out of school. The larger impact has been continued focus on the graduation rate. With the addition of Roanoke City Public Schools' Forrest Park Academy—geared toward helping older students who have fallen behind in school complete their studies and receive a standard diploma—Roanoke City Public Schools, under the leadership of more recent superintendent, Dr. Rita Bishop, has increased their graduation rate to 80 percent. This has been helped along by an increased sense of urgency for school accreditation and the employment of internal intervention specialists in addition to the Forrest Park Academy. Referrals to TAP's Project Recovery program have fallen from four hundred per year to under one hundred. The current strategic plan calls for an increase in the graduation rate by a minimum of three percent per year in addition to full accreditation of all schools.

Surfing for Change

I have often thought that creating social change is like surfing. It is hard to surf without a wave. No wave, no surfing. At the same time, you will never be able to catch a wave unless you are out there on a board. Social change frequently requires a trigger issue to create opportunity for the support needed to deal with problems that otherwise are ignored. Like taking advantage of the wave, you have to be ready to take advantage of the trigger issue. The Rental Inspection Program and the Drug Market Initiative Life College are a couple of examples of how projects start by early involvement in an issue.

The Rental Property Inspection Program

When I was the director of inner-city ministry for Montgomery Presbytery and working in Southeast Roanoke, I remember being called to the home of an elderly couple. The husband had just died, and his casket was in the living room. The woman was in tears. The social worker at the Roanoke City Department of Social Services had prematurely stopped payments to the home, cutting off a vital means of support for the couple. The situation was exacerbated by the fact that the plumbing in the rental apartment had not been working for some time. I caught up with the social worker at the Department of Social Services, and she became so nervous in the course of our discussion that she broke the pencil she was holding in two. The elderly woman got her check. The financial issue was solved, but the plumbing was still defective. After meeting with an obstinate landlord who refused to make repairs, I contacted a young attorney, George Harris—who later became a municipal court judge—and asked him to take the case pro bono. George was eager to help. With his assistance, we put the rent payments in escrow, showing that the woman was not trying to dodge her rent obligations, prevented the landlord from evicting her, and took him to court. The courts had a tradition of backing landlords no matter what, since there were no local building codes that prevented them from renting slum housing. The judge threw the case out of court and asked that the landlord be paid the money that was in escrow. Some repairs were made, but the overall situation of substandard housing was not addressed.

In 1985, an elderly woman named Mrs. Tate froze to death on a January evening in her home because she had no heat. In 1995, grandmother Goldie Christie Duncan and four children in the Leftwich family (Mark, six; Clyde, five; Patrick, four; and Nancy, three) died in a fire because of faulty wiring in a substandard rental apartment in Southeast Roanoke. The house also lacked requisite fire walls (to prevent the spread of fire between apartments) and smoke alarms.

Since TAP was well known in the city, especially in the low-income neighborhoods surrounding the downtown area, and since we had worked with most community leaders, TAP's neighborhood development staff called a meeting of leaders of the neighborhoods. Together, we petitioned the City of Roanoke to enact code enforcement measures to bring all rental housing up to code and prevent what happened to the Leftwich children from happening to others. The city, more concerned with the property rights of landowners and nervous about opposition from owners of downtown rental housing, was reluctant to take action.

At the next meeting of the Regional Housing Network, which had been set up to deal with the provision of affordable housing, I made a presentation on the research I had done on rental inspection programs in the Virginia cities of Lynchburg, Charlottesville, and Virginia Beach, proposing a rental inspection program for residential rental property in the City of Roanoke. A group of eighty landlords organized to oppose the imposition of an inspection program.

After continued persistence on the part of TAP and the coalition of neighborhood groups—under the banner of the "Leftwich-Tate Certificate of Compliance Coalition"—and a supportive resolution by the Roanoke Regional Housing Network, the City of Roanoke created a rental inspection taskforce that brought together members of the Regional Housing Network, TAP, neighborhood organizations, and the local landlord association to hammer out the provisions of a local rental inspections statute.

In 1996, Roanoke City Council passed a statute that set up a program for the inspection of inner-city neighborhoods. The city attorney had taken a conservative approach, citing the Dillon Rule, which prevented Virginia localities from exercising authority that had not been specifically delegated to them by state action.[20] The 1996 Roanoke Rental Inspection Program was voluntary unless a renter initiated a complaint.[21] The City of Lynchburg had alternatively argued that the presence of the state building code required local authorities to mandate that all residential properties meet that code.

In July of 2005, Virginia's governor signed into law legislation authorizing localities to establish "rehabilitation districts" in which a rental inspection is mandatory. Today the City of Roanoke has eleven inspectors who conduct mandatory inspections every four years. The large majority of landlords in the district comply. Together with housing rehabilitation, new construction, and the rental inspection program, TAP has greatly improved the condition of housing in Roanoke's inner-city neighborhoods.

The Drug Market Initiative Life College

The Drug Market Initiative (DMI) was a program developed in High Point, North Carolina, to take drug dealers off the street and reconnect

---

20 Fairfax County, "Dillon Rule in Virginia," http://www.fairfaxcounty.gov/government/about/dillon-rule.htm (accessed March 29, 2015).

21 David Reed, "Fire Fatalities Prompt Calls for Rental Unit Inspections," *The Free Lance-Star*, January 25, 1996.

with communities victimized by the drug trade. The program involved undercover work by the police to gain the necessary evidence on the dealers that would stand up in court. Those with long rap sheets were charged by the prosecutor and convicted. Those who were not hardcore were brought before their families, community leaders, and public officials, and given a chance to clean up their act, enroll in school or get a job, and change their lives. The program, created by an anthropologist, had received high acclaim.

After reading about the program, I approached local authorities to see if we could replicate it in Roanoke. At the time, the relationship between the commonwealth attorney and the chief of police was not at an all-time high. As a close working relationship was required for program success, nothing was done. Shortly after, Chris Perkins, an anthropologist by training, became chief of police. He decided that the initiative was worth bringing to Roanoke. TAP's experience with the offender population was well established, so as a creative expansion of the program we worked with Chief Perkins to create a "life college" for those who chose a better life than going to jail. As a result, Roanoke's DMI program, with the addition of TAP's "life college," has had the best success of any program nationally with the rehabilitation of low-level dealers.

In the case of the rental-inspection program, the sad deaths of Mrs. Tate as well as the grandmother and small children of the Leftwich family was wave upon wave. In the case of DMI, the wave was a new police chief and working relationship with the office of the prosecutor. In both cases, TAP was in the position to take advantage of the opportunity for the good of the community.

Replicate and Enhance

Part of working for (or in) the nonprofit sector is doing one's best to make sure every effort has the greatest possible impact. There are many situations in which the needs of one community are needs shared by others. Often there are solutions to those needs that can be adapted elsewhere. In those instances, there is no need to start from scratch. It only requires one to recognize what is being done somewhere else and replicate it. Let's look at a few of the ways TAP has made this strategy work.

Youthbuild

Youthbuild is a nationally successful program that enrolls young people, ages sixteen to twenty-four years, who have dropped out of school and have been unemployed. The program pays them a stipend while they complete their GED, learn construction skills, graduate with a Construction Trade certification, and build a house for a first-time homebuyer. TAP is now in its fourteenth year as a Youthbuild project sponsor. Three hundred and sixty students have assisted in fifteen complete builds and worked on a total of forty homes. In the last few years, we have partnered with Habitat for Humanity in the Roanoke Valley, which has recruited new homeowners, provided construction financing, and allowed our students to work as part of their crews on active job sites. Youthbuild helps to provide affordable home ownership and transforms the lives of the workforce.

Certified Nurse's Aide Training

TAP's Nurse's Aide Training Program provides students with intensive classroom and clinical training experience to prepare them for employment in the health care field. This program is of incredible value in the Roanoke Valley, where the health care industry is the number one provider of jobs and the area's fastest-growing industry. TAP's nurse's aide students attend classroom training for twenty-five hours per week for six weeks, engaging in a curriculum specifically designed to prepare students for the Virginia Board of Nursing's Nurse's Aide Certification Exam. This curriculum is put together with national nursing standards firmly in mind, as well as employer input provided through TAP's Nurse's Aide Advisory Council. After completing classroom training, students receive an additional forty hours of clinical training at actual health care sites, allowing trainees to learn hands-on skills in a real work environment.

TAP's training program differs from other nurse's aide programs in the Roanoke Valley in that it instills valuable life skills in students. Achieving success as a certified nurse's aide requires more than just nursing knowledge. Individuals must know how to manage stress, find work-life balance, and communicate effectively. At TAP, students are taught valuable job readiness, financial literacy, and life skills, including stress management exercises like meditation, yoga, and tai chi. They are also given access to supportive services including case management, counseling, and emergency assistance. By going the extra mile, TAP ensures that its nurse's aide graduates not only have the professional skills to find a job, but also the life skills to keep it. Finally, TAP works closely with industry employers, which has enabled it to successfully place nearly all of its graduates into employment. The Nurse's Aide Advisory Council also gives health care employers an opportunity to provide input on graduates' performance and upcoming employer needs.

TAP has also partnered with local colleges to provide opportunities for students interested in continuing their education. In 2013–2014, TAP's CNA program was approved as a training site and had a 94 percent certification pass rate, a 95 percent employment rate, and a 91 percent employment retention rate.

Learning from Others

In the quest to find projects that have worked elsewhere that might address needs in your area, I have learned that it is extremely important to learn from the best in the business. The nonprofit industry is full of very talented leaders. I continue to be amazed at the tremendous work done by so many. There are many great organizations and even more that qualify as good. There's hardly an organization from which you can't learn something.

For instance, visits to Cleveland Works formed the basis for TAP's This Valley Works. A visit to the California offices of the Center for Employment and Training in Northern California raised the bar as to what to expect in a first-class employment skills training program. A firsthand look at Delancey Street in San Francisco, the nation's premier reentry program for those involved in drug rehabilitation, helped to inform the development of Virginia CARES. The two-generation approach to Head Start in Tulsa, Oklahoma, is a model that we will seek to replicate in the year ahead. The Washington, DC, Head Start program that had implemented the Tools of the Mind curriculum created the incentive to pilot the program in our own classrooms.

You may not be able to replicate every project. There may be special circumstances that enable another nonprofit to install solar energy systems on the roofs of other nonprofits, develop a credit union, or turn a local mountain into a major economic development project. Nevertheless, contact with leaders of this caliber raises your vision of what is possible and encourages you to broaden your horizons and leads to the development of new ideas.

One Success Triggers Another

It is often the case that success breeds success. In the life of a nonprofit, this is often experienced. A successful project can open the way for other successful projects, extending the reach of the organization, allowing it to have greater impact in the same arena or a different one. TAP's successful expansion in the area of Early Head Start is a good example of expansion in the same arena. The story of how a performing arts center led to the development of a 187-unit affordable housing complex is a useful example of how success in one project can lead to opportunities in a different arena.

Head Start

In 1964, the nation's leading child development experts had already figured out that if poor children were going to have a chance to compete with children from more privileged backgrounds, they had to have an opportunity for a quality preschool education. Head Start was launched to provide that quality experience, including language development; social-emotional education; nutrition; health and dental care; and physical development with special attention to speech, language, special physical disabilities, mental health, and parental involvement. Head Start was TAP's first program. As the body of research on early childhood grew, (in particular the research surrounding what constituted best practices in early childhood education), it became clear that in order to make a difference, you had to start with infants and toddlers. As a community organizer, I had frequently seen toddlers in playpens or walkers—in a room with no lights to save electricity—who had been left in front of a TV to serve as a surrogate babysitter; an ineffectual foundation for later learning at best. As a result, Early Head Start for infants and toddlers was created. It was left up to local Head Start programs whether they would take advantage of competitive funding to include infants and toddlers. In 1999, after two failed submissions, TAP received funding for its first Early Head Start program. In 2009, we won a $3,000,000 award for the expansion of Early Head Start. On December 10, 2013, President Obama announced the winners of an additional Early Head Start expansion. TAP's award was $2.7 million.

The Dumas Center and the Terrace Apartments

The largest community development project undertaken by TAP was the transformation of the Dumas Hotel on Henry Street into the Dumas Center for Artistic and Cultural Development. Henry Street is a two-block street located in the heart of the oldest neighborhood in the City of Roanoke, separated from downtown Roanoke and the more affluent communities of Southwest Roanoke City and southern Roanoke County by the Norfolk Southern railroad tracks. In earlier years, the tracks represented the hard dividing line between predominantly African American and white residential areas.

During segregation, Henry Street was the social, political, commercial, and leadership hub of the African American community. Like similar areas throughout the South, the advent of desegregation caused Henry Street to fall into decline. The hotels closed; and the barbershops, attorney's office, and ice cream parlors were replaced with illegal drinking and gambling "nip joints" and pool halls. The decline was accelerated by urban renewal and the removal of five African American residential areas surrounding Henry Street, which worked to cut the links between African American residents and African American-owned businesses. In 1970, the Roanoke Redevelopment and Housing Authority took ownership of the entire two-block area, going so far as to demolish the offices of the historic African American paper, *The Roanoke Tribune*, before the Whitworth family—who owned the paper—was able to remove all of the business documents.

One of the two hotels, the Palace Hotel, eventually crumbled to the ground under its own weight. The Dumas Hotel, owned by the Barlow family, had previously been the place to stay for the great African American entertainers who, even though they performed in the City of Roanoke, could not stay at any of the all-white hotels. These entertainers included Cab Calloway, Duke Ellington, Count Basie, Dizzy Gillespie, Louis Armstrong, Sarah Vaughan, Little Richard, the Harlem Globetrotters, and more.[22] The Roanoke Chapter of the NAACP was founded in 1909 on Gainesboro Road, a few blocks away from the Dumas Hotel, according to Al Holland, a ninety-eight-year-old friend of mine.

With the encouragement and support of the African American

---

22 Shareef, Reginald, PhD. The Roanoke Valley's African American Heritage: A Pictorial History. (Virginia Beach, VA: The Donning Company/Publishers, 1996), p. 148.

community, TAP was granted title to the Dumas Hotel for the purpose of a major renovation before it too collapsed. TAP put together a resource package of a Health and Human Services federal grant and no-interest loans of $250,000 and $300,000 from the Head Start Regional Administration to renovate the structure into a modern Head Start kitchen serving all of TAP's Head Start centers. The renovations included a large downstairs community room that would accommodate the incubation space for an all-African American theater whose productions would include *The Wiz, The Colored Museum, For Colored Girls Who Have Considered Suicide When the Rainbow is Enuf*, and *The Piano Lesson*. Years later, Harry Belafonte would be invited to a breakfast in this space, witness an excerpt from the Dumas Drama Guild's production of *Colored Girls* and speak of his own involvement with the arts, which changed his life forever. It was an electrical moment.

A second $4.1 million renovation in 2004 would again transform all three floors of the Dumas Center into a 188-seat modern theater and dressing rooms with complete video technology, a top floor for the Downtown Music Lab (an exciting training and production site for young musicians), and office space. Today, the theater is the home of the successful Roanoke Children's Theater.

Our consultant on the Dumas project, Susheela Shanta, later made us aware that the two-hundred-unit Terrace Apartments (built in the 1950s and located in the heart of Roanoke) were up for sale, and that a Richmond, Virginia, company was willing to sell the option that they had purchased. Since the Dumas Center had provided us experience with both historic and new markets tax credits, TAP took on the Terrace complex. The buildings are located in a beautifully landscaped area near one of the premier public parks in the community, on the bus line, and within walking distance of the Grandin Village, one of the most successful commercial areas in the City of Roanoke. The Roanoke city manager opposed the sale, arguing for a plan to demolish the structures and replace them with upscale housing that would strengthen the city's tax base. TAP then leveraged its assets to purchase the buildings and worked to acquire $27 million of low-income tax credits to completely renovate the structures, ultimately decreasing the unit density to make the apartments larger and outfitting them with modern conveniences like air conditioning, new heating units, dishwashers, and new interiors. The Dumas project ended up creating the opportunity to preserve affordable housing in two of the strongest neighborhoods in the City of Roanoke.

The Quest to Make a Difference: Launching a Project Take-Aways

- What are the outstanding unmet needs in your community?
- Who are the people most invested in solving that need in your community?
- What are the current options for a solution to those unmet needs?
- Who will "package" the solution to elicit support from others to create the resources necessary to implement the solution?
- Who are the key people in your community who would constitute a leadership team for moving the project forward?
- What plans have been made for evaluation of the solution?
- Are there factors in the environment that could impact the delivery and sustainability of the solution?
- What is happening in your community that might provide a "surfing" opportunity to provide additional impact?
- What projects have been done elsewhere that could be replicated by your agency or in your community to address unmet needs?
- What program success have you had that might yield expanded programming?
- Who are the top leaders in the nonprofit arena that you admire and from whom you could learn if you had increased contact?

Profile in Excellence:
Jayne Thomas

In 1972, with her fourth marriage—to a major league baseball player—going south, Jayne Thomas, the daughter of an African American physician, took her eleven-year-old son and left Indiana, where she had worked for a community action agency. She was out of work and about to be evicted from her motel in Washington, DC, when she reached TAP's Executive Director Bristow Hardin, Jr. on the phone at the advice of a friend. Bristow welcomed her to TAP and informed me that she was now on my training staff as a consultant.

Jayne came from an upper-middle-class family. The house servants that assisted the family were white. Jayne was used to relating to people in authority as equals, and her ability to find some quality she liked in everyone made her a natural connector. She worked equally well with low-income neighborhood leaders and high-level public officials.

In 1975, Roanoke's city manager asked for TAP's help in curbing juvenile delinquency. Within a year, Jayne—by then Director of TAP's Youth Services—had built a million-dollar youth division from twenty-two sources of new money. This would fund a summer Earn and Learn program that combined work and education; a Latch Key program to engage children of working parents; an alternative education program for children having difficulty performing in Roanoke City Schools' classrooms; a GED program for dropouts; a shopping cart retrieval program led by young people; an Aid to the Elderly program in which young people helped low-income seniors; a weightlifting and karate program for young people; and a fresh-air camp for kids during the summer.

That same year, one of my first actions as the new TAP Executive Director was to appoint Jayne to the position of Director of Special Projects and ask her to work with Mrs. Thompson, the leader of the Northwest Investment Council, to renovate the Harrison School (mentioned in Chapter Two). The renovation of the school into the

Harrison Museum for African American Culture and the annual Henry Street Festival were an outgrowth of Jayne's leadership.

Some years later, Jayne and outreach worker Pam Irvine began talking to me about food banking. I told Jayne and Pam, "I really don't understand what you just told me, but if you think it is important, make it happen." That was the beginning of Southwest Virginia Second Harvest Food Bank (now Feeding America Southwest Virginia) under TAP's umbrella.

Jayne would go on to join the Roanoke City School Board that hired Superintendent Frank Tota, who brought new and creative leadership to Roanoke City Public Schools. She would then move to Richmond to serve as the first Director of the State Office of Community Services. Since her death in 1987, Jayne inspired the Jayne Thomas Award to be given by the National Community Action Partnership to the local grassroots leader who has contributed the most to the War on Poverty.

Chapter 3:

Making a Larger Difference: Scaling Up and Collective Action

Individual commitment to a group effort—that is what makes a team work, a company work, a society work, a civilization work.

~ Vince Lombardi[23]

Two terms that are everywhere in the twenty-first century nonprofit world are *scaling up* and *collective action*. *Scaling up* frequently refers to the idea of addressing the same issue in a larger geographic setting. *Collective action* refers to the need of nonprofit, public, and private entities to work together to do what no one organization can do by itself. It goes beyond simple partnerships and requires a broader commitment of time and resources. The Virginia Water Project, Virginia Community Action Re-entry System (CARES), the Comprehensive Health Investment Program (CHIP), and Feeding America Southwest Virginia were initiated by TAP in the Roanoke Valley of Southwest Virginia, and they started as local projects. These were scaled up to address the issues on a statewide basis with the assistance and collective action of the thirty independent community

---

23 "Famous Quotes by Vince Lombardi," http://www.vincelombardi.com/quotes.html (accessed May 8, 2015).

action agencies across the Commonwealth of Virginia whose mission was broadly the same as TAP's.

The Virginia Water Project

The Need: TAP's earliest community organizing efforts were in the rural communities surrounding the urban centers in the Roanoke Valley. Five hundred families in the counties of Roanoke, Bedford, Botetourt, and Rockbridge listed the lack of potable running water and sanitary waste disposal as their number one need and priority. As a young pastor in the Pico community, I had previously known families who bailed their water from a creek or borrowed water from a neighbor's front-yard spigot. To use the restroom, you were guided out back to the ubiquitous outhouse. The lack of both water and wastewater disposal facilities (which were available to the vast majority of Americans) had a clear impact on those who were without. The water they used was often contaminated with bacteria, leading to poor health. The inconvenience of bailing water from a creek and using the outhouse in the back was exhausting and demeaning. Addressing the lack of water and sanitary waste disposal would have a ripple impact on educating the young, employing adults, developing economy of the area by improving family health, reducing the time dedicated to mere survival, and improving the way families saw themselves compared with their neighbors.

The Solution: Build small water systems that served clusters of houses in five communities. Access to water and technology were not the issues. Water was plentiful in the aquifers. The engineering needed to drill wells, transport the water to homes, and provide for drainage fields was standard. The training for managing and maintaining a private water system was well known. The resources were lacking to finance the building of the water systems and provide the management and maintenance training to the residents to operate their systems.

The Leadership Team: TAP's first Executive Director, Bristow Hardin, appointed Margo Kiley, one of his assistant directors, to head up the project. Margo assisted the leaders of these rural communities in meeting with officials in the Washington, DC, headquarters of both the Office of Economic Opportunity (OEO) and Farmers Home Administration (FmHA) to request grants and loans to build the systems. A separate corporation, the Demonstration Water Project (DWP), whose board was made up of leaders from each of the newly assembled neighborhood organizations, was created.

Packaging the Solution and Institutional Commitments: TAP's planning staff developed proposals and sent them to OEO, which was looking to assist projects developed by low-income communities, and to FmHA, which was concerned with rural housing. The result was a funding formula in which FmHA provided 50 percent of the financing in loans and 30 percent in grant subsidy with the remainder provided by OEO and DWP. Prior to this project, OEO had never been involved in hardware projects of this complexity and magnitude. The involvement of these two federal agencies, along with support from county boards of supervisors and our congressional representative, constituted the necessary *institutional commitments* to carry the project to fruition.

The Implementation: DWP hired a team to manage building the new systems, training the neighborhood leaders in maintaining each independent water system, including system finances. The board selected Joe Van Deventer as executive director, J.C. Reynolds as neighborhood management trainer, Ed Weingard as field operator, Wally Johnson as construction manager, and Elaine Stinson as financial manager.

The Evaluation: The Demonstration Water Project was so successful that it expanded from the original five communities to fourteen, serving more than a thousand families who had been living in third-world conditions in the richest country in the world.

The Adaptation: With the passage of the Safe Drinking Water Act in 1974, stricter standards and the need for more professional operators encouraged local county governments to absorb these companies into their developing water utility operations.[24]

Scaling Up and Collective Action: Scaling up made sense since the lack of access to potable water and sanitary waste disposal was an issue for hundreds of thousands of Virginians across the Commonwealth and millions of Americans across the nation. Scaling up required the collective action of others who could generate both the person power to address the issue and the political support to draw the attention of state leadership to provide funds necessary to carry the work forward. The Virginia Council Against Poverty was the trade association that brought together the community action agencies from across the state five times a year to focus on poverty issues. Their adoption of what would become the Virginia Water Project and the commitment of staff to help implement the program in their locality would be key to bringing two hundred forty thousand water and wastewater connections to low-income Virginians.

The project was later scaled up on a national level to the National Demonstration Program, and then to the National Rural Community Assistance Project, providing access to potable water and sanitary waste disposal to low-income rural families in all fifty states.

Virginia Community Action Re-entry System

The Need: The Virginia CARES initiative started as the outgrowth of TAP's realization that poor men, especially those who are African Americans in the Commonwealth of Virginia, often tragically end up in prison. For the most part, they are poorly educated with poor work histories and are often involved in drug and alcohol addiction. While society talks about locking them up and throwing away the key, in reality, the vast majority of those who serve jail and prison time are released back into the community at some point. Before 1980, other than the criminal element on the street, there was no reentry system

---

24 Cobb, Edwin L. *No Cease Fires: The War on Poverty in Roanoke Valley.* (Cabin John, Maryland: Seven Locks Press, 1984), p. 126.

in Virginia to receive those coming out of the state penal institutions. Offender Aid and Restoration pilots begun in 1968 worked only with local jail inmates.

To verify that those who were in prison saw a pre-release program as helpful, the TAP training division had begun working with the inmate population in the local Roanoke City Jail. We began by taking a life-planning exercise developed for company executives and adapting it for male inmates at the jail.

This simple plan consisted of five exercises:

1. Participants took a piece of blank newspaper and, with a magic marker, drew a line illustrating their life's ups and downs from birth to the present, indicating key events in their lives.

2. Participants then explored their values by repeatedly answering the question "What is important to you?" and writing each response on a quarter-sheet of 8½" x 11" paper. They were then asked to tape these responses together, putting the most important one at the top.

3. Participants forecasted their death and wrote their obituary.

4. Participants developed a life plan of where they would like to be in five to ten years and indicated five positive steps to help get them there.

5. Participants shared their life plans and received feedback from the other participants. Every exercise required that each participant stand in front of the group and share what they had written.

The response was overwhelmingly positive. The majority of the inmates had never really looked at their lives from a long-term perspective. Poverty is a crisis-to-crisis experience in which dreams for the future are lost, immediate gratification is cherished, and an overwhelming sense of powerlessness over the long-term future becomes a reality. Simply completing these exercises and receiving positive feedback represented an optimistic and encouraging step for the inmates. We then expanded this format into a year-long self-awareness group at medium-security State Prison Camp 25 in Troutville, Virginia, helping inmates identify and express feelings, seek better ways of dealing with anger and frustration, and improve their ability to handle conflict.

A pilot reentry program, Stop Gap Jobs, was also developed with a grant from the local Comprehensive Employment and Training Act Consortium. The project paid a stipend to enrollees who participated in life planning, communication skills, and team-building training. In addition, they learned to fill out a job application, prepare a résumé, and conduct themselves during an interview. The participants were then enrolled in one of three teams: The "store front team" provided peer counseling and helped to hustle clothes, work tools, bus passes, and job leads that would help those stopping by for assistance. The "job research team" met with local business owners and company human resource directors to discover local job opportunities for those coming out of prison. The "community education team" made public appearances before service clubs to speak on the needs of those coming out of prison. And the beauty of it? This program helped those coming out of prison adjust to a work environment and make positive connections with the public at large.

The Solution: Create a permanent pre- and post-incarceration reentry system, one that prepares inmates for reentry before release and continues support after release. Post-release services would help ex-offenders access identification, housing, employment, substance use and mental health treatment, health care, and transportation. These are all requisites necessary to make a satisfactory and legal adjustment to the outside world.

The Leadership Team: Lin Atkins had been the Director of Women's Programs at Hegira, the residential drug treatment program in the City of Roanoke. She joined the TAP training department and was promoted to Director of Rehabilitation Programs. Lin's staff, themselves ex-offenders, were extraordinarily devoted to her. They included Shaheed Omar, who would graduate with both a bachelor's and master's degree while at TAP; Correlli Rasheed, who on his off-hours would help build the local mosque while working with the program; and Cynthia Martin, who was at one time a clothes buyer for a local department store chain but had gone to federal prison for distributing counterfeit currency. Cindy would become the second executive director of the statewide effort.

Packaging the Solution: With the help of Dr. Tom Coffman, Professor of Social Psychology at Roanoke College, TAP published a thirty-six-page white paper called "Going Straight in America" that detailed the cost of crime and criminal relapse. This included the inadequacies of the traditional solutions to reentry (probation and parole, halfway houses, and work release) and proposed a reentry system headed by Virginia community action agencies to deal with the transition shock of coming from a prison culture to an outside world culture. The paper was directed at the Community Services Administration (CSA), the successor to OEO. CSA awarded a planning grant of $106,000 to TAP, guided by an advisory board of twenty-six Virginia community action agencies.

Institutional Commitments: This project depended on the commitment of the twenty-six local community action agencies to work together in spite of the urban, rural, racial, and personality factors that sometimes divide local organizations. These agencies were fully aware of the impact that imprisonment had on the entire family when a member was incarcerated. They were also aware of the reality that those with money got preferential treatment before the bar of justice. Because of the respect that these agencies had garnered with elected state and federal representatives, the community action agencies were important allies. I vividly remember how nervous I was when we presented the project to the Virginia Association of Community Action Agencies, and the elation I experienced when the project was endorsed. Without the support of these important institutions, the project would have been dead in the water.

Though CSA had funded the planning grant, the agency declined to entertain the $3 million implementation proposal. The Office of Demonstrations, a division within CSA, didn't want to tackle a less-than-popular venture. Water and wastewater for hard-working folk was one thing. Money for criminals and ex-cons was an entirely different matter.

Enter Charlie Tisdale. Tisdale had been the executive director of the community action agency in Bridgeport, Connecticut. He had also gone on to be Bridgeport's director of community and economic development, bringing millions of federal dollars into the city. Charlie had come to Washington, DC, after a stint with World Vision in Texas to work with Monsignor Baroni, the head of U.S. Department of Housing and Urban Development's (HUD) Self-Help Program. He was now working for the Carter White House assisting Rosalynn Carter with her Cities and Schools project. I knew Charlie well from meetings with the National Association of Community Action Agencies, at a time when the organization went to court and prevented President Nixon from dismantling OEO.

Charlie Tisdale was an extremely forceful personality with great physical and intellectual presence. An African American, he was built like a boxer and had rugged good looks that could command attention, whether in an executive boardroom or a tough public housing community late at night. Charlie was a straight shooter and not easily intimidated. He understood immediately what we were doing. Without any White House authorization, Tisdale courageously called together representatives of the Department of Labor (DOL), CSA, the Law Enforcement Assistance Administration (LEAA), and the Veterans Administration (VA), and worked out a deal that was signed in the Executive Office Building. Each department pledged their part of a $3 million grant over three years, administered by the Department of Labor, to fund the Virginia CARES network. The deal included the CSA director of demonstration projects who had previously turned the project down.

The Implementation: Virginia CARES was launched in 1980. Pre-release programs were operated in every major Virginia penal institution, and the majority of Virginia community action agencies had new, fully staffed post-release centers. The Virginia CARES

Board of Directors, representing the local agencies, elected Lin Atkins to guide the program as Executive Director.

The Evaluation: Virginia CARES has been evaluated by the Virginia Department of Corrections, comparing those who have received Virginia CARES services with those who have not. Virginia CARES participants show lower rearrest, reconviction, and reincarceration rates than the control group. A more recent two-year study of TAP Virginia CARES clients demonstrates a seven percent relapse rate compared to a 23 percent rate for non-client former inmates over one year. The data also shows that if a person remains out of prison for three years post-release, he or she is not likely to relapse. Although the results were impressive, both of these studies were never published.

The Adaptation: Virginia CARES's first year coincided with the election of Ronald Reagan. The next year, Reagan eliminated the DOL department that funded Virginia CARES and Jesse Jackson's PUSH organization. Lin kept the program alive with a grant of $125,000 from the Virginia General Assembly, with local community action agencies picking up the balance of the funding for local programs. Year after year, the funding increased through the Virginia Department of Criminal Justice Services. Today, Virginia CARES is in a coalition of pre- and post-incarceration service providers and continues to operate 65 percent of the local reentry programs in Virginia with an annual budget of $1.2 million.

Scaling Up and Collective Action: Unlike the Virginia Water Project, which began with a serious federal commitment by the Office of Economic Opportunity and the Farmers Home Administration to establish the Demonstration Water Project, TAP's Stop Gap Jobs was financed by limited resources from a local workforce grant and limited in addressing the full dimension of the problem. TAP leadership knew that a statewide pre- and post-release reentry system was needed for all prisoners across Virginia, since a person imprisoned in far Southwest Virginia might end up being released back home to Tidewater, Virginia—hundreds of miles away. Furthermore, the project had to be big enough to eventually attract state funding. The success of the Virginia Water Project created the relationships among the state's community action agencies that encouraged them to work together on yet another venture. What was even more challenging about this project was that it addressed persons who would elicit less public sympathy than law-abiding rural Virginians whose only crime was to be poor. Hence it was agreed that the planning grant would be overseen by an advisory board of twenty-six Virginia community action agencies to ensure that the project had maximum statewide backing and involvement as early as possible.

The planning grant resulted in a 205-page proposal for a comprehensive reentry system including both pre- and post-incarceration services, operated by local community action agencies and administered by a new statewide corporation, Virginia CARES, Inc. This formed the basis for the agreement that Tisdale forged with DOL, CSA, LEAA, and the VA.

The Comprehensive Health Investment Program (CHIP)

The Need: In 1986, Douglas E. Pierce, a prominent pediatrician in the Roanoke Valley medical community, was concerned about the welfare of poor children in the area. Having grown up in a rural section of eastern Tennessee, Dr. Pierce was well acquainted with poor families who struggled to make it, and he had witnessed the ways the community helped ease their struggles while helping to maintain their dignity. He was concerned with the fact that many pediatricians and family practitioners were limiting the enrollment of Medicaid patients, and that poor children often had nowhere to turn for medical attention other than the hospital emergency department. The emergency room was not geared toward the long-term care of children, nor was it helpful in educating parents about their role in helping their children maintain a healthy lifestyle. It was also extremely expensive. Dr. Pierce approached TAP Founder and Board Chairman Cabell Brand and asked for his help to address this need.

The Solution: At Cabell's suggestion and with the help of TAP staff, a meeting was called at the Hotel Roanoke. Brand and Pierce extended an invitation to local physicians and leaders of the Roanoke City Department of Social Services, the Roanoke City Health Department, and TAP. They first addressed why many local physicians were limiting the admission of new Medicaid patients or simply refusing to take Medicaid patients at all. Prior to the meeting, physicians explained that Medicaid reimbursements were too low to pay the cost of the visit and the medical care rendered. It appeared on the surface to be a matter of dollars and cents. However, after further discussion, it became clear that the problem was not really the Medicaid repayment rates. Medicaid patients frequently did not show up for their appointments, cancelled at the last minute, and more often than not, did not follow the doctor's recommendations or take medication that had been prescribed.

The Leadership Team: Out of that first meeting at Hotel Roanoke, a task force was formed. Dr. Pierce and Cabell Brand served as joint coordinators and held monthly meetings. The superintendent of the Roanoke City Department of Social Services, the director of the Roanoke City Health Department, the leader of the local nursing association, and TAP staff served on the task force. TAP helped facilitate meetings and kept a record of the minutes of each session. The key TAP staff person dedicated full-time to the project was Angie Francis, the wife of an emergency room physician, who served on TAP's planning staff.

Packaging the Solution: After a year of meetings, Angie developed a proposal to the Kellogg Foundation, based on studies of projects across the nation addressing medical services to children of low-income families. The project proposed a three-prong solution:

1. Eligible children age seven or below would have a private-practice medical home of physicians recruited to support the program.
2. A health department nurse would assist in making appointments, which would help spread the client population

and prevent overload on any one practice. The nurse would also prep the family to ask questions to ensure they understood what was being said and help the family in following through on the doctor's advice, including the acquisition of the approved medication.

3. A family service worker would assist the family with non-health issues that might have health implications, which could include transportation, employment, and/or housing issues such as adequate heat during the winter, the presence of lead paint, or conditions that contributed to asthma problems. Virginia Tech was brought on as a program evaluator for the project.

Institutional Commitments: In 1989, the Comprehensive Health Investment Project (CHIP), whose board was initially composed of task force members, received a $1.2 million grant from the Kellogg Foundation. Cabell had been instrumental in making contacts with the medical director of the branch awarding the grant, who was on leave from the faculty of the University of Virginia Medical School. At first, the family service workforce was managed by TAP; however, it became obvious that it was more efficient to have the whole CHIP team managed under one person, so all staff became CHIP employees managed by CHIP's executive director.

The Implementation, Evaluation, and Adaptation: In its twenty-fifth year under the long-term leadership of Executive Director Robin Haldiman and a blue ribbon board of directors, CHIP of Roanoke continues to serve over one thousand children per year with an annual budget of $1,800,000 and an endowment of $1,000,000. Local medical providers now consider CHIP patients, whose cost is still reimbursed by Medicaid, to be among their best. CHIP services have expanded to deal with asthma conditions, application of dental fluoride to children ages three to six months, and mental health issues. Dr. Pierce has received numerous awards for his role as founder. These include The Virginia Chapter of the American Academy of

Pediatricians President's Award, the Humanitarian Award from the National Council of Christians and Jews, and the Medical Society Foundation's Salute to Service Award for service to the poor and uninsured. In 2005, CHIP was one of six finalists for the Monroe E. Trout Premium Cares Award, a national competition that recognizes measureable, innovative solutions for providing health care to the nation's medically underserved.

Scaling Up and Collective Action: CHIP of Roanoke is now the flagship of a network of eight CHIP projects across Virginia, serving twenty-seven jurisdictions supported by a mix of state, foundation, and individual contributions. While CHIP of Roanoke is generously supported by local donations, it is also supported by a state contribution that is targeted through CHIP Virginia, Inc. TAP's experience with both the Virginia Water Project and Virginia CARES, and the collaboration of the collective action of community action agencies across the Commonwealth, were extremely important in building both the advocacy and delivery base for the CHIP project. It is instructive to note that Angie Francis who designed the initial CHIP or Roanoke project would go on to become the first CEO of the statewide entity, CHIP of Virginia, Inc. In the case of CHIP, from the beginning, collective action brought together local physicians, health departments, community action agencies, and departments of social services to support and embrace the program and its goals.

Feeding America Southwest Virginia

The Need: Nothing is more basic than the need for food. The paradox is that in the land of plenty, millions of Americans go hungry each night. This was one of the earliest issues that TAP confronted. I remember TAP community organizer, Shirley White, telling me of how as a little girl going to school without breakfast, she would rub her stomach so that she could overcome hunger pains in order to concentrate on her assignments. The scattering of insufficiently stocked church pantries did not come close to scratching the surface of this problem. Even today over one hundred fifty thousand people in Southwest Virginia struggle with hunger.[25]

The Solution: In its early years, TAP experimented with a number of different initiatives to address the hunger issue. Among these were:

1. The development of food-buying clubs where community members worked together buying in bulk and then sharing the purchases of basic foodstuffs.
2. The distribution of surplus commodities through the local departments of social services.
3. The creation of small food co-ops owned and run by the members.

It was clear than none of these were large enough in scope to distribute the food necessary to meet the demand. In 1981, TAP heard about the food bank movement and proceeded to organize the first region-wide food bank in Southwest Virginia.

The Leadership Team: Pamela Irvine had been hired in TAP's Department of Neighborhood Services as a temporary "work experience" employee with money from a Department of Labor grant. Growing up in a poor, dysfunctional family with a history of interpersonal violence, she knew firsthand about poverty. She knew intimately about hunger as a young mother on public assistance with barely enough to survive, and having to choose between paying a light bill or buying food to feed her family. She felt deeply for others who were in the same condition and faced the same dismal choices.

Packaging the Solution: Pam came back from a conference that talked about the new food bank movement that provided tax credits to food wholesalers and retailers for food they were going to have to throw away. Food banks acted as brokers between those in the food industry and local food pantries, increasing their stock to distribute to those in need in their area. In exchange, the local pantries paid the food bank a greatly reduced price to cover administration,

---

25 Feeding America Southwest Virginia, "Fast Facts for Fiscal Year 2013," https://www.faswva.org/wp-content/uploads/2014/05/Fast_Facts_FY2013.pdf (accessed May 7, 2015).

storage, and distribution costs. It was Pam, supported by Jayne Thomas and Alvin Nash, who led the development of the Southwest Virginia Second Harvest Community Food Bank from the ground up. Beginning with a small warehouse with one loading dock at the TAP building on Shenandoah Avenue, Pam helped expand Second Harvest to its modern complex with multiple loading docks and three tractor-trailers in Salem, Virginia.

Institutional Commitments: To provide oversight of the operation and community support, Pam created the Food Bank Board of Commissioners. Jim Pearman, the owner of Partners in Financial Planning LLC, embodied the same passion to fight hunger. Using his business connections, he brought together business leaders from across the community to assist in the mission to fight hunger. Jim has served as chair of what has become Feeding America Southwest Virginia for the last twenty-four years. He is widely regarded, alongside Pam, as the leader for food justice in Southwest Virginia.

Evaluation and Adaptation: Feeding America Southwest Virginia continues to expand and provide basic nutrition to hundreds of thousands of low-income residents in a twenty-six-county, twelve-thousand-square-mile area, and one hundred fifty-one thousand food-insecure residents.[26] To make things worse, Southwest Virginia also has had high unemployment for decades. "Food insecurity" is "a lack of access to adequate, nutritious food."[27] The food bank works with nearly four hundred food pantries. In 2013, thousands of volunteers (contributing 37,022 volunteer hours) and local organizations distributed almost 20 million pounds of food.[28] Its $3 million annual budget supports a modern, state-of-the-art warehouse, two distribution sites, and forty full-time staff. Pam Irvine chairs the Federation of Virginia Food Banks, composed of the Virginia and

---

26 Ibid.

27 "Hunger and Poverty Fact Sheet," *Feeding America,* http://www.feedingamerica.org/hunger-in-america/impact-of-hunger/hunger-and-poverty/hunger-and-poverty-fact-sheet.html (accessed May 10, 2015).

28 Feeding America Southwest Virginia, "Fast Facts for Fiscal Year 2013," https://www.faswva.org/wp-content/uploads/2014/05/Fast_Facts_FY2013.pdf (accessed May 7, 2015).

Washington, DC, food banks located in ten strategic locations. She is a member of Feeding America national committees, the Business Solutions Council, the Contract Task Force, and is an elected member of the National Advisory Council. In 2014, Feeding America awarded Pamela Irvine the Dick Goebel Public Service Award for outstanding commitment to ending hunger in her community and across the country. In her spare time, Pam received her ministerial ordination and now pastors a small church, Solid Rock Ministries, in her hometown of Covington, Virginia.

Scaling Up and Collective Action: In the case of TAP's fight against hunger, Pam Irvine and Jim Pearman realized that TAP's effort needed to become part of the emerging national food bank movement. TAP could then negotiate with national food chains on behalf of the local food bank organizations. Only through collective action could the local food banks generate the strength to make that connection effectively. Subsequently, TAP's food bank became part of the national Second Harvest Community Food Bank organization, which later became Feeding America, Inc. Over the course of the next three decades, Feeding America Southwest Virginia would create modern distribution sites in Salem and Abingdon, Virginia. As the Food Bank grew, it would be spun off into a separate corporation, with TAP's blessing, with Pam Irvine as its president and CEO and Jim Pearman as its board chair.

The value and impact of many good projects can be increased with a wider application. As shown in this chapter, these projects can be scaled up, increasing their impact and long-term benefit to those in a broader community.

Making Things Happen: Scaling Up and Collective Action Take-Aways

- What projects that you have been involved in would be best served if they were scaled up to address a larger geographic area?

- What collaborations are important to produce the desired impact?
- What associations of other nonprofits can be relied on for helping to scale up the project and bring collaborations that result in additional resources and advocacy to better serve the population that your nonprofit is addressing?
- Is there a way to channel the energy of competing organizations into a collaborative structure in which everyone benefits and the clients are better served?

Profile in Excellence:
Wilma Gene Casey Warren

Wilma Warren, the secretary at Roanoke's West End Elementary School, was the second person hired in 1965 by Bristow Hardin, TAP's first executive director, who had previously been the principal of that school. Wilma, who had grown up in Bridgewater, Virginia, enjoyed being an elementary school secretary. She treasured her connection with the children, parents, and teachers. In addition to working as a secretary, Wilma, whose husband sold insurance for Shenandoah Life, was a suburban housewife with three small children. Previously content with her life, Wilma had a life-changing experience at an Episcopalian retreat and could no longer pursue suburban detachment from the suffering of African Americans and the poor. When Bristow Hardin told her that she was joining him at TAP, she initially balked and then caved to his insistence.

Cabell, TAP's Founder, was dumbfounded by Bristow's suggestion to hire Wilma and said, "Bristow, Wilma's just a secretary." Bristow responded, "I know who she is, and Wilma is who I want." Wilma was an essential part of the team that applied for TAP's first grant and was the first person Bristow consulted on all major decisions. Her personal caring for others, positive demeanor and passion for justice, and sense of the big picture earned her respect from everyone she touched. Wilma would accompany Bristow on all state and national community action meetings and was beloved by all. Years later, when OEO officials were curious about who was who at TAP, the newest member of the team asked, "What is Wilma's role?" The lead representative, Louise Hodeling, who had been involved with TAP since the beginning, said, "Oh, Wilma is Bristow's alter ego." So important had Wilma's role become that Louise mandated that if Bristow did not raise Wilma's salary she would terminate the OEO grant to TAP. Wilma got her raise.

Wilma Warren, the former elementary school secretary, would become Executive Director of the Virginia Water Project, determined to bring water to every rural home in Virginia and the United States. Her leadership resulted in over two hundred thousand low-income rural homes in Virginia receiving access to potable drinking water and sanitary waste disposal.

It was her compelling vision, passion, and ability to speak to the heart that encouraged the other community action agencies whose residents had water and wastewater access needs to support the new project. Immediately, she held workshops with outreach workers from twenty-eight agencies that became part of her dynamic statewide team.

Wilma became well known and respected by the delegates and senators of the Virginia General Assembly, which voted to grant an appropriation of over $100,000 to the new project and contribute millions of dollars more over the lifetime of her leadership. When the program grew into the National Rural Community Assistance Program, Wilma would chair its board of directors.

Wilma never sought a role or position out of personal ego needs, but she loved the title she bestowed upon herself, "Wilma Gene the Water Queen."

Chapter 4:

CREATING A VISION

Where there is no vision, there is no hope.
~ George Washington Carver[29]

Chase the vision, not the money, the money will end up following you.
~ Tony Hsieh, cofounder, Zappos[30]

An absolute key to nonprofit success is the presence of visionary leadership. Visionary leadership involves someone able to see beyond the present to a world that could be, and who has the interpersonal skills to transmit that vision to others and involve them in the visioning process. The person may be on the board of the organization; if so, it is often the board chair or the CEO. I am convinced that Theodore White is correct in his book, *The Making of the President*, that history is not merely led by the events of the time but by individuals who are able to communicate an understanding of the times, a vision for the future, and a pathway into that destiny.

29 "George Washington Carver," *African American Quotes*, http://www.africanamericanquotes. org/george-washington-carver.html (accessed May 8, 2015).

30 Harrison, Kate. "The Best Startup Advice From 14 Tech Heroes," *Forbes*, January 9, 2014, http://www.forbes.com/sites/kateharrison/2014/01/09/the-best-startup-advice-from-14-tech-heroes/ (accessed May 8, 2015).

The presence of a person of vision is the defining factor that separates the good and great nonprofits from those that are at best mediocre. After my more than forty years of nonprofit leadership, I am convinced that it is the essential factor in determining which organizations lead the way in their community and in their particular area of service. Often that person is the founder of the organization. Sometimes it is a new CEO. My good friend Rob Goldsmith, CEO of People, Inc., whose headquarters is in the town of Abingdon in far Southwest Virginia, took over a small ailing agency thirty years ago and made it a powerhouse in housing and economic development. Nothing is truer in our business than the proverb "Where there is no vision, the people perish" (Proverbs 29:18). To me, there is no greater example in my own life of the power of vision than Cabell Brand.

A Businessman with a Mission

By the time of the passage of the Civil Rights Act in 1964, Cabell Brand was forty-one years old. He had already been a military school graduate, World War II veteran, business leader in the Roanoke Valley of Southwest Virginia, and a member of the Roanoke Valley Council of Community Services, a community services planning organization. As a result of his war experience, he had committed to spending 20 percent of his time making the world a better place.

Over six feet tall with a strong, handsome face, polished attire, intense eyes, a warm broad smile, down-to-earth manner, intellectual curiosity, independence, and tremendous confidence, Cabell was a force of nature. No less an attribute was his wife, Shirley, a blond beauty once described as "soft as a cloud and tough as a diamond," who could work a room with grace, making everyone feel as if they were the most important person there—even those on the opposite side of the political spectrum. They were a power couple whose home was frequented by governors and senators.

Cabell had been a cadet at the Virginia Military Institute, class of 1944, when World War II broke out. VMI's commander asked his class to leave school and enlist in the war effort. Most did. Cabell went through basic training twice, first in the Army infantry and then as a member of the Signal Corps. He served in France after the initial American invasion, where he was responsible for ensuring communication between three infantry divisions and headquarters—work that earned him the Bronze Star. Following the war, Cabell served with the State Department as an economic analyst. He saw firsthand the contrast of economic systems between East and West Berlin at the time of the Berlin Airlift. In addition, he witnessed the early development of the Marshall Plan that would rebuild Germany and Japan.

Cabell's tour of service brought him face to face with tyranny, German Nazism, Italian fascism, and Soviet communism. The release of prisoners from Auschwitz imprinted the horror of racism on his conscience in a profound way and gave him a firsthand look at the devastating human and material waste of war as a poor option for solving problems. In addition, the political and governmental efforts of the Marshall Plan revealed the possibility of government playing a vital role in assisting with rebuilding a free-market economy and encouraging the democratic institutions that could lift an entire nation.

Cabell returned to VMI after the war with one hundred other servicemen to complete his degree in engineering, finishing first in his class. He returned to Salem, Virginia, where he turned down a position with the General Electric affiliate in the area and bought the family business, Orthovent Shoe Company, which his father was prepared to dissolve. The company sales at the time were $150,000 with a $2,000 profit. In five years, Cabell had rebuilt the organization, renamed it the Stuart McGuire Company, and transformed the business into a publicly traded, national direct sales company that generated $250,000 a year. Eventually, the search for quality merchandise at the best price would take Cabell all over the world. At the height of business, the company was worth $556 million. Stuart

McGuire was the first American company to import shoes from China. At the end of the century, Cabell would sell his modern order-processing warehouse in Salem to the Home Shopping Network.

Cabell was a compulsive goal setter who established self-imposed benchmarks including five-year plans, one-year plans, and monthly expectations. He followed the same behavior with his business and family. Years later, Wilma Warren, Executive Director of the Virginia Water Project, told him, "Cabell, I can only meet with you every six months. It takes me that long to accomplish your assignments from the previous meeting!"

In 1964, Cabell was in attendance at a monthly meeting of the Council of Community Services of the Roanoke Valley. One of the members came to the board meeting, furious, brandishing a news article about Johnson's War on Poverty and the development of the Economic Opportunity Act that, among other things, was establishing community action agencies across the country. The purveyor of bad tidings described the federal initiative as the "greatest pork barrel waste of money" in US history and asked for an immediate vote against the program and a veto to any such initiative in the Roanoke Valley. Cabell had found himself philosophically and politically at odds with the maker of the motion and persuaded the Council to take some time to study the matter.

Immediately, Cabell contacted Sixth District Congressman Richard Poff and requested a copy of the legislation. He found himself in sympathy with the legislation whose "Findings and Declaration of Purpose" (section two, page 508) states:

> Although the economic well-being and prosperity of the United States have progressed to a level surpassing any achieved in world history, and although these benefits are widely shared throughout the Nation, poverty continues to be the lot of a substantial number of our people. The United States can achieve its full economic and social potential as a nation only if every individual has the opportunity to contribute to the full extent of

his capabilities and to participate in the workings of our society. It is, therefore, the policy of the United States to eliminate the paradox of poverty in the midst of plenty in this Nation by opening to everyone the opportunity for education and training, the opportunity to work, and the opportunity to live in decency and dignity. It is the purpose of this Act to strengthen, support, and coordinate efforts in the furtherance of that policy.[31]

The Economic Opportunity Act of 1964 went on to establish Youth Corps, work training programs, work study programs, urban and rural community action programs, adult basic education programs, voluntary assistance programs for needy children, special programs to combat poverty in rural areas, employment and investment incentives, and work experience programs. The Act was accompanied by companion legislations that established Head Start, Medicare, Medicaid, and community health centers. The timing of the Economic Opportunity Act, its purpose, and the expanse of its program initiatives fit Cabell's vision of making a substantial difference in a manner similar to the Marshall Plan in Europe, in which the government worked with the private sector to strengthen the economy and democracy.

At the next meeting of the council, Cabell suggested that hearings be held in all of the jurisdictions of the Roanoke Valley to assess poverty issues and the level of interest in the formation of a community action agency to address those concerns. The motion passed, and Cabell took six months off from his business to hold those public meetings. The support for a community action initiative was so strong that, at a later meeting of the council, Total Action Against Poverty (TAP's previous name) was launched. For the next thirty years, Cabell would serve as TAP's chairman of the board, representing a seat jointly appointed by the City of Salem and the County of Roanoke, contributing 20

31 Economic Opportunity Act of 1964, Pub. L. No. 88-452, 78 Stat. 508 (1964).

percent of his time to the antipoverty effort in Virginia and around the country.

Cabell gained the donated use of a forty-thousand-square-foot warehouse to house TAP's operations, wrote TAP's first grant for $87,000, and traveled to Washington, DC, to submit the proposal. In the corridor of the new Office of Economic Opportunity, he introduced himself to Sargent Shriver, who invited him into his office. Shriver told Cabell that the new antipoverty organization needed a Head Start program, directed him to visit the new Head Start operations in Chicago and New Haven, and then submit a TAP proposal to establish Head Start in Roanoke. That meeting precipitated a life-long friendship between Cabell and Shriver.

Cabell believed that everyone can make a difference and that in a democracy everyone should have access to the highest levels of government. Wilma Warren, one of the first staff members at TAP, remembers Cabell telling her, "Call the White House and ask for . . ." Wilma was astonished that Cabell thought you could simply call the White House and ask to speak to someone. Nevertheless, she did and the party got on the line and talked with Cabell. Wilma said, "In that instance, I learned the potential power of being a citizen in the United States. I learned what democracy was all about. We are all capable of connecting with the most powerful persons in our government if we only have the nerve and persistence."

When I recently asked Cabell where he learned the science of marketing, he smiled and replied, "In high school I was on the state championship debating team. I won public speaking awards and was editor of the high school newspaper. I guess I am a born salesman." No wonder that Shriver wrote in a note to Cabell, "Had we had four businessmen like yourself we would have won the War on Poverty."[32]

As chairman of the board for thirty years, Cabell's contributions to TAP have been well documented in Edwin Cobb's 1984 book on TAP, *No Cease Fires*, and Beth Brand's 2000 book, *Community Action at*

---

32 Note from Sargent Shriver to Cabell Brand, part of the Cabell Brand Collection, Salem Museum Historical Society.

Work: TAP's Thirty Year War on Poverty. These contributions include but are certainly not limited to:

- An instrumental role in the development of four statewide community action programs: the Virginia Water Project, Virginia CARES, the Comprehensive Health Investment Program (CHIP), and Project Discovery.
- The development of the Shepherd Poverty Program at Washington and Lee University, which has been replicated in twenty-two other universities.
- Maintaining relationships with key contacts within Congress, Virginia's state government, and various foundations (e.g., the Kellogg Foundation, which provided over $1 million to start the CHIP program) to secure funding for TAP and all Virginia community action agencies.
- Acquisition of the Lindsey Robinson building, TAP's first headquarters, and The Crystal Tower building in downtown Roanoke in 1990.

In 1987, Cabell Brand's address "America the Strong" won the Paxton Lecture Competition award as the best Torch Club speech in the nation. In that address, Cabell argued that it is not enough for a nation to have a strong economy and a strong defense. It must have a "strong society" which ". . . is one that not only provides opportunity and the means of success for most of its citizens, but one that provides opportunity and the means of success for all of its citizens. Hence, a strong American society is one that finds a solution to the poverty of a large minority of its citizens, an America free from hunger, homelessness, ignorance, and curable illness." Cabell's address goes on to refute the detractors of the antipoverty effort, and to address solutions that include education and training programs, health care for the poor, targeted programs to special segments such as rural homes without running water, the large number of ex-offenders who will relapse without help, and support for community action, which Cabell describes as having ". . . been at the forefront in offering a cost effective way back to the main track in American society . . . for twenty-six million needy persons in their community . . ."[33]

Cabell's address speaks to the indispensable role of government in this effort:

> The primary question today is "what is the role of government?" No one questions that defense of our nation is a proper role of government. But we have been assaulted with the belief that government is the problem and what is needed is less government. And yet, who is going to build and rebuild roads, the bridges, dams, harbors, water supply systems, sewage systems, and mass transit projects? Who is going to educate our people? Who is going to protect the environment on our beautiful and fragile planet where the water is in danger and the air carries deadly acids? Who is going to protect the poor and the helpless?
>
> It certainly will not be private industry even though there are many things business people and corporations can do to help. Unless funded by someone else, there is no money to eliminate acid rain. There is no money to help the poor to stand on their own feet. The poor have no money. They cannot buy their way out of poverty.[34]

After retiring to the position of TAP board chair emeritus, Cabell opened the Cabell Brand Center, whose mission is to work with local and regional organizations promoting sustainable economic and environmental development. The center's main goals are poverty reduction, water and energy sustainability, and peace through conflict resolution. In 2010, Cabell published a second edition of his book, *If Not Me, Then Who? How You Can Help with Poverty, Economic Opportunity, Education, Healthcare, Environment, Racial Justice and Peace*

---

33 Brand, Cabell. "America the Strong," *The Torch Magazine*, Fall 1987, p. 3.

34 Brand, *America*, p. 4.

Issues in America. The book calls on its readers to pick up the torch and answer the question, "Why are you here?" and seeks to engage others in the struggle to build a better America and a better world.

In recognition of his role as a visionary, over his career Cabell had received a list of awards spanning two pages that includes an Honorary Degree as Doctor of Humane Letters from Roanoke College in May 1997, an Honorary Degree of Doctor of Letters from Washington and Lee University in June 1999, an Honorary Degree as Doctor of Humanities from Ferrum College in June 2005, and an Honorary Degree as Associate in Human Letters from Virginia Western Community College in June 2005. Yet of all the awards he has received, the one that is closest to his heart is an award, given at the Kennedy Center in 1978, for the businessman who had most contributed to helping the poor in America. President Carter, who was to present the award, was called away at the last minute. Instead, the award was presented by the Secretary of the Treasury. Others who were presented awards at the same ceremony for contributions in their fields were John Denver; the trio Peter, Paul and Mary; and the president of the AFL-CIO.

A Vision Begins With Asking the Right Question

Cabell Brand exemplified the power of having a large vision. His commitment to social justice and belief in striving to create a more equal society spanned five decades and spurred the creation of at least three major agencies or initiatives dedicated to furthering those ends. He never stopped learning, never stopped questioning, and never stopped believing that change—while sometimes painfully slow—is indeed possible. Cabell's vision began by his asking what he could do to build a stronger society. It is the task of the nonprofit leader to ask the question or questions that lead to a vision that directs and empowers the organization's work.

Ten years ago, I was invited to address a Radford University MSW (master's of social work) graduate studies class. These were students close to graduation who would one day be leaders in their field. I have a great respect for the social work profession because of the potential of both clients and social workers themselves. Social workers around the world do amazing work rescuing at-risk kids, assisting those who face homelessness, providing comfort and support in old age, and helping low-income families access critical programs like food stamps, Medicaid health coverage, social security disability, and the like. My dear friend, colleague, and collaborator Corinne Gott, Director of the City of Roanoke's Department of Human and Social Services, exemplified the best of the profession. For more than forty years, she was a tireless advocate for the poor, a critic of a society with vastly unequal opportunities, and a defender of the poor against a society too quick to lay all the blame for their impoverishment on their shoulders. She had a clear vision of the kind of society she was working to establish.

Yet, I was also aware that in social work, as in nonprofit leadership, a calling can quickly become a job and a paycheck if you lose sight of why you're here, in this place, at this specific time. Many social workers find themselves dealing with a maze of regulations that change yearly, serving folks with inadequate resources, and over-stressed with the behavior of clients. In some cases they may, in frustration, join the chorus of those who blame the victim, their clients.

The question I posed for discussion to that class of budding social workers was "What kind of world do you want this to be?" The twentieth-century philosopher John Rawls, in his classic work, *A Theory of Justice*, poses the following hypothetical thought exercise: "No one knows his place in society, his class position or social status, nor does anyone know his fortune in the distribution of natural assets and abilities, his intelligence, strength, and the like. [This would of course include race, gender, health, life expectancy, and all things in which we are different from one another.] The principles of justice are chosen behind a veil of ignorance."[35] After a vigorous discussion, I told the class, "Your focus on this question will, more than anything, determine the nature of your career, your experience, and the energy that you are able to give to the people you will help."

The answer to this question indicates the kind of world that you are willing to strive for or settle for. There are many prerequisites for nonprofit organization leadership. Among them are the ability to write well and to speak, the ability to listen and build consensus, a basic understanding of finance, and some supervisory and management experience. However, the most important is a vision of how you want the world to be. That vision is the fire that fuels the passion to make something happen.

Whether we are aware of it, everyone answers John Rawls' question of what kind of world we want this to be even if we don't entertain his thought experiment. The answer to that question determines our vision for the future and informs our view of our place in that vision. The vision that we bring to our role as nonprofit leaders determines our level of passion and the depth of our actions. In fact, frequently you can get a sense of both the answer to the question and a person's vision by their leadership of their organization and role in the broader community.

No vision at all, or too small a vision, is apt to be reflected in the view that nonprofit leadership is basically a job. All we have to do is satisfy our board and maintain modest financial and public support. A larger vision is more likely to inspire behavior that seeks to measure progress on the goals that have been laid out, adapt to better ways of operating, adjust to changes in the needs that present themselves, create a learning community in which there is interaction with the best in the industry, partner and collaborate with others toward making a greater impact, and build an organizational culture that inspires its members to dare to be great. A big vision seeks not only to perform a service but to reform the systems that often create

---

35 Rawls, John. *A Theory of Justice.* (Cambridge, Massachusetts: The Belknap Press of Harvard University Press, 1999), p. 11.

or exacerbate the problems being addressed. A big vision attracts and develops added-value leaders throughout the organization who will go beyond their job description and do whatever it takes to get the job done.

Nonprofit leadership involves realism: sharpening your mission, facing tough decisions, constant evaluation of what you can do and what lies beyond your capacity. Nevertheless, having a big vision of what you are seeking to achieve, even if you play a small part in accomplishing that vision, is empowering. When he came to pastor High Street Baptist Church, the Rev. Dr. Noel C. Taylor was refused service in the dining room of the Hotel Roanoke because of his race. Before his career ended, he served as mayor of the City of Roanoke from 1975 to 1992 and was the most popular elected official in the Roanoke Valley. Dr. Taylor encouraged others to always dream big. "Aim for the heavens," he preached, "and if you fall short, you fall among the stars!"

So, what kind of world do you want it to be and what is your role in that vision?

Creating a Vision Take-Aways

- Who have been the past visionaries for your organization?
- Who are the visionaries currently on your board and staff?
- What is your answer to John Rawls' thought experiment? How does it relate to the work of your organization?
- If you were writing an impact analysis on your organization ten or twenty years from now, what would you want it to say?
- If you were writing your own obituary, what would you want it to say about what you have contributed to your organization?
- What is the long-term impact that you want for the organization you serve?
- What visioning activity could you develop that would create a corporate vision for the future?

Profile in Excellence:
Jeri Rogers

Jeri Rogers, then Jeri Nolan, is characteristic of many talented individuals who have happened on TAP's doorstep where they gained traction for their lives and made an incredible contribution. Jeri grew up in El Paso, Texas. Her father, a World War II pilot and Distinguished Flying Cross recipient, attended Teachers College and became a school principal in an area populated by the Tigua Indians. Jeri's growing experience with Native Americans and Mexican immigrants would help her understand a minority perspective. Jeri gained an appreciation of the arts from her mother, a California show girl who had appeared in movies with Ginger Rogers and Fred Astaire.

Jeri put herself through Texas Western College, graduating with a degree in Political Science. She witnessed Texas Western defeat the top-ranked University of Kentucky all-white basketball team for the NCAA Men's Division I Basketball championship on March 19, 1966—winning 72 to 65 in front of an all-white crowd, including the referees. Texas Western was the first college team ever to start five African Americans in any game. That NCAA championship broke through the color barrier in college sports for all time.

Having tried and outgrown various careers, Jeri was determined to pursue a career in photography and use the camera for social change. She answered TAP's advertisement for a new Director of Women's Programs. TAP had just received a grant to do a study on women's issues and create a Women's Resource Center to empower women, especially poor women, and to provide counseling to those who were involved in abusive relationships. During the interview, Jeri made it clear she didn't want to abandon photography. Bristow Hardin, Jr., then the director of TAP, assured her a grant for her photography if she took the job. She could pursue photography, empower women, and counsel at the same time. It was a dream job she couldn't turn down.

TAP's 1975 Annual Report reported that "In its first year of operation the Women's Center assisted 2,196 women with problems ranging from physical abuse at home to housing, from assertiveness training to getting food stamps; from finding employment to dealing with alcoholism—their own or their partner's or husband's." Under Jeri's leadership, The Women's Center developed the first twenty-four-hour counseling program for women fleeing domestic violence in the Roanoke Valley and—with the help of the Brambleton's Women's Club—the first residential safe haven for victims of domestic violence.

At the end of The Center's first year, TAP co-sponsored a display of Jeri's photographs of Appalachian women in a show entitled "Season of Women: An Exposition of Women" at the Roanoke Fine Arts Center. The exhibit featured portraits of women—young and old, African American and white, urban and rural, privileged and poor—whose common thread was their quiet strength.

Inspired by writing workshops she started in her second year of leading The Women's Center, Jeri launched *Artemis*, a Celebration of Women in the Arts, in 1977. Women from Roanoke and the Southwest Virginia area provided the visual-arts exhibit, food, coffee, poetry, music, drama, and dance for this weeklong Artemis festival. Soon after, the publication *Artemis* hit the stands, the product of a group of writers and visual artists celebrating the work of women. By the third year of publishing its annual issue, the contributors included men after mistaken acceptance of a poetry submission. The expanded journal continued showcasing contributions from area artists and writers, including writer's workshops and gallery shows, until *Artemis* suspended publication in 2000.

Since then, Jeri has established her photography career and expanded her knowledge of visual arts to video and film at Hollins University's Masters of Arts and Liberal Science program. Her thesis led to *Wounded Sky*, a movie documenting the theme of battered women and their recovery. *Wounded Sky* was picked up by public station WBRA and Jeri co-produced the video, which aired on the station.

In 2014, Jeri revived *Artemis* with an eighty-page publication of exceptional beauty. Photographer Sam Krisch was the cover artist. Seventy-seven area artists and writers were featured in the publication, which was dedicated to celebrated poet Nikki Giovanni, whose work is also included. Rave reviews for *Artemis* led to the momentum needed to continue publication, giving voice to artists and writers of the Blue Ridge Mountains and beyond.

Chapter 5:

EXECUTIVE LEADERSHIP

I'm the ultimately responsible person in this organization. Other people can pass the buck to me, but I can't pass the buck to anyone else.

~ Harry S. Truman[36]

The final test of a leader is that he leaves behind him in other men the conviction and the will to carry on.

~ Walter Lippmann[37]

In an organization, leadership is everything. Leadership establishes the organization's reason for being, the seriousness of its mission, the horizon toward which it is moving, its ability to evaluate progress, the norms and values that make up its culture, and its emotional tone.

In his book, *Good to Great*, Jim Collins describes the "Level 5 leader" as someone totally committed to the organization, with low ego needs, who in the darkest periods of the organization's history is able to make the tough decisions and maintain optimism about the future. Collins describes the Level 5 leader as "a study in duality:

---

36 "Quotes from American History," http://faculty.polytechnic.org/gfeldmeth/histquotes.html (accessed May 8, 2015).

37 "Great Leadership Quotes," *Holden Leadership Center*, http://leadership.uoregon.edu/resources/quotes (accessed May 13, 2015).

modest and willful, humble and fearless."[38] In addition, he or she maintains a "ferocious resolve, an almost stoic determination to do whatever needs to be done to make the company great."[39] They "are fanatically driven, infected with an incurable need to produce *results*."[40] "When things are good, the Level 5 leader looks out the window to attribute success to factors other than themselves. When things go poorly, however, [Level 5 leaders] look in the mirror and blame themselves, taking full responsibility."[41] "Level 5 leaders . . . are incredibly ambitious—but their ambition is first and foremost for the institution and not themselves."[42] Level 5 leaders "maintain unwavering faith that [they] can and will prevail in the end, regardless of the difficulties, *AND at the same time* have the discipline to confront the most brutal facts of [their] current reality, whatever they might be."[43] It was my privilege to work under just such a person, the first Executive Director of TAP, Bristow Hardin, Jr. His leadership exuded a confidence that no matter what, the organization would prevail.

Cabell Brand laid the foundation for that confidence. As founder of TAP and its longest-serving board chair, Cabell Brand provided the initial vision and the "big hairy audacious goal"[44] for the organization. In Cabell's mind, TAP was an integral part of a war on poverty, and the object of a war is to win! He was dead serious about the elimination of poverty in this land of plenty, and those of us on the staff fully believed him. We joked about which country Cabell would turn his attention to after eliminating poverty in the United States. As chairman of the board for three decades, he always had a hand in deciding the next skirmish, be it college access for African Americans

---

38 Collins, Jim. *Good to Great: Why Some Companies Make the Leap . . . and Others Don't.* (New York: HarperCollins, 2001), p. 22.

39 Ibid., p. 30.

40 Ibid.

41 Ibid., p. 39.

42 Ibid., p. 21.

43 Ibid., p. 13.

44 Ibid., p. 202.

(whom the newly integrated secondary schools were often failing), or the need for primary health care for children whose only medical access was the emergency room. Adding to his leadership ability, Cabell would often use his contacts as a businessman to help sell a project to a foundation or get a foot in the door with an influential bureaucrat, financial institution, or public official.

After receiving the initial $87,000 grant to get TAP on its feet, Cabell searched for the right person to lead the new organization. Starting a responsible, dynamic, multimillion-dollar organization from scratch in an area where there were not many models had its challenges. Procedures for financial systems, personnel, planning and evaluation, program development, and staff training had to be developed and established.

Roanoke reporter Charlie Cox and his wife, Leila, good friends of Cabell's, told him that he ought to look at a fellow named Bristow Hardin, Jr., who was then the principal at West End Elementary School. Wilma Warren, Bristow's secretary at the school and later his right hand at TAP, loved to recount stories of Bristow as principal of West End. Students knew that the worst thing you could do was to lie to Mr. Hardin. He had a pinwheel on the end of a little stick that, as a student began to lie to him, would magically revolve counterclockwise and only begin a clockwise rotation when the student began to tell the truth. In short order, Bristow was hired as TAP's CEO.

Physically, Bristow Hardin, Jr. was a big man. In later years, adorned with a red beard, he would be mistaken for Burl Ives, the popular folk singer. In addition to an imposing physical presence (to put it lightly), he had a voice like Orson Welles and the same ability to project when he found something funny or irritating. A veteran of the Navy, Bristow was fond of an expressive enlisted man's vocabulary. When he walked into a restaurant or airport, eyes would inevitably turn toward him. He was, as Virginia Delegate Chip Woodrum described, "A mammoth stimulus on the horizon."

Bristow identified with the powerless. Wilma said Bristow, even as principal, never forgot what it was like for a little kid to be cooped up in a classroom. At the end of a long rainy day, he would dash into a classroom and begin a duel with the teacher using long cardboard tubes. The two would leap over desks, dueling up and down the aisles. At the end, he would make the children beg for mercy so that he would not expel the popular teacher from the school. Bristow always kept an arsenal of water pistols in his office (another of his jovial antics), and was known for starting water fights with teachers and staff to help bring laughter to the school. The superintendent of schools told him, "Bristow, every school system needs somebody like you, but only one."

The many bureaucratic techniques often used by other organizations to keep the average citizen at bay irritated Bristow, especially the use of secretaries to screen calls for their bosses. If a TAP manager's secretary made the mistake of asking Bristow his name and reason for his call, the manager had one warning before he was terminated. One day, Bristow placed a phone call to Roland Lafayette, the Washington, DC, leader of the national Head Start program. Mr. Lafayette's secretary asked the caller for his name. Bristow exploded over the phone, "God." The perplexed secretary, suspecting that she must have misheard Bristow, asked if he would spell his name. Bristow boomed, "G-o-d. God!" Nonplussed, the secretary dutifully inquired, "Mr. God, can you tell me the reason for your call?" Bristow replied, "S-e-x. Sex!" That did it. The secretary responded, "Just a minute, Mr. God, I will put you right through to Mr. Lafayette."

From the beginning, Bristow thought big. The first decision made was to write a program that would fund TAP's administration, the Head Start program, and yet-to-be-determined program initiatives. When Cabell suggested a $1,000,000 budget, Bristow said, "Let's go for $2,000,000." He frequently hired others who had served as executives of smaller nonprofits to provide the needed administrative capability to expand TAP's programs.

Bristow also insisted that everyone was responsible for their own behavior. He had little tolerance for whining, excuse-making, and blaming. Everyone was ultimately responsible for their own thoughts, feelings, motivation, and actions. One day I entered his office in a funk, and Bristow asked if he could do anything to help. After complaining that I was not sure what was wrong or what to do to correct it, Bristow exploded, "I'll give you twenty-four hours to figure out what is wrong and find a solution or I'll fire your ass!" The results were amazing. The next day I was on fire with enthusiasm for my life and my job.

A key to Bristow's charm was that he never pretended to be something he wasn't. Indeed, he downplayed his importance. His traditional garb of baggy pants and shirt that hung outside his trousers led visitors to mistake him for the janitor. In addition, he was known as Bristow rather than Mr. Hardin. One day, he was making a collect call from out of town to the TAP switchboard. The long-time receptionist was told by the operator that there was a Mr. Hardin on the line and asked if TAP would accept a collect call. The receptionist replied, "I'm sorry, we don't have a Mr. Hardin here." Over the voice of the long distance operator, Bristow's voice boomed, "Teresa, honey, this is Bristow. Accept the damn call."

Bristow had a great sense of humor. During one radio interview, after describing the work of TAP, the journalist asked Bristow what he did. Bristow paused for a moment and then said, "I am sure you are familiar with organization charts. At the top of any organization is a small box of who's in charge. I fill that box."

"Yes, but what do you do?"

"Why, (stuttering to come up with an answer) I make the big decision and then the big decision comes rolling down the pike. All of Roanoke can be comforted to know that Bristow Hardin Jr. is here to make the big decision."

Bristow also did not pretend to know something he did not know. Apart from an education program, Bristow initially knew that he did not have a clue what it was that TAP should be doing. So he reached out to University Research Corporation to train the non-Head Start staff in how to involve the poor in discerning local needs and addressing them. A team, led by Larry White and John Sabean, trained staff and volunteers to develop local neighborhood community organizations who defined their needs, goals, and strategies, and gave shape to reform efforts in the Roanoke Valley.

Bristow believed in telling the truth. When our first Head Start enrollees were only African Americans, OEO representatives criticized TAP for running a segregated school system. Bristow responded, "We not only admit it but we claim it!" He went on to explain that low-income whites were not used to an integrated school system and that we were not going to run two Head Start Programs, one African American and one white. We intended to run a fully desegregated Head Start program, and he told the officials that we had every confidence that our recruitment efforts would pay off.

In 1968, Bristow was interviewed by a WSLS TV reporter who was tracking down a rumor that an unidentified TAP neighborhood worker was allegedly responsible for a fire bombing incident. Bristow responded that he had fully investigated the allegation and was certain that, unless there was something that had not come to his attention, no staff member was responsible for throwing a firebomb. No one had made, thrown, or taught someone to make or throw a firebomb. It was the TAP strategy to suggest only positive, legal steps to solving a problem. TAP not only did not condone violence, but worked for peace, harmony, love, and justice. The reporter then got down to an issue that he thought had legs, saying, "We are told that TAP hires felons." Bristow responded, "Of course we do. We are in the business of rehabilitation. We require that they have served their time and are on parole. What would you have us do, shoot them or put them on welfare?"[45]

Bristow got along with the press because he was always accessible to them and always told the truth. After Bristow's death at fifty-two,

45 "Bristow Hardin, Jr., Executive Director of Total Action Against Poverty, Defends His Employees Against Accusations That They Are Involved in Fire Bombings," The WSLS-TV News Film Collection, 1951–1971, released September 17, 1968, http://search.lib.virginia.edu/catalog/uva-lib:2220592, (accessed April 22, 2015).

ten years into his work at TAP, *The Roanoke Times* news editor Forrest Landon wrote:

Bristow never hesitated to "use" the press. Unlike most other would-be manipulators he readily acknowledged his purpose. Where others failed in that objective, he succeeded. Why? Because he never lied to a reporter or editor; because he freely admitted blunders, ineptitude, dishonesty, and bureaucratic inertia; because he genuinely cared about the role of the press in a free society; because he demanded intelligence and fairness of the journalist and nothing more.

How was it that a hometown newspaper—one with an editorial-page tradition of political conservatism, hostility to growing centralization of government, skepticism of social welfare programs—openly supported Bristow's objectives? Partly, no doubt, because Roanoke was and is, as Bristow said: a community with a conscience.

Largely, however, it was a personal tribute to Bristow—his honesty, his pragmatism, his openness, his decency.[46]

Bristow was an expert at reading people and handling difficult situations. There was a time when an irate white parent demanded to see Bristow. He was angry because his little girl was sitting next to an African American child and told the secretary he was bringing a gun. Bristow welcomed the man into his office, and the two talked for more than an hour. After the conversation, when the door opened and the two walked out, Bristow's arm was around the man's shoulders. Later when asked what had happened, Bristow said that the man was really worried that his daughter, who was an excellent student, would discover that he could not read or write. That was his real issue.

---

46 Forrest Landon, *The Roanoke Times*, week of June 24th, 1975.

When a group of young African Americans asked Bristow to come to the Black House, a vacant store next to the Lincoln Terrace Public Housing Community that had been converted into a community education center on African American history and issues, to discuss their concerns, Bristow showed up late. One of the young men put a knife to Bristow's throat and demanded that TAP fund their initiatives. Bristow told him that he would not make a commitment but would assign a staff person to work with them. They agreed to meet the next week. The leader, Ivory Morton, who carried a brace of bullets around his chest, remarked about Bristow, "He's the first white man who never lied to me." Bristow helped Ivory continue his schooling and secure a job in Roanoke City Public Schools' maintenance department, where Ivory made it a point to encourage every African American student he encountered, particularly in the elementary schools. Today, the Rev. Ivory Morton is the pastor of the Reed Street Baptist Church in Vinton, Virginia.

While he was pragmatic and did not recommend "making waves" unnecessarily, Bristow was not easily intimidated. Cabell had once arranged for some twenty members of the prestigious Young Presidents Organization, made up of successful business leaders from across the United States, to come to Roanoke for a week-long educational seminar on poverty. To prepare for this seminar, six senior staff members had assembled around Bristow's desk in his office, planning a program that would include: individual luncheon interviews with a woman on Aid to Families with Dependent Children who would tell the business leaders about poverty first hand, participation in a poverty simulation game that I had created, a full-day tour of TAP programs, and a closing discussion.

Suddenly, there was a loud knock on the door to Bristow's office. Bristow had an open door policy, but the rule was that if he did not answer it meant that he was busy and the person wanting his attention should go away and come back at another time. No answer. Knock . . . knock . . . knock . . . knock . . . "All right, you son of a bitch,

if you want to come in so badly slip your ass in under the door,"
Bristow finally said.

The door opened, revealing a clean-shaven, white-haired man in
a business suit and trench coat. When Bristow asked who he was, the
visitor answered, "I am Agent Settles of the FBI, and I am not used to
being treated in such a fashion."

Bristow shrugging apologetically, but with his feet on the desk,
replied, "Well, it happens. What can I do for you?"

"It is imperative that I meet with you on an important matter!"

"Well, I am busy now and don't have time to meet today."

"This is a serious matter of national security."

"I guess I can give you ten minutes," Bristow said.

The rest of us were glad to get out of the room. Rumors were that
there were FBI files on all antipoverty workers.

After Agent Settles had laid out the evidence that TAP was in the
business of starting a Black Panther organization with federal funds,
Bristow sent the following letter to J. Edgar Hoover of the FBI:

> *Dear Mr. Hoover: Agent Settles has accused TAP of starting
> a Black Panther organization with federal funds. The evidence
> is an endorsed TAP check for $11.87 for some Black Panther
> literature. I would like to assure you that if we are involved in
> such an undertaking this will be the most cost effective Black
> Panther organization in the country costing only eleven dollars
> and eighty seven cents. I am hereby recommending Agent
> Settles for early retirement.*

There was no reply.

Bristow relished the experience of being alive. Early on in my
career at TAP, Bristow's usual travel companion, Wilma Warren,
had declined to go with him to a community action conference on
the West Coast. When I volunteered, Bristow explained to me that
I could go if I agreed to take some vacation time and pay my own

expenses to take a one-week trip with him to Mexico first. Bristow, who made sure to maximize the full value of a business trip by tying it to an experience to live life fully, once sent Manpower Director Al Hill to an employment conference in Florida because he knew that Al loved to fish. He was disappointed to hear that Al had spent morning, afternoon, and evening in seminar meetings. Bristow, with exaggerated disapproval, exploded, "Well, Al, that's the last damn time I send you to a Florida conference. Man, get your priorities straight!"

I desperately wanted to understand what he knew about people, organizations, the use of power, and dealing with conflict. I had long ago decided that Bristow was my equivalent of a PhD education, and I enthusiastically made travel plans. For the next week we traveled throughout Mexico, ending up in Oaxaca, a place that Bristow referred to as "Ox-tale." On the second evening of our stay in Acapulco, I persuaded Bristow to leave the comfort of the air-conditioned hotel. He suggested a bullfight held in the local stadium.

Now, a bullfight, despite Ernest Hemingway's glorification of its savagery in his *Death in the Afternoon,* is a rather depressingly brutish exhibition of man's power over nature. The bull is psychologically stressed by the matador's cape, which holds no target. The muscles in his neck are pierced and torn by the picadors' lances, which remain embedded in the bull. The majestic animal is confused by the yelling in the stadium and physically fatigued by exertion and loses focus. The matador then seeks permission to kill the bull and slays it by coming over its head, embedding his sword between the animal's shoulder blades, and piercing the bull's heart.

The first three bulls went through the customary ritual and were summarily dispatched. Each time, a rope was lassoed around the horns of the dead animal, which was dragged by a horse out of the ring. It was another matter with the fourth bull. On one of the passes, the bull dodged the matador's cape and caught the matador around the leg and rolled him across the stadium. Bristow, twice the size of the average Mexican there, was immediately on his feet, screaming,

"Bravo, El Toro! Bravo, El Toro, Ole!" Fans across the stadium stared perplexed at this drama developing in the stands. Having just finished *The Ugly American,* I tried to dissociate myself from Bristow by turning away.

The matador brushed himself off and resumed his trade. Again, the bull caught him around the leg and rolled him to the other side of the ring. Bristow was on his feet with a tirade of approbation for the bull. To my astonishment, fans across the stadium began to stand and yell for the bull. Sensing that things were getting out of hand, the matador signaled the judges to be allowed to slay the bull and regain his dignity. Permission was granted, much to the objection of Bristow and his followers who were now imitating Bristow's two-handed, thumbs-down gesture. By now I felt it safe to join and was on my feet. However, when the matador's sword attempt hit shoulder bone, the sword bent like a toothpick and bounced across the stadium floor. Bristow had the crowd on its feet in a tumult of derision for the matador and praise for the bull. When the humbled matador again asked permission from the judges for another kill attempt, everyone was on their feet screaming at the top of their lungs and displaying the thumbs-down gesture. That was the day that Bristow Hardin Jr. saved the bull in Acapulco.

Wilma said that Bristow loved to recite a poem entitled "Awaken," (written in the late 1700s by Lawrence Tribble) that spelled out Bristow's philosophy of change: "One man awake, awakens another. The second awakens his next door brother. The three awake can rouse a town by turning the whole place upside down. The many awake can cause such a fuss it finally awakens the rest of us. One man up with dawn in his eyes surely then multiplies."

I saw it happen in Acapulco.

Bristow Hardin had a profound optimism about TAP and its mission. That optimism was fed by a dual conviction in American fairness and his deep Christian faith. When the community action honeymoon of the sixties came to an end, and the backlash to the civil rights and antipoverty movements gained traction, accompanied by deep budget cuts, Bristow held tight to the conviction that TAP would not only survive but "survive gloriously!"

Among his academic achievements, Bristow had earned a Master's of Fine Arts from the University of Texas. He was also an actor and had originally come to Roanoke in 1954 to be the radio and TV coordinator for Roanoke City Schools. For many summers, he was part of the cast of the outdoor theater production of *The Common Glory*, produced in Tidewater, Virginia. It was from the live theater that many of his management principles were taken. Heading the list of those admonitions were:

The play's the thing! Nothing was more important than the end product, the reason for being. In the theater, it was the performance. At TAP, it was our mission to side with the poor in their effort to extricate themselves from poverty. We were there to side with the single mother, the family who had no running water, the ex-offender trying to get on his feet, the resident of slum rental housing, the unemployed without job skills.

No shoddy performances! Excellence was the only acceptable standard. In the theater, it meant perfection each and every night. At TAP, it meant going the extra mile to make sure that there was real positive impact on the low-income individuals, families, and communities for which we were responsible.

No prima donnas! On the stage, it was the responsibility of each actor to do her best and to work in concert with the other actors to put on their best performance. At TAP, there was no room for showboating and undercutting another staff person in order to promote oneself. At the end of a theatrical performance, everyone bows together.

There can only be one director! At TAP, as in the theater, all suggestions were encouraged. However, when a decision had to be made, the director had to make it. The other members of the team were expected to support that decision. The executive would either spend his or her time struggling for control, or establish control and be able to share that power and authority with talented leadership. Bristow did not intend to struggle for control. Bristow made that clear when he told Cabell, "You run the board and I'll run the staff." Those two decisions created TAP's organizational framework. There would be a clear division of leadership responsibility between the founder and chairman of the board and the new executive. To Cabell's enormous credit, he did not fall prey to the founder's syndrome[47] that encourages overreach into staff decisions and prevents his exit at an appropriate time.

The decision of who was to do staff hiring was reinforced when Bristow told Cabell he was going to hire Wilma Warren, his school secretary at West End Elementary School, as his top assistant. Cabell was incredulous. Wilma started the following week.

The principle that there can only be one director would be challenged. It would be tested when the director of training and her assistant organized a coup on the grounds that Bristow was not deemed serious enough about the War on Poverty. Frustrated that the overthrow never materialized, the exhausted proponents left for other jobs. When the leadership in the planning department thought that Nixon would kill community action, they designed a separate project, a group foster home called Tree House, under a separate corporation as a lifeboat for themselves. All who were involved were invited to leave. Bristow knew that to share power you had to maintain it. There could only be one director.

At all costs, avoid unnecessary bureaucracy! Bristow's style of management was one of confidence. He said that if you had to choose between over-management and under-management, it was always better to choose under-management. His trick was to choose capable people and let them do the job without micromanaging. Bristow had been annoyed before by the bureaucracy of the public school systems, which centralized all hiring in a single personnel department, restricting a principal's ability to hire his own staff. Bristow wanted all positions to be hired by the supervisor at the lowest possible level.

---

47 Jowdy, Jeff. "9 Ways for Nonprofits to Overcome 'Founder's Syndrome'," Fundraising Success, January 30, 2013, http://www.fundraisingsuccessmag.com/article/9-ways-nonprofits-overcome-founders-syndrome/1 (accessed March 29, 2015).

Likewise, the purchasing of office supplies should not be tied up through a cumbersome system of authorization upon authorization. He had no patience for dealing with unimportant issues. One day, while still working for the school system, he interrupted a principal's meeting with the suggestion that they immediately turn their attention to the paramount issue of whether the cafeteria should serve chocolate or vanilla ice cream.

Bristow had sometimes described his management style as a "beneficent dictatorship." It was no democracy. His was best described as a "consultative" leadership style. On most issues of substance, he solicited and received input from the widest number of persons involved. He encouraged vigorous debate and expression of opinions among the strong-minded staff that he had hired. However, once everyone had given their best arguments, he reserved the right to make the decision and expected everyone to fall in behind the position he had taken.

During this tumultuous period of history, as the forces of change were confronted by the forces of reaction, the future of the antipoverty movement, community action, and the TAP organization were by no means certain. Indeed, well before President Nixon tried to dismantle the Office of Economic Opportunity and support for more than a thousand local community action agencies, there were public outcries against the community action movement. In spite of the uncertainty, Bristow had a deep sense that in siding with the poor to bring opportunity and fairness, TAP was on the right side of history and would prevail. Not only did he not join others in worry and handwringing, but he insisted that TAP's future was secure. I remember introducing Lin Atkins (who had just joined my training staff) to Bristow as he passed by in the hallway. I explained who Lin was and said that she was a little worried that TAP might go under and she would lose her job. Bristow drew close to her, backing her up against a wall and bellowed, "Are you after my job? It's my job to see TAP survives, not yours!" and then stormed down the hall with a smile on his face.

Bristow died in the early summer of 1975. The following article was written in *The Roanoke Times* (then called *The Roanoke Times And World News*) on June 24th:

Bristow Hardin, who left his imprint on the valley's Total Action Against Poverty with all the heft, personality and passion he could muster appropriately left a huge legacy: the lesson that people come first.

He learned, in the first few months with TAP, that no administrative text-book, no set of managerial principles, no "helpful hints" would do him much good in his search for a solid program for the valley's poor. So he flew by the seat of his ample, baggy pants: cajoling, blustering, demanding loyalty from those under him and earning begrudging admiration from those who had dealings with TAP of those early days.

But always, people came first: the poor, because they had been on the "outs" so long that they needed far more than money alone; businessmen, because their support gave the program a local impetus that all the federal money couldn't provide; TAP workers, because their devotion alone could turn a potential bureaucratic jumble into a believable instrument.

TAP has always had to both discover and toe that fine line between success with the poor and "respectability" with the rest of the population; Bristow Hardin may well have been the only one willing to play that kind of game.

Another administrator, perhaps with more raw administrative talent and less dramatic flair and determination, would have quit out of sheer exasperation or exhaustion. A slick, public-relations type might have scored well among the affluent, but would have bombed among [African Americans].

Anyone less than a person with a mission—and that is what TAP was for Bristow Hardin—would have turned the organization into a perfectly proper efficient, "model" antipoverty agency . . . that wouldn't have accomplished a thing.

He was outlandish, bumptious, controversial and idealistic; but he was also pragmatic and ingratiating. If he was the center of TAP, life—throbbing and teeming— was at his center. What TAP will need to replace him is not just a head, but a heart.[48]

In the estimation of the TAP organization, especially those closest to him, Bristow was a giant. To be sure, he was a flawed giant. The fact that he admitted it made him all the more loveable and sometimes frustrating. Planning Director Jim Stamper would say, "Bristow thinks that just because he admits he's a bastard it is all right to act like one. I could go off sailing in the middle of the week if I had someone like me to do the work!" His attention span was short lived and his attention to detail was sporadic. However, in a world of dramatic change, the backlash to the Civil Rights and Great Society programs, criticism of the excesses of the community action movement and financial uncertainty, Bristow was the high seas captain who could successfully navigate during periods of gale winds and avoid the shoals of disaster. Suddenly, the unthinkable had happened. Bristow had died.

In hindsight, it is obvious that Bristow Hardin Jr. was the right person to lead the organization in the 1960s. He was a man who realized that we were at historic societal crossroads. The 1954 Supreme Court decision and the Civil Rights legislation of the 1960s marked a point from which there was ultimately no turning back. In addition, the Great Society legislation further extended the New Deal legislation of the 1940s, reaching out to include those who were not embraced by American postwar prosperity.

Bristow had left the relative comfort and security of a job as a

---

48 Editorial, *Roanoke World News*, "Bristow Hardin: Lesson in Living," June 24, 1975.

public school principal to take on a new agency, positioned at the forefront of change, whose future was precarious. He combined a lack of pretense about needing to have all the answers with the courage to tell the truth to the press or to an African American radical who put a knife to his throat. When the young women of the African American Hollins Community decided to picket the local newspaper over the newspaper's refusal to put the pictures of African American brides on the social pages, Bristow's phone rang off the hook from community leaders and clergy urging him to call off the picket, which might lead to social disorder. Bristow replied that it was not his decision to make and that TAP encouraged local community leaders to identify areas of concern and take action. He then joined the march. He had a keen eye for talent and attracted the best. He loathed bureaucracy, could live amidst uncertainty and disorder as TAP tried to gain its footing, and never made an enemy unnecessarily.

Cabell Brand would become the standard by which all community action agency founders would be measured. Yet, had it not been for Bristow, the history of TAP would have taken a very different turn.

After Bristow's death, Cabell Brand called all of the TAP staff together and gave his assurance that the work of TAP was just beginning. In Bristow's words, we would not only survive but "survive gloriously." Under Cabell's lead, the TAP board posted the job, did a national search, and held interviews.

After a series of interviews, I was chosen by the board of directors to succeed Bristow. Clearly, I was no Bristow Hardin, Jr. No one took notice as I entered a restaurant or walked through an airport. A "mammoth stimulus on the horizon" I was not. However, during his last ten years I had learned a great deal from Bristow and his dealings with people that we were exposed to during his life, and I believed deeply in our mission. Although I had flirted with a couple of other opportunities, working for TAP and Bristow was a powerful magnet that quickly pulled me back. I was deeply humbled by the offer from the board of directors and have never in the last forty years aspired to anything else. Any other position would have been a demotion.

Bristow's Influence in a Post-Bristow Era

Great leadership creates a culture of values. Without values, when principled leaders and staff leave, the organization falls apart. The lessons that I had learned under Bristow ("The play's the thing!" "No shoddy performances!" "No prima donnas!" "There can only be one director!" "At all costs, avoid unnecessary bureaucracy!" "We would not only survive but 'survive gloriously!'") would be my management guide. Over the next forty years, there would also be some changes. There would be increased organizational discipline. TAP would develop strategic plans. We would cease to emphasize programs that maintained people in poverty through emergency assistance and focus on programs that provided a way out of poverty. TAP would increase its areas of influence and program development in the realms of education and career development, affordable housing and community development, and business and economic development. The budget would grow from $6.5 million to $20 million. Staff sophistication in the areas of finance, personnel, and planning would evolve tremendously. We would adapt to the growing world of technology. TAP programs would implement evidence-based practices in all fields of endeavor, from Head Start to homeless initiatives. Three new state projects would be piloted and then developed statewide.

I would follow Bristow's lead to avoid bureaucracy and micromanagement, choose highly self-motivated staff willing to learn and get the job done, and give them the authority to do so. I also made sure each program area worked as a small business responsible for program development, funding, and evaluation. Although each component must work together and within an overall agency framework, they were led by persons with an entrepreneurial spirit and energy.

Above all, Bristow was always on message, and we have carried on believing we should, above all, remember the mission. We work for the poor. Every day it is our job to help them build a future for themselves and their families. We have no other reason for being.

Until I retired at the end of January 2015, I had a framed picture over my work desk of Bristow Hardin Jr. looking down on me, reminding me of my responsibility to carry on his legacy of leadership over the agency that he loved and was devoted to. In April 2015, the TAP Board of Directors chose Annette Lewis, a veteran of the organization, to carry on that legacy and ensure the agency was in excellent hands. I believe Bristow would have been greatly pleased with that decision. I question whether my leadership has consistently matched the Level 5 category over the last four decades. I am sure I have fallen short on many occasions. Nevertheless, I agree with the conclusions of Collins's research team: "Whether or not we make it all the way to Level 5, it is worth the effort. For like all basic truths about what is best in human beings, when we catch a glimpse of that truth, we know that our own lives and all we touch will be the better for the effort."[49] I would never have accomplished what I have done without the experience of knowing and working for Bristow Hardin Jr.

Executive Leadership Take-Aways

- Does the CEO of the organization: Embrace the characteristics of a Level 5 leader? Have absolute commitment to the mission of the organization? Show a long-term commitment of service to the agency? Display a continual attitude of optimism toward the future of the organization? Boast a proven record of hiring and developing leaders in the organization? Have the ability to adjust to a changing environment?
- Where do you stand on Bristow's core organization principles (The play's the thing, No shoddy performances, No prima donnas, After much input there can only be one director,

---

49 Collins, *Good to Great*, p. 38.

Under-management is preferable to over-management if there has to be a choice)?

- What can you do to be more of a Level 5 leader and pave the way for a Level 5 successor?
- Is there a clear division in your organization between the policy role of the board and the executive role in administering that policy, including responsibility for staff?
- Does the personnel policy give the CEO the necessary authority to discipline staff and reorganize staff positions in order to carry out the mission of the organization?
- Does the CEO hire others who, because of their work, become respected leaders in the community?
- Does the CEO create the opportunities for full input on important decisions affecting the organization?

Profile in Excellence:
Annette Lewis

Upon the announcement of my resignation as TAP CEO in 2014, Annette Lewis was named the President and CEO of TAP by the board of directors on the recommendation of an executive search committee. Annette Lewis is a statuesque African American woman known for her tasteful changes in hairstyles as the notion hits her. Her sharp eyes and strong face belie a deep intelligence, confidence, and integrity. She is warm and engaging, has a commanding personal presence, and inspires respect. Annette approaches issues with an open mind and without a hidden agenda. She is a keen judge of character and her laughter is infectious. Annette is the kind of person of whom it is said, "If you can't get along with her, it is a good sign that you have a problem." She speaks with authority.

Annette grew up in Dallas, Texas, and earned a BS in Social Work from West Texas State University. She migrated to Roanoke with her husband, Lee, who is the beloved pastor of Morning Star Baptist Church. After working as an underwriting unit manager for Allstate Insurance Company, she began work with TAP Youth Services as a youth counselor and GED instructor. In 1992, Annette supervised all of the family services and parent involvement staff for TAP's Head Start program.

In 1993, TAP expanded its education and career development program to young people and adults. Annette became the program architect for This Valley Works, which supports premier education and employment programs in the Roanoke Valley. Program participants include secondary school dropouts, GED students, middle and high school low-income students who will be first in their family to attend college, out-of-work veterans, ex-offenders just released from prison, estranged fathers seeking to reconnect and engage with their children, women escaping domestic violence, and those seeking a Certified Nursing Assistant certification.

Annette has also functioned as the COO of TAP, in her capacity as vice president of Program Coordination. When there have been management failures in other programs, Annette has taken them under her wing, where they have thrived. In addition, she has served as state director of five Center for Employment Training programs across the Commonwealth. She is well known and respected in the Virginia General Assembly. In the absence of the TAP president, Annette had assumed all responsibility for the TAP organization.

Annette has a strong leadership presence in the Roanoke community where she has coordinated the Southwestern Virginia Regional Job Fair for the past eleven years and co-coordinated the Southwestern Virginia Education Classic for thirteen years, bringing attention to the dropout issue and raising money for dropout retrieval. She has led the Walk-a-Mile event, which pairs local legislators with recipients on public assistance and asks legislators to live on a welfare food budget for a week. She also serves on the Roanoke City School Board, the Higher Education Board of Authority, the Virginia Tech School of Medicine Community and Diversity Board, and is a lifetime member of the NAACP. Annette has been the recipient of numerous awards, including the 2013 Workforce Development Professional of the Year, the 2009 YWCA Woman of Achievement Award in Business, and an honorary doctorate from Bethlehem Bible College.

Annette Lewis is a woman of deep religious faith that infuses her with a sense of confidence and hope as well as respect for others and fair play. She is a fighter and a survivor. In her personal fight against cancer and in her professional fight to expand the programs under her purview, she is unrelenting. She is an embodiment of the quote at the end of her emails that she attributes to her daughter Patrice: "I choose to love. I choose to communicate. I choose not to quickly pass judgment. I choose to hope. I choose to find solutions. I choose to help others regardless of their differences from me. I choose to be part of positive change. I choose to forgive. I choose to dream. I choose to believe. Who will join me?" Annette has already proven herself to be a Level 5 leader.

Chapter 6:

BOARDS OF DIRECTORS

Governance and leadership are the yin and the yang of successful organi[z]ations. If you have leadership without governance you risk tyranny, fraud and personal fiefdoms. If you have governance without leadership you risk atrophy, bureaucracy and indifference.

~ Mark Goyder[50]

The fiduciary agent of any nonprofit organization is its board of directors. An organization is only as good as the quality of its board. The quality of board leadership, members' commitment to the organization, the experience and skills that they bring to their service, their willingness to make external contacts for the agency, the seriousness with which they take their responsibilities on board committees and the board as a whole, their commitment to the people the organization serves, and their ability to work together all vitally affect the future of the organization.

There are two major functions in an organization: The setting of policy and the execution of that policy. The task of the board is to set policies that include but are not limited to the mission, budget, work

50 Corporate Governance Quotes," http://www.corporate-governance.co.za/Home/ CorporateGovernanceQuotes/tabid/148/Default.aspx (accessed May 8, 2015).

plan, financial operation (budget reporting and oversight, audits, and the operations manual), and personnel policy. It is the task of the executive to carry out the policies of the board of directors, including the hiring and management of staff and coordination of volunteers.

This chapter covers all major aspects of an outstanding board of directors, including:

1. The importance of strong boards
2. The necessity of business community involvement
3. Board organization and commitment
4. Selection of a board attorney
5. Ensuring board involvement
6. CEO selection and contract
7. Boards of commissioners
8. Strategic planning
9. Board training
10. Reunions of past board chairs

The Importance of Strong Boards

There are really only two kinds of organizations: Those with weak boards and weak executives and those with strong boards and strong executives.

Some executives may appear to be strong, taking charge of the entire operation, assisted by a weak, rubber-stamp board. A very large organization in Virginia experienced just such a crisis when its executive stayed past her prime and lost touch with the organization. The organization then had an overspending crisis and had its largest program taken away, damaging the budget, program, and reputation of the organization. The prominent executive, though she appeared strong, was weak and shortchanged the organization by not helping to recruit strong board leadership with fiscal and management expertise.

Likewise, some boards that are actually weak may appear strong when they begin to usurp executive functions and assume day-to-day management of the organization, including the hiring and promotion of staff. This often happens after failed executive leadership. A weak board that was previously asleep at the wheel, not asking questions that would have yielded information that might have helped prevent the collapse of finances, programs, and reputation, then decides to take over and run the entire operation.

My experience is that weak boards hire weak executives, and weak executives perpetuate weak boards that will not call them into question. Likewise, strong boards hire strong executives, and strong executives help to recruit strong board members who are fully engaged in helping to formulate policy and ensure that the executive properly carries them out.

The TAP organization, which I have served for four decades, began with a strong board chair, its founder, Cabell Brand. A distinctive feature of a community action agency board is its diversity. Drawing from all segments of the community helps to enlarge the view of all members of the board and dispel stereotypes that perpetuate problems and prevent solutions. TAP's board, like all community action agencies, is made up of representatives from all of the local governments in its service area, poor communities, and the civic and business communities.

I have been proud to work with TAP board members who have been influential leaders in the greater community. Some are unforgettable. Georgia Meadows was a six-foot-one-inch-tall African American woman who represented the Botetourt Improvement Association. She had been a reading teacher in Botetourt County Public Schools for four decades. She completed all of her course work for her PhD, but because of racial jealousy was denied a leave of absence with assurance that she could continue in her job. At the time no one else in the recently desegregated school system had a PhD, and few, if any, (besides Mrs. Meadows) held a master's degree. Even during segregation, she had instilled optimism in her students of what they could become. At a ceremony celebrating her leadership, one successful businessman who had been her student apologized to her that he had let her down. The reason? He had not yet been elected President of the United States!

At a county board of supervisors meeting, Georgia requested a contribution to a senior citizen transportation project. When a local plant owner objected to the request based on his notion that the use of government money just encouraged idleness and dependency, she rose to her full height, thanked the gentleman for his concerns for seniors, and asked him for a private donation to the cause. When a representative from the Virginia Department of Transportation arrived at her home to tell her that VDOT was considering taking a second parcel of her land, she went into her house and reappeared with her shotgun, sending a message to his supervisor to reflect on whether he wanted to be buried on the same patch of land. Ms. Meadows was exactly the type of person we needed on the TAP Board of Directors: intelligent, strong, an advocate for our clients, and not afraid to challenge leadership by asking hard questions and demanding satisfactory answers.

Brenda Hale is another one of those larger-than-life leaders who has served on the TAP Board. A veteran Army nurse retiring as a Sergeant First Class, she has held numerous leadership positions including secretary for the Virginia State Board of Nursing and member of the Jefferson College of Health Sciences Board of Directors. Ms. Hale has been the dynamic executive director of the Roanoke Chapter of the NAACP for more than a decade, combining a zeal for justice with the ability to work well with others for change. She possesses an incredible will, reflected not only in her work, but her ability to emerge from three bouts of life-threatening illness after months of rehabilitation. As soon as she has emerged from rehabilitation she is back on her walker or motorized scooter, never missing an important meeting or appointment. She is tireless in her insistence that TAP keep its focus on its mission to this day. Always willing to listen, she is just as intent on asking critical questions about the organization's operations. Her leadership has attracted support from many quarters.

The Necessity of Business Community Involvement

Cabell's strong role in the business community meant that, from the beginning, TAP would recruit members of the business community whose board service could be relied on to ensure an involved and well-rounded board of directors. Cabell served in that capacity for the first thirty years of TAP's history. After that, I have made it a priority to work with the board to continue to involve strong leadership from the business community as well.

Cabell's commitment to the agency had no equal in terms of long-term commitment. The next chair, Ted Feinour, partner of a prominent investment firm and former chair of the Roanoke City School Board, agreed to a two-year term. Of the following eight chairs, all have been members of the business community with the exception of one prominent community leader. In addition to knowing how to run a strong board organization and meetings, all have brokered contacts and connections with other leaders in the community, including important public officials in local, state, and federal government. Their business backgrounds have brought strong knowledge in the areas of finance, law, development, and construction, all of which have been important to TAP and its undertakings. Furthermore, their involvement in the organization has further enhanced our reputation throughout the community. When you are an $18 million dollar corporation, nonprofit or not, you are most definitely a business. A perfect place to recognize that fact is in the selection of board members.

I can think of two major instances in the past five years alone that underscore the importance of business acumen in board leadership. After the financial crash hit with full force in 2009, TAP found itself with an eight-story office building that was bleeding money and a $30 million apartment complex that was piling up construction loan debt without a closing date in sight. John Williamson, then the CEO of Roanoke Gas Company and one of the most respected businessmen in Southwest Virginia, was TAP's board chair. Before heading up the gas company, John had served as county administrator for Nelson and Botetourt Counties. He was well acquainted with the ins and outs of local government. His steady hand led us through the financial maze of competing interests that included bankers, lawyers, investors, and tax credit syndicators (those who broker tax credits so investors can put up equity) that allowed the organization to emerge successfully from those financial straits.

Lee Wilhelm retired in September of 2014 as the most recent TAP board chair. Lee is a prominent business leader who has been in the construction industry. In addition to his previous service as Vice President of Turner Construction Company, a major construction firm in the area, Lee owns his own company specializing in green roofing and also manages facility development for a large Salem, Virginia, nursing home. Lee has served in a leadership position on many prominent Roanoke-area nonprofit organizations, including the Roanoke Council of Community Services, a large inner-city YMCA, the Roanoke Chamber of Commerce, and the Roanoke Valley Convention and Visitor's Bureau. Three years ago, he was awarded the prestigious Citizen of the Year award by the City of Roanoke. Lee has led the TAP Board in making judicious financial decisions that have strengthened our bottom line and brought sound advice to many property matters, reducing the number of properties that were losing money without abandoning other promising construction opportunities.

The one difficulty in drawing from business talent in the community is the danger of a conflict of interest. Sometimes a business is given preferential treatment because of its representative's position on the board. However, if the mere presence of a business representative denotes a conflict of interest, you could never have someone representing a major utility on the board. In many communities, it might limit participation from a banker, attorney, builder, or architect. To allow for participation of influential business leaders and avoid a conflict of interest, the bylaws must require a board member to indicate where they have a conflict of interest and refrain from speaking or voting on the matter.

Board Organization and Commitment

Any way you cut it, serving on a nonprofit board, if it is done well, requires a time commitment. From my experience, that means a monthly board meeting to deal with an organization's business. At a minimum, a well-run meeting will review the minutes from the previous meeting, include decision items brought by the board committees, discuss areas needing board input, and present reports from the CEO and appointed staff. The decision agenda should always include reports and recommendations from the major board committees.

A strong board of directors will always have a strong committee system. Since accounting for money is always a key issue, a finance committee is imperative. The finance committee's job is to stay on top of expenditures, hire an auditor and receive the audit report, ensure positive cash flow, authorize and monitor necessary lines of credit, and build a financial base that guarantees—at a minimum—three months of wages, benefits, taxes, and nonpersonnel costs. It is important to note that no two auditors are alike. While money is always important, it is often better to pay a little more to get the most thorough auditor who will present a full report on management weakness as well as compliance. I know of one auditor whose failure to properly fill out an agency's IRS 990 report (which is like a nonprofit's tax return) triggered an unnecessary IRS audit that consumed almost a month of management time even though there were no findings.

Also important are a property committee, especially if property ownership is involved, and a human resource committee that governs policy in those important areas. In addition, the board should have standing committees on the bylaws, membership, and marketing. To ensure board diligence, I recommend quarterly meetings of an executive committee that includes officers of the corporation, the immediate past chair, and heads of all standing committees of the organization. The executive committee thus formed constitutes the board leadership team of the organization. From time to time, an extended executive committee meeting with invitations to other board members can serve as a board retreat, giving time for more long-term planning.

Ensuring Board Involvement

At TAP, the board of directors meets monthly, with the exception of February, when it predictably snows in our area, and August, when folks are most likely to take vacations. During February and August, the executive committee meets to take care of the business of the organization. Most people do their life planning on a monthly calendar. I have found that holding board meetings every two months or quarterly will result in board disengagement and, ultimately, a weak board.

In most cases, a well-organized board meeting can accomplish all that has to be done in an hour. Meetings should last an hour and a half at most, unless a crisis requires more time. On the other hand, start a meeting with no time limit and people will find a way to fill up the time. The best definition of hell is a committee without a chair and no adjournment in sight.

Board members should also be informed. The more they know about the organization's work, the better. A popular first item in the TAP board agenda is hearing from a program participant who has succeeded in improving their life and that of their family through the opportunity afforded them by the organization. Another strategy that has worked well is to have the board divide itself into teams corresponding to the major divisions of the organization's work. Each team familiarizes itself with the work of a division and shares their findings with the entire board at a subsequent meeting. The findings will include their perceptions of program strengths and weaknesses and recommendations for improvement.

There is nothing like a tour of operations in which board members see the work that is being done firsthand, meet the program participants, and hear their stories from their own lips. TAP conducts monthly tours for board members, community leaders, and interested citizens.

Selection of a Board Attorney

A nonprofit organization is a legal structure that has legal responsibilities to a wide range of groups and individuals. It assumes legal liability if it abrogates its contracts with those parties. The nonprofit needs a corporate attorney to solve problems and refer staff to lawyers with specialization depending on the need. Over the years, TAP has dealt with attorneys specializing in personnel, labor, tax, property, and incorporation matters, to name a few.

Charlie Fox III, a partner in the prominent Roanoke law firm of Fox, Wooten, and Hart, became TAP's corporate attorney at its inception. He came on board when most attorneys did not want to be associated with this radical new agency promoting desegregation and a stronger voice for the poor. Charlie wholeheartedly believed in TAP and its mission. For most of the three decades he served as TAP's corporate attorney, he never billed for his time. When he referred TAP to lawyers dealing with specialized issues, he referred us to the best and asked them to keep their costs as low as possible.

Charlie loved to solve problems. When the TAP board wanted to elect a nonboard member as chair because of his support of TAP and strong community presence, I took the matter to Charlie. Fox, poised at his Jeffersonian stand-up desk, chuckled. "That's simple. Just change your bylaws. There is no requirement that a nonboard member cannot be an officer. They can be officers as long as they don't vote!"

A key task of an executive is to do whatever it takes to avoid lawsuits; however, we live in a litigious society. Anybody can sue anyone, and a lawyer can be found for even the most frivolous cases. TAP was sued for gender discrimination by a man who was fired by his female supervisor. He was terminated for cause, but he sued on the grounds that he was fired because his superior disliked men. His evidence was that she was overheard in an unrelated conversation saying, "Men are dogs." The suit failed to win support in court after court but was later appealed to the Supreme Court of the United States, even though there was no chance that it would be heard. It wasn't. Having a good corporate attorney on board—in this case, Charlie Fox's successor, Jonathan Rogers—allows an agency to do its job and not be intimidated by the mere threat of a lawsuit.

CEO Selection and Contract

The first responsibility of the board is the selection and evaluation of its chief executive officer. This is a major area where nonprofit and for-profit boards differ. Members of for-profit boards are usually paid for their involvement and can measure the performance of the CEO in terms of the company's earnings over a period of time. Employment contracts usually spell out specific benchmarks and timetables that the CEO must meet. The contracts also often call for reevaluation after a certain period of time, during which the board can choose to extend or renew them. This procedure is also common with city or town managers and superintendents of public education. Nonprofits, however, generally do not use a contract spelling out expectations and time limits.

The lack of a contract between the board of directors and the CEO leaves the organization in a precarious position because of the nature of most nonprofit boards. Nonprofit board members are all volunteers who join the organization out of compassion for that organization's clientele and a desire to promote good in the community. They are reluctant, for the most part, to terminate an executive even if the organization needs and deserves more. There is always the concern of creating additional organizational instability or doing more harm than good with a leadership change. Furthermore, without strong retirement or severance packages, which is the case with most nonprofits, termination of the CEO is difficult from a human angle. In addition, the last thing that volunteer board members are interested in is a legal, and potentially very public, battle over a CEO termination. Finally, unless the organization has a strong strategic plan with measurable outcomes, it may be hard to critique whether a particular CEO should stay or go.

For this reason, I asked to be put on a contract by the TAP Board of Directors in 1991. Usually the contract was for a five-year period of time, but I gave the board of directors full authority to terminate my employment if I did not fulfill the leadership requirements of a CEO. Our bylaws were then revised to require a contract with all future CEOs and preclude that person from having another full-time job. I am all too familiar with nonprofit CEOs who use their public position as a leader of a community-based organization to run for public office and take additional positions, such as mayor of a city or chairman of a board of supervisors. In every case of which I am aware, their agency suffered—both during their time of service and after their departure. I have also seen rural organizations hire clergy that also have a full-time job as pastor. In every case, the community nonprofit that they serve gets short shrift. Unless a board of directors takes its role seriously in selecting, evaluating, and, if necessary, terminating its CEO, in time they will get a weak CEO who will drive away their talented board members and recruit those whom they can manage (or strong-arm). This underlines why it is absolutely essential to have a strong board that isn't afraid to make a hard decision and take hard action when necessary.

I have been impressed by the process many churches, especially mainline churches, use to select their clergy. In nearly all cases, they visit the church, synagogue, or mosque that their prospective candidate has served. Moreover, they do not select merely on the basis of a paper résumé or interview, and they don't rush. Increasingly, these organizations will hire an interim pastor or minister for a period of one or two years in order to give the board sufficient time to make the right decision. Most often, the interim is hired with a contract that eliminates them from serving as pastor once their term is completed. When an organization needs some time to think through the type of leader they want to attract, the use of an interim is a good model to follow. If an organization is to hire from within, it is important that the board establish a well-thought-out succession plan to ensure competent future leadership for the organization. I know of a major organization with a budget in excess of $20 million and more than four hundred employees without a succession plan. This organization has twice, in desperation, hired the secretary of the previous executive to replace the CEO, with disastrous long-term consequences.

Boards of Commissioners

In addition to board committees, from time to time, TAP has developed "boards of commissioners" that have taken on concerns requiring more community input and attention. TAP's This Valley Works Board of Commissioners oversees all of TAP's youth and adult education, training, and employment programs. Its commissioners represent area education and training partners, local Departments of Social Services and Juvenile Probation, and local businesses. Another example, TAP's Alleghany Highlands Board of Commissioners, includes representatives appointed by the City of Covington, the town of Clifton Forge, and Alleghany County, enabling greater participation and input from the areas farthest removed from the City of Roanoke, the site of TAP's central office. While the boards of commissioners report to the TAP board, the title "board of commissioners" seems to help members feel a deeper commitment and responsibility than the more traditional term "advisory board." It has sparked them to undertake activities that have enlarged the impact of the organization in their area of operation.

Strategic Planning

The old adage, "If you do not have a plan, you plan to fail" works for organizations as well as individuals and families. The organization should have a strategic plan that, at a minimum, covers a two-year period. The best strategic plans can be summarized in a brochure. If the plan is so long that it cannot be viewed at a glance, then no one will continue to read it and it will cease to guide the organization. The best strategic plans have three categories: focus area, strategic priority, and success indicator. Recently, one of TAP's focus areas was to ensure agency financial stability. Among the strategic priorities was the sale of all properties with a financial loss. The success indicator for that priority was the sale of the Crystal Tower office building, scattered rental units, and single-family homes that we had constructed. This kind of strategic plan is clear, direct, and can be measured by whether or not the success indicators are met.

In preparation for the development of a strategic plan, it is important to do an annual assessment of the organization. The most frequently used tool is a SWOT analysis that includes an assessment of an organization's *"strengths, weaknesses, opportunities, and threats."*[51] My only reluctance is that the SWOT analysis can often be experienced as a downer, with so many weaknesses and threats that it takes the wind out of people's sails, leaving leaders overwhelmed with the negative. Given that the brain has a well-established negativity bias (which we'll discuss later), the SWOT analysis lends itself to reinforcing that negativity.

The SOAR model of strategic planning is a reaction to that feature of the SWOT analysis. This model concentrates on *"strengths, opportunities, aspirations, and results."*[52] Clearly this is a very positive model. My biggest concern with this model is that it may not take into

---

51 Berry, Tim. "What is a SWOT Analysis? Definition, Purpose, and Examples," Bplans.com, http://articles.bplans.com/how-to-perform-swot-analysis/ (accessed March 29, 2015).

52 SOAR Strategy, "What is SOAR," http://www.soar-strategy.com/index.php?f=what-is-soar &PHPSESSID=05d61aef696c203ea2f47e09938a9710 (accessed March 29, 2015).

account weaknesses and threats that are important in being brutally honest about the issues facing the organization.

I prefer the SCORE model that I have developed, which includes an analysis of *strengths, challenges* (weaknesses/threats that must be overcome), *opportunities,* needed *results,* and recommendations of where board and staff must focus their *energy* to achieve the needed results. Its comprehensive approach moves past analysis with an eye toward results and resource allocation, both of which dovetail directly into the development of a strategic plan with its focus, strategic priority, and success indicators.

In the allocation of resources, assignment of tasks is a major decision. One of the suggestions in the book *Good to Great* is that you "put your best people on your biggest opportunities, not your biggest problems."[53] This is the kind of thinking that will move an organization forward.

Board Training

The issue of board training is an important one. Over the years, we have used a number of formats: training specifically for new board members, training of the entire board on a specific topic during a regular board meeting, and training done in focus groups. The latter was by far the most effective form of training we have used—it gave leadership and staff an opportunity to hear from board members about their experience on the board. We held the focus groups during a breakfast or lunch meeting in order to accommodate board members' schedules. We asked what they liked, what they did not like, and what recommendations they had for the future. The second half of the meeting was an opportunity for the officers of the corporation to share information on the mission of the organization, its history, the role of the board, board member expectations, the corporation's bylaws, board committees, and the strategic plan. This

---

53 Collins, *Good to Great*, p. 58.

format had the benefit of a smaller group setting, which encourages more sharing on the part of each board member. Often, the questions and suggestions of focus group participants helped to improve the agenda of our regularly scheduled board meetings.

Reunions of Past Board Chairs

Finally, we have found it helpful to have periodic meetings of all of TAP's board chairs, past and present. These are people who have committed four years or more to serving on the board of the organization. They know the organization better than anyone else, identify with its mission, and are proud of the impact they have had through the organization's work. Moreover, they continue to be ambassadors throughout the community on behalf of the agency and its clientele. These past board members appreciate being brought up-to-date on what the organization continues to achieve and some of the issues with which it is wrestling. Frequently, they are willing to help in some capacity to move the organization forward.

In Summary

To sum things up, a great organization is going to have a very strong and dedicated board whose membership is populated by persons important to the mission of the organization. Among those who should be considered are members from the business community. A dedicated board will optimally meet on a monthly basis, have a strong executive committee composed of officers and chairs of key committees, and create standing committees to deal with the issues of finance, human relations, property, bylaws, and other important matters such as the development of a strategic plan. The selection of a CEO and the establishment of a CEO contract is as important for nonprofits as it is for private for-profit and governmental organizations. Involvement of the board can be strengthened by firsthand experiences in the work of the organization, evaluation of program areas, and service on "boards of commissioners." The use of board focus groups has proven to be a great way to gain information from board members and to do board training. Reunions of past board chairs are an excellent way to continue involvement of those who remain deeply committed to the organization.

Boards of Directors Take-Aways

- How strong is your board? Beyond the minimum level of activity necessary to fulfill the bylaws, are the members the best that you can find from your community? Do they have the kind of leverage that will garner the required support from other individuals and institutions necessary to fulfill the mission of the organization? Are they strong evangelists for your organization?
- Does the board fully carry out its responsibility for hiring and evaluating the CEO, approving of the strategic plan, budget, and important policies that include bylaws, personnel regulations, financial manuals, and audits?
- Does the board overstep its bounds by involving itself in the hiring, disciplining, and termination of staff?
- How strong is your CEO? When was the last time the CEO was evaluated? Did the evaluation contain benchmarks to be achieved in order to form the baseline for continued evaluation?
- Is your CEO under contract? If you were free to choose the best person to lead your organization, would you choose your present CEO?
- What do you do to ensure board involvement? Have you considered dividing the board up to perform in-depth evaluations of programs?
- When was the last time you did an analysis (SWOT, SOAR, or SCORE) in preparation for a new strategic plan?
- Are there areas of work that might be served more effectively by a board of commissioners that reports to the full board?

- What have you done to develop an alumni association of past board chairs or past board members in order to continue to ensure their support of the organization?
- Have you considered using focus groups to improve board involvement and board training?

Profile in Excellence:
Alvin Nash

Alvin Nash, who grew up in Northeast Roanoke, saw his community displaced by the 1960s City of Roanoke urban renewal program. Alvin, his mother, father, and five siblings could only find affordable housing in the newly developed Hurt Park public housing complex. An accomplished karate student, he would travel to full-contact tournaments in towns where no African American man was expected to beat a white opponent. Eventually, he became national full-contact karate champion. A copy of a newspaper article showing his well-wired physique hung in a neighborhood café. While working as a draftsman for a local architectural firm, he was recruited to TAP by Jayne Thomas to run her gym for young people.

In 1978, Alvin succeeded Jayne in becoming director of TAP Youth Programs. He had an amazing ability to read people, gain their confidence, and negotiate differences. When the Second Harvest Food Bank central office sought to deny TAP's food bank national recognition because TAP was not a single purpose agency, Alvin convinced them to make TAP an exception. When TAP's director of housing was failing in our effort to rehabilitate twenty homes in the Hollins community, I asked Alvin to manage the program and ensure its success. His efforts earned TAP a strong reputation in housing rehabilitation. In 1987, he went on to manage all of TAP's housing programs including weatherization, emergency home repair, and rehabilitation and housing counseling.

In 1997, with support from TAP, Alvin became the CEO of the Blue Ridge Housing and Development Corporation (BRHDC). Alvin continued to manage TAP's housing programs and BRHDC evolved into a major player in inner city, low-income housing rehabilitation and construction in Roanoke. BRHDC's very first project was a successful low-income housing tax credit application for the renovation of five vacant houses into apartments for forty-three homeless persons in the city. The City of Roanoke had reached out to TAP after a private contractor had failed in the effort. From 1997 until 2011, BRHDC built and rehabilitated a total of 146 homes in the City of Roanoke. In 2005, BRHDC won the Virginia Municipal Award for its "South East . . . By Design" project, which was the first concentrated use of Community Development Block Grant (CDBG) dollars (mentioned in the next chapter) to impact a single low-income neighborhood in Southwest Virginia. In addition, Alvin served three and a half years on the Roanoke City School Board and one year on the Roanoke City Council. Between 1985 and 2002, Alvin also served as a facilitator of anger management classes for men involved in domestic violence through Family Service of Roanoke Valley.

Alvin's negotiating skills were called on in a number of circumstances in which he made a distinct difference. In 1993, he took a leave of absence from TAP to work for the City of Roanoke, which had come under fire for not involving local and minority contractors in the rehabilitation of the landmark Hotel Roanoke. Through Alvin's leadership, the project ultimately included the participation of 26 percent local firms, 13 percent minority firms, and 5 percent female-owned firms. In 1998, when Roanoke County sought to persuade local residents of the all-African American community of Pinkard Court to sell their property to Lowe's for the building of a new superstore, the county sought Alvin's negotiating talents. During that process, Alvin helped to negotiate a more than fair value for the property, which left residents able to buy property elsewhere.

Alvin Nash is a talented leader whose company, Blue Ridge Housing and Development Corporation, made a significant difference. Hard times exacerbated by some bad business decisions forced the firm to go out of business after a strong history of accomplishments. A stronger board might have provided improved oversight and checks and balances that very likely would have averted the agency's closing. Today, Alvin is Director of the Housing Department and the Housing Authority in Dubuque, Iowa, where he continues to make a significant impact.

Chapter 7:

MANAGING FOR RESULTS

Teamwork is the ability to work together toward a common vision. The ability to direct individual accomplishments toward organizational objectives. It is the fuel that allows common people to attain uncommon results.
~ Andrew Carnegie[54]

The only justification for a nonprofit organization's existence is to get results. Achieving those results entails:

1. A results orientation
2. Concern for both advocacy and service
3. A dual focus on the work (task) and people doing that work (maintenance)
4. A focus on the task by doing the job
5. A focus on the people using motivation and the Johari Window
6. Building effective teams within the organization
7. Shared leadership, not designated leadership
8. Creating a learning organization

---

54 Stephen R. Nehls, "Commentary-Teamwork," October 9, 2007, http://www.mildenhall. af.mil/news/story.asp?id=123072534 (accessed May 8, 2015).

A Results Orientation

The recipient of the most honors by the Harvard Business Review and the Presidential Medal of Freedom, Peter Drucker, remains an icon on business leadership. His books *The Practice of Management* and *Managing the Nonprofit Organization* are essential guides for leadership. His unrelenting emphasis in his books on managing for results is a mantra for nonprofits as well as for-profit businesses. With increasing scarcity of funds from private and public coffers, there is a growing demand for results in the nonprofit sector. Today, results are measured in terms of both outputs and outcomes. *Outputs* refer to the actual services that are provided: the number of children receiving quality preschool experiences; the number of people provided housing and counseling in a transitional living facility; the number of homes that were provided energy efficiency measures through weatherization. *Outcomes* refer to a change in a recipient's behavior, the improvement of a recipient's situation or an increase in a recipient's knowledge because of the services rendered. An emphasis on outputs alone misses the mark. Everyone in today's marketplace is interested in not just what you do, but what the effects of your programs and services are. What happens as a result of what your organization does? What are the outcomes? Outcomes help you gauge the effectiveness of the organization's programs and provide much-needed data to communicate to the public at large.

The gold standard for outcome measurement is a control group. Unfortunately, funders rarely provide the necessary resources to set up a scientifically designed and implemented control group study. However, when the opportunity for such a study is available, its results can often have a powerful positive impact and help bolster future funding applications and plans for program replication. Such was the case when the Virginia Department of Corrections (DOC) decided to do a control group study on the effectiveness of the Virginia CARES reentry program as measured by rearrests, reconvictions, and reincarcerations (mentioned in Chapter Two). The DOC matched participants receiving Virginia CARES services with those who did not receive Virginia CARES services. In spite of the fact that it was a mismatch (the control group had far fewer African Americans, with less time served and less severe crimes), the Virginia CARES group had a statistically lower rearrest, reconviction, and reincarceration rate than the control group. Currently, TAP Head Start, in partnership with the United Way of Roanoke Valley and the Virginia Tech Research Institute, is collaborating with Roanoke City Public Schools and two other local school districts in an innovative data-tracking project. This will allow TAP Head Start to track the progress of children who have graduated from its program in recent years and entered the local school systems. In both years studied to date, TAP Head Start children were more likely to be ready for kindergarten [as measured by the PALS (Phonological Awareness Literacy Screening) PreK assessment[55]] than was the general population of kindergartners, many of whom came from significantly more advantaged homes.

When the gold standard of a control group study is not available, there are other ways of validating outcomes. The first is by using research that has already been compiled on services similar to what you are providing and in areas comparable to yours. The second is by using evidence-based practices in the delivery of services that have been shown to provide demonstrable outcomes. Virginia's Department of Corrections uses an evidence-based curriculum called *Thinking for a Change* with inmates returning to society. The curriculum focuses on the impact of thinking on behavior, the practice of social skills, and applying problem-solving analysis to everyday life. All of the staff in our This Valley Works component (who work with ex-offenders and low-income students) are trained in the administration of that curriculum. In addition, as we plan for the development of a

---

55 "PALS-PreK is a scientifically-based phonological awareness and literacy screening that measures preschoolers' developing knowledge of important literacy fundamentals and offers guidance to teachers for tailoring instruction to children's specific needs. The assessment reflects skills that are predictive of future reading success," PALS PreK Assessment, http://pals.virginia.edu/tools-prek.html, (accessed March 26, 2015).

Care Transitions program to prevent costly readmissions of Medicare patients, we have trained transition coaches in the evidence-based program developed by Dr. Eric Coleman.[56] Use of evidence-based practices increases the likelihood of program success and potential funding for program continuation.

Finally, wherever possible, it is important to tie the delivery of these services to a cost-benefit analysis that shows how the services are resulting in savings in public expenditures.

You must make sure that your program chooses the most relevant outcomes. An example of what happens when you don't is Project Discovery. This college-access program that we piloted and replicated across Virginia in 1986 has helped over ten thousand first-generation, college-bound low-income students, predominantly African American, go to and be successful in college. It's been my experience that most college graduates do not raise poor children and grandchildren. Unlike the cycle of poverty and poor school performance, in which the uneducated too often raise children, Project Discovery produces a generational cycle of success extending for the foreseeable future. Although the program has shown that its students graduate at a higher rate than the average college entrant, staff at the state Project Discovery office discovered too late that the desired outcome metric had shifted from college entrance to college completion. The program's failure to keep in touch with the times has resulted in an outdated program design that does not emphasize college completion. It has lost its credibility with funders and is now on the defensive, trying to regain the footing that it lost.

At the same time that nonprofits are measuring outcomes, it is important not to forget outputs. This is especially true for organizations that solicit and operate programs based on government and private foundation grants. TAP's strength has been meeting the goals and objectives of all contracts and outperforming our competitors. In one

---

56 Eric A. Coleman, "The Care Transitions Program: Health Care Services for Improving Quality and Safety During Care Hand-offs," http://www.caretransitions.org/ (accessed March 29, 2015).

instance we were called to task by federal bean counters for exceeding our goals and asked to justify our success! Our results (both in terms of outputs and outcomes) enable our continued success in reapplications to secure funds for early childhood development, education and job training, weatherization and emergency home repair, and business development projects. While outputs do not necessarily predict outcomes, the failure to comply with contracted outputs will foster doubt about an agency's capabilities in funders' minds, leading to a lack of credibility that, if not corrected, will ultimately spell disaster when it comes to securing necessary funding.

Since documentation of both outputs and outcomes relies on the accuracy of accumulated data contained in participant files, we have implemented our own periodic internal audit of those files to ensure their completeness. Not performing these audits is a guarantee that when grantor agencies come to audit programs, or you are looking for the data on which to evaluate your programs' effectiveness, that the files will not be complete. As a best practice, I recommend instituting a similar internal file auditing process to ensure that nonprofits have access to reliable and complete data for a variety of purposes.

Advocacy and Service

Forces for Good by Crutchfield and Grant listed being involved in both service and advocacy as core features of the best nonprofits.[57] Some "start with service and add advocacy."[58] Others are advocacy organizations to begin with and then become invested in service. The following story was told in my first training session as a volunteer with TAP:

> Picture this mental image: you're hiking with a group of friends in the beautiful Blue Ridge Mountains on a spring day. The sun is shining. The flowers are blooming. The

---

57 Crutchfield and Grant, *Forces for Good*, p. 32.

58 Ibid., p. 37.

birds are singing. New leaves are sprouting on the forest trees. The group comes upon a large blue-green pool of water fed by an incredible waterfall. It is midday, so the group breaks for lunch. Suddenly, bodies come hurtling from the top of the falls and dash themselves on the rocks below. Quickly, members of the group rush to the aid of the victims, pulling them out of the pool, resuscitating them, and binding their wounds. But bodies continue toppling over the falls in spite of the efforts down below to save them. Finally, one of the members of the team calls out to the others, "While some of us stay below helping those who are drowning, why don't some of us go up to the top to figure out who or what is throwing them in?"

The moral of the story is that changing an organization's systems, along with tending to the victims, is what is needed to solve many problems. The optimal goal is to create institutional change to prevent problems from appearing in the first place. The very nature of community action agencies encourages them to focus on both systems change and tending to victims. From its inception, one of TAP's guiding principles has been to call into question unjust, unfair, and/or inadequate systems that result in human tragedy and try to get those systems fixed.

Many of TAP's projects showcase this service and advocacy model. One example is our dropout prevention effort. Not only do we work to prevent students from dropping out, we also help those who have dropped out come back to the classroom. In addition, we've helped Roanoke City Public Schools improve its graduation rate from 58 percent to 80 percent with the goal of increasing it by an additional three percent per year for the foreseeable future. We are proud of pilot projects such as the Demonstration Water Project, but even more satisfied by developing the six Rural Capacity Assistance Programs that will, in time, eliminate all houses that lack indoor plumbing, in cooperation with the federal and state agencies who have backed that mission. The development of a rental inspection program in the city of Roanoke will eventually eliminate all substandard housing in that municipality. TAP's Virginia CARES program was the first organization to put the automatic restoration of rights for felons on the state ballot. Today, we're campaigning to "ban the box" that requires job applicants to note prior criminal convictions on their applications, the effect of which is to limit their opportunity for interviews. In each of these situations, TAP has been promoting systems change for the institutions serving our communities.

A Dual Focus: Task and Maintenance

Two concerns challenge both for-profit and nonprofit organizations: doing the job and soliciting the best effort from the people driving the work. These two concerns are referred to in group dynamics as "task" and "maintenance." Organizations are most productive when they focus on both issues. An organization's sophistication in dealing with both the work to be performed and the human factor will determine its productivity and long-term viability.

Blake and Mouton, in their book *The Managerial Grid: Key Orientations for Achieving Production Through People*, created a classification system based on the attention that organizations paid to these two functions. They theorized that organizations fall into one of four positions on the grid (shown below) with respect to task-focus and people-focus. Allowing for a bit of exaggeration on my part, high task/low people-focused organizations (9,1) are concentrated exclusively on task and have little time for people concerns. People are essentially replaceable widgets. There is a job to do. If those responsible do not do their job then they can hit the road. Low task/ high people-focused organizations (1,9) are all about keeping people happy even if the organization does a mediocre job. Trying to hit a middle road between being task focused and people focused (5,5), some organizations switch back and forth between the two. When the organization is behind on meeting its goals, it is entirely production oriented. When the toll gets too great for the employees or volunteers, it stops and does something special to soothe their frustrations and discontent, then it swings back, attempting to make up for lost time on the job. Blake and Mouton suggest an alternative. The ideal and most productive organization is one that is focused on both task and people concerns at the same time (9,9). These organizations succeed by involving the labor force in the decision-making process (e.g., when wrestling with difficult situations or discussing how to improve production). When individuals connect their contributions to improving the success of the organization, they are much more willing to do what it takes to succeed.[59]

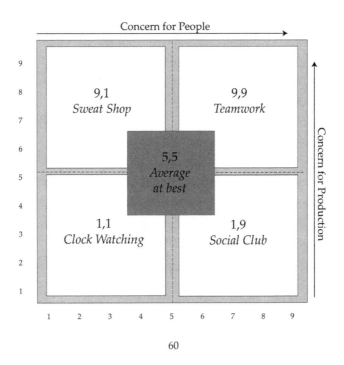

60

59 Blake, Robert R., and Jane Srygley Mouton. *The Managerial Grid: Key Orientations for Achieving Production Through People*. (Houston, Texas: Gulf Publishing Company, 1964), p. 11.

60 Ibid., p. 10.

Task Focus

Let's look at the task and maintenance aspects of an organization, in turn. Focusing on task above all else depends upon disciplined thinking. Disciplined thinking and action involve continually returning to these questions:

- "Why are we here?"
- "What should we do?"
- "What should we stop doing?"
- "Who is going to do what to whom?"
- "What are the indicators of success?"
- "How are we going to measure our success or failure?"
- "What changes are we going to make based on that data?"
- "How and by whom will these adjustments be made?"

Three resources have been extremely helpful in improving TAP's disciplined thinking on these matters. They are: David E. K. Hunter's *Working Hard—and Working Well: A Practical Guide to Performance Management*; Jim Collins's *Good to Great and the Social Sectors*; and Mario Morino's *Leap of Reason: Managing to Outcomes in an Era of Scarcity*. Let's take a look at some examples from the books.

David E. K. Hunter tells the story of taking leadership of a psychiatric clinic. Believing that the best strategy for discovering the current state of affairs was walking the halls, he just showed up unannounced with no external identification at a hospital for emotionally disturbed patients. No one bothered to ask his name as he went through the front doors and walked the corridors at will. Unattended patients were strewn about. The staff was unconcerned and no one appeared to be in charge. Patients remained hospitalized for extensive stays, largely without progress, and hospital staff declined new admissions. When he asked about responsibility for patients, the psychiatrists, nursing staff, and social workers passed the buck to one another, indicating that they could not do their job until someone else had done theirs. Professionals blamed union members who indicated that they could not do anything without a reduction in the untenable level of violence.[61]

Hunter immediately took charge. He created a leadership team and gave them the alternative of working together or being terminated. He opened the doors wide to new admissions and created a daily evaluation system for every patient in conjunction with their recovery plan. He also tasked union members to come up with suggestions for stemming violence, asking them to withhold grievances until the suggestions were put in place. Violence was reduced by 75 percent. Lastly, he expanded therapy options from individual to group therapy and introduced evidence-based "dialectical behavioral therapy"[62] classes for patients, educating them in behavioral options in order to help them take responsibility for their behavior.

Hunter had created a "theory of change, [which] is best thought of as an organization's blueprint for success. It is the guide whereby the organization structures its daily activities to achieve its strategic goals and objectives. It also provides the framework within which an organization can examine what works and does not work within its own programming, and manage performance for continuous improvement."[63] This blueprint linked patient needs to the hospital's mission, a set of goals and objectives (or milestones), and actions to be performed by the staff. Then he instituted an evaluation system to measure and determine results.

These interventions produced the following results: Patients got better more quickly, with the average stay dropping from forty-five days to seventeen and a half days. Once discharged, patients stayed in the community 50 percent longer before returning to the hospital. The hospital transformed a locked ward into a day treatment

---

61 Hunter, David E. K. Working Hard — and Working Well: A Practical Guide to Performance Management for Leaders Serving Children, Adults, and Families. (Hamden, Connecticut: Hunter Consulting, LLC, 2013). Chapter 2, "Why I Take Performance Management Personally," p. 13–23.

62 Hunter, Working Well, p. 20.

63 Ibid., Chapter 4, p. 42.

program, with a graduated reentry program that reduced the number of necessary staff. A combination of data collection, research, and training effort reduced the level of violence well beyond the promised 75 percent. A hospital once threatened with the loss of accreditation was accredited with commendation.[64]

Hunter created a framework other organizations can use:

Day one: Review mission, strategic goals, objectives, and identify target population.

Day two: Identify short-term, intermediate, and long-term outcomes.

Day three: Evaluate programs as they stand now; determine what to add, discard, or keep; decide who will do what, when, where, to whom, and for how long.

Day four: Decide what data should be gathered, how to gather it, who will gather it, and how and by whom it will be used to increase accountability.[65]

Hunter spends a great deal of time with his clients in helping them to hone their mission statement to something that is concrete, measurable, and achievable. In the same vein, Ken Starr of the Mulago Foundation proposes in his article, "The Eight-Word Mission Statement:" "As investors in impact, we . . . don't want to wade through a bunch of verbiage about 'empowerment,' 'capacity-building,' and 'sustainability'—we want to know exactly what you're trying to accomplish. All we want is this: A verb, a target population, and an outcome that implies something to measure—and we want it in eight words or less. Why eight words? It just seems to work. It's long enough and short enough to force clarity. Save kids' lives in Uganda. Rehabilitate coral reefs in the Western Pacific."[66]

On the basis of a three-day planning session in 2014 using the

---

64 Ibid., p. 19–24.

65 Ibid., Chapter 4, p. 50–106.

66 Kevin Starr, "The Eight-Word Mission Statement." *Stanford Social Innovation Review,* September 18, 2012, http://www.ssireview.org/blog/entry/the_eight_word_mission_statement (accessed March 13, 2015).

Hunter format, the TAP Board of Directors approved a three-year plan developed by the agency management team. This plan included the following:

- A rewrite of the agency's mission statement: We reduced a mission statement a half page long to *TAP helps individuals and families achieve economic and personal independence through education, employment, affordable housing, and safe and healthy environments.*

- Development of a data system to measure improvement of economic and personal independence of all TAP program participants.

- Implementation of service bundling[67] so that 100 percent of clients are referred to internal components and outside agencies, 75 percent of clients follow up on referrals, 70 percent of clients receive services through TAP or other organizations, 45 percent of clients access benefits through online submission or referral to Public Access Benefits programs, and 45 percent of clients receive financial literacy education.

- Quarterly outcome reports by all TAP divisions (Head Start, This Valley Works, Housing, Financial Services).

- A commitment to continued agency financial stability through the sale of nonproductive properties and management of program expenses.

- Implementation of the "Tools of the Mind" curriculum[68] in six Head Start classrooms and a two-generation[69] approach to coordinating resources of Head Start family service workers and This Valley Works staff.

---

67 Annie E. Casey Foundation, Early Findings in "An Integrated Approach to Fostering Family Economic Success," January 2010, http://www.aecf.org/m/resourcedoc/aecf-CWFfosteringFES3modelsites-2010.pdf (accessed March 22, 2015).

68 Tough, Paul. *How Children Succeed: Grit, Curiosity, and the Hidden Power of Character.* (Boston: Houghton Mifflin Harcourt, 2012), p. 194.

69 Teresa Sommer et al., Abstract, "Early Childhood Education Centers and Mothers' Postsecondary Attainment: A New Conceptual Framework for a Dual-Generation Education Intervention, *Teachers College Record* 114, no. 10 (2012): 1–40, http://www.tcrecord.org/library/abstract.asp?contentid=16678 (accessed March 22, 2015).

- Expansion of programs central to TAP's core mission that also generate increased funding for the organization.
- Improvement of TAP's Information Technology in the areas of security, operations, and an intranet system for staff.
- The development of a 2015 signature event that will raise at least $50,000–$100,000 in discretionary income.
- Compliance with all certification benchmarks and continued status as a low-risk auditee.

Selecting and Pursuing the Right Task

Jim Collins, in his book *Good to Great*, offers an extremely helpful matrix for nonprofit business analysis called the "Hedgehog Concept." The hedgehog is an animal that hunkers down and plods along on a steady course, as opposed to the fox, which is prone to jumping around and going off in one direction after another.[70] The Hedgehog Concept consists of three intersecting circles similar to the Olympic rings.

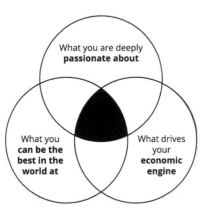

71

The first ring is the response to the question "What is the organization's passion?" Simply put, "Why are you here?" The

70 Collins, *Good to Great*, p. 90–91.

71 Collins, Good to Great, p. 96.

answer to that question defines the mission of the organization and fuels the energy to persist in spite of all of the obstacles and external forces that try to thwart that mission.[72]

The second ring is the response to the question "What do you do better than anyone else?" The answer to this question helps to assess the organization's niche. It is the gauge to measure where to put the organization's energy. It helps the organization sort out what it needs to stop doing and what opportunities it should pursue.[73]

The third ring answers the question "Where is the money?" What is the economic engine that will fuel individual activities or the organization as a whole? Where are the resources, whether human or financial?[74]

Without "religious focus on the intersection of all three circles," the organization can neither do its work nor expect to build a brand that is going to garner support. All activities need to be measured and reevaluated on a continuing basis by adherence to the Hedgehog Concept.[75]

Martin Eakes of Self Help, an organization that has created mortgage opportunities for low-income families and led the way in promoting legislation to curb predatory lending in North Carolina, describes the role of mission and resources as two wheels of a bicycle. The front wheel is the mission that you allow to steer you. The back wheel is the financial resources. It is the two together that allow for major impact.[76]

TAP has had to make adjustments in its mission over the years, too. Three decades ago, TAP was involved in a great deal of emergency aid. We distributed food, clothing, assisted with housing bills, and vetted applicants for aid from local churches that also provided assistance. While emergency aid is important, in many

72 Ibid., p. 108–110.

73 Ibid., p. 97–100.

74 Ibid., p. 104–108.

75 Ibid., p. 124.

76 Crutchfield and Grant, *Forces for Good*, p. 65.

cases the result did not encourage self-reliance, self-determination, or strengthen and empower its recipients. It did not fit our mission and passion. Ironically, while the American public does not want its tax dollars used for emergency assistance, that is very often, in my experience, the major target for considerable voluntary giving. Programs like the Rescue Mission and Roanoke Area Ministries became the major distributors of emergency assistance in our area. TAP made a deliberate decision to honor our passion for helping people escape poverty. As a result, we redirected our resources to expand Head Start and Early Head Start; develop our education, training, and employment programs; increase affordable housing programs; and focus on our small business assistance programs. It was a pivotal point in TAP history.

As a result of this decision of where to focus our efforts, TAP has been in the job training business. Its first programs under federal Manpower legislation provided remedial education and career development through Neighborhood Youth Employment programs working with in-school and out-of-school youth; New Careers, training aides who desired to move forward with their entry-level careers in the school system, local government, and police departments; and Mainstream, programs that hired adults to build campsites in state parks. TAP created a local Opportunities Industrial Council (OIC), which provided training in secretarial skills, auto repair, brick masonry, and manufacturing assembly, while at the same time enabling participants to attain their GEDs. As government funding shifted, TAP has continued to invest in job training and placement. In 2014, TAP's This Valley Works graduated 757 youth and adults, preparing them for the world of work. In addition, 782 clients were placed on jobs; and TVW's Certified Nurse's Aide program had a state certification rate of 94 percent, an employment rate of 95 percent, and an employment retention rate of 91 percent.

TAP has also worked hard to improve affordable housing opportunities for thousands. TAP's weatherization program, home repair, and new construction programs have improved the quality of housing for hundreds of families each year. For homeowners, TAP's investment has shored up the worth of their dwelling. For those who have rented housing with affordable rates, they have been able to stretch their income to meet other needs.

TAP's Individual Development Account program offers an opportunity to participate in a matched-savings program where the savings can be invested in educational advancement, purchase of a home, or starting a business. Business Seed Capital, Inc. has a loan portfolio of $1,450,000 for small businesses owners whose credit was too low for traditional bank funding. In 2014, TAP's Free Tax Clinic helped 606 individuals earn $639,280 in Earned Income Tax Credits.

To date, the focus on education and career development, affordable housing, and financial services all fit the hedgehog principle. Because they match TAP's passion, what TAP excels at, and are sustained by available resources, these programs go a long way toward managing for results.

Maintenance Focus

Maintenance has to do with creating a highly motivated workforce and an environment of trust that promotes teamwork, creativity, and initiative. Dr. Jim Goodnight, the founder of SAS, a company recognized as an international leader in the development and sale of analytic software, and listed next to Google as the best place to work in the world,[77] has said, "Creativity is especially important to SAS because software is a product of the mind. As such, 95 percent of my assets drive out the gate every evening. It's my job to maintain a work environment that keeps those people coming back every morning. The creativity they bring to SAS is a competitive advantage for us."[78]

---

77 Lauren K. Ohnesorge, "SAS Trails Google in International 'Best Place to Work' List," (blog), *Triangle Business Journal*, October 23, 2014, http://www.bizjournals.com/triangle/blog/techflash/2014/10/sas-trails-google-great-place-to-work-institute.html (accessed March 24, 2015).

78 "Jim Goodnight, Chief Executive Officer, SAS," http://www.sas.com/en_us/company-information/executive-bios/jim-goodnight.html (accessed March 24, 2015).

When talking about capital, most people think about financial capital. Equally important, though often overlooked, is human capital. It has been estimated that only three out of ten American workers have their heart in their job.[79] Dr. Goodnight recognizes that the key to his company's financial success is his people.

Over the years, I have noted that there are two types of leadership styles: those who lead by building relationships and those who lead by control and intimidation. I am always amazed at control-type personalities that end up as university presidents or city managers and last far longer than they should. Nonprofit leaders often do not have the clout to rule by fear and are more likely to draw leaders who build relationships (though not in all cases). There is always the sad case of a nonprofit leader who maintains control through screaming and threatening. The result is staff that does no more than necessary, takes no risks, and can't wait to get home at the end of the day.

Bristow Hardin, TAP's first executive director, didn't see what it would look like years later. At the beginning, he was not even sure, beyond Head Start, what TAP would be doing. The one thing he was certain of was that we were in the people business and that our success would be determined by how we worked with one another. A staple of training in human interaction and group dynamics was participation in training groups, often offsite, in which we learned to express our feelings and ideas, listen to others, ask for and offer behavioral feedback to one another, negotiate differences, build on others' ideas, and recognize the perceptions, biases, and stereotypes we bring to our interactions. The model for the human interaction, group development, and organization development sessions was the "learn by doing" model. Training-group participants would explain their experience in an organized manner. From the very beginning,

---

79 Adams, Susan. "Unhappy Employees Outnumber Happy Ones By Two To One Worldwide," *Forbes.com*, October 10, 2013, http://www.forbes.com/sites/susanadams/2013/10/10/unhappy-employees-outnumber-happy-ones-by-two-to-one-worldwide/ (accessed March 24, 2015).

TAP has been a learning community open to increasing behavior that facilitates personal and organizational effectiveness.

Early in my career, I was asked by a supporter, "How do you motivate people?" After some thought, I replied that motivation takes three things. The first is an *opportunity*. If a person has experienced a whole life of closed doors, it is hard to hope that things can be different. The second is a *decision* to set a goal and muster the courage to dare to do something significant, even if it might mean failure. The third is the *support* of someone in your corner cheering you on, helping you to pick yourself up and get back on course when your path is blocked or you fall. Every time a TAP participant succeeds, he or she credits someone at TAP who has seen something in them that they have not seen in themselves—who stood by them through thick and thin until they moved into an affordable apartment, graduated from college, remained sober for a year, started their own business, or got a good job. It was not TAP who helped him or her, but Corelli or Sharon or Sarah who made all the difference. Creating those supportive relationships is an essential element in helping others to have the courage to make positive changes in their life and sustain those changes.

In order for staff to be of help, they have to be excited about their job and the organization that they serve. They have to enjoy coming to work and creating an environment that gives support, tough love, and encouragement to those in need. The workplace itself must be a place of optimism, warmth, understanding, encouragement, and challenge. Rather than those eight hours or more being the worst part of someone's day, they can be the best part of the day if the staff communicates their energy and excitement to the program participant or customer.

Building a staff's social-emotional relationship skills is as critical as technical skills development. Decades ago, Karl Rogers and his colleagues spelled out the core features of a healthy and healing relationship. In sum, these features include:

- Empathy: the ability to understand the other person's deepest feelings and connecting with the other person's experience while suspending judgment.

- Respect: appreciation for the worth, strength, and ability of the other person to make his own decisions.
- Genuineness: the ability to respond honestly rather than being detached or playing an artificial role.
- Concreteness: the ability to stay focused on the issues with which the other person is concerned.[80]

I recall reading a study many years ago that compared the success of clients who received counseling with those who were on a waiting list to receive counseling services. Those on the waiting list did as well as those who found counseling. It would be easy to assume that the counseling was ineffective. It would be just as easy to assume that many on the waiting list found "that the therapeutic effectiveness of professional help is obscured by the fact that the normally existing 'non-profession[al] help' of friends, acquaintances, clergymen, bartenders, etc., is *also* (equally) therapeutically effective."[81]

More recently, Daniel Goleman, the author of the groundbreaking book *Emotional Intelligence*, argues that emotional self-awareness, the ability to manage emotions, harnessing emotions productively, reading emotions, handling relationships through problem solving, communication, and conflict-resolution skills contribute to a more productive environment.[82] Leaders with high self-awareness, self-regulation of moods and impulses, empathy, and social skills that help to build rapport with others tend to outperform those who are just technically or intellectually proficient.[83]

---

80 Carkhuff, Robert R., and Bernard G. Berenson. *Beyond Counseling and Therapy*. (New York: Holt, Rinehart, and Winston, 1967), p. 26–30.

81 Truax, Charles B., and Robert Carkuff. *Toward Effective Counseling and Psychotherapy*. (New Brunswick and London: Transaction Publishers, 1967), p. 13.

82 Goleman, Daniel. *Emotional Intelligence: Why It Can Matter More Than IQ*. (New York: Bantam, 1995), p. 283–284.

83 Goleman, Daniel. "What Makes A Leader," *Harvard Business Review*, January 2004, vol. 82, no. 1.

The Johari Window

Relationship skills are the key to building high-trust environments that stimulate creativity and productivity. In my very first human interaction training session in the late 1960s, I was introduced to the Johari Window. Here is how it was presented: In 1955, Joseph Luft and Harry Ingham developed a theory for the self in relationship with others that has become a staple of human development and human relations training since that time. The Johari Window has four panes: *open, hidden, blind,* and *unknown.* The *open* pane is what is known to both you and me about me. It relates to those aspects of me (gender, age, race, appearance) that are quite apparent. The *hidden* pane is information about my past, my personal history. It also includes internal aspects of me that may not be apparent, such as my thoughts and feelings at the moment, my belief system, and perceptions. The *blind* pane is what is known to you but not to me in our interaction. It constitutes your perception of me and my behavior, your reactions to what I say and do, and who I am. The *hidden* pane is reduced when sharing is encouraged. The *blind* pane is reduced when constructive behavioral feedback is promoted. When the *hidden* and *blind* panes are reduced, the *open* pane is enlarged. The *unknown* pane constitutes that part of each of us that is potential yet to be actualized. It relates to hidden abilities, talents, and gifts that will only be discovered during situations where there is personal sharing and feedback that results in a high-trust environment in which both of us are willing to take risks.

Johari Window

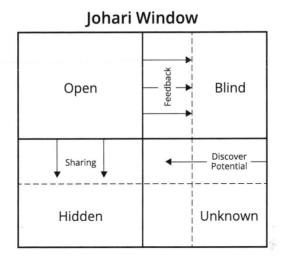

Building superior human interaction is about creating a high-trust environment. High-trust environments are created through high levels of personal sharing and feedback, both of which imply the ability to listen to one another. We learn things about one another through opportunities to share. The more we know what others think of us, how they feel about what we do and say, and what we do that makes them comfortable or ticks them off, the freer we are to express ourselves. In contrast, environments low in sharing and feedback lead to fear-based environments fueled by calculation, interpersonal manipulation, or avoidance and blame. High-trust environments encourage risk-taking, which often allows us to discover new potentials in ourselves that we never knew existed. High-fear environments lead to playing it safe, covering your ass at all costs, and finding someone to blame, none of which are conducive to discovering your potential.

Low	Trust
Open	Blind
Hidden	Unknown

High	Trust
Open	Blind
Hidden	Unknown

Neither sharing nor feedback will occur naturally without structuring the opportunities for these skills to be learned and exercised. Both of these skills have to be built into, and practiced in, the workplace. These skills are rarely learned in schools, even at the highest levels. In fact, educational institutions are frequently good examples of high-fear environments in which punishment is the primary enforcer of behavior.

The focus on maintenance issues is as important as the focus on task issues. Most often, nonprofits are dealing with people, which requires human interactions that provide understanding, encouragement, and support. Those interactions require empathy, respect, genuineness, and the ability to deal with concrete situations. This begins with leadership that creates a climate in which emotional intelligence is honored and nourished. Organizations with high degrees of personal sharing and feedback produce high-trust environments that lead to high satisfaction, high creativity, and discovery of latent talents.

Building Effective Teams Within the Organization

The creation of work teams that continue to focus both on the task and maintenance concerns leads to building an environment that promotes trust, creativity, and productivity. The building of successful teams is the key to building a 9,9 organization which combines maximum focus on both production targets and the people who do the work.

This does not happen without creating the necessary structure for team building.

The best example of a team is the family. As a licensed counselor, I am aware that the way to instill a healthy set of values in a family is through family rituals. One of the key rituals is how a family eats. When a family is able to eat together around the dinner table and share what has been happening without the intrusion of TV or cell phones, the family is more likely to build individual members' capacities for listening, respect, genuineness, problem-solving, and honoring those healthy values. The family that shares in preparing the meal, setting the table, and cleaning up creates both a work ethic and a sense of mutual support. The family ritual that has everyone eating in their own space, tuned into their own electronic world, and then leaving the cleaning up to one member creates a whole other value system.

The family unit in a nonprofit organization is the team. At TAP, everyone is part of a team. Whether you are a teacher in a Head Start center, an auditor on a weatherization project, or a staff member on a Virginia CARES reentry program, you are part of a team. In fact, the organization is a complex web of interlocking teams, beginning at the top with the team of program directors led by the CEO. In turn, each director is in charge of a component or division team that reports to him or her. The division team carries out the work of the various programs and functions that are part of its responsibility. The division director in effect becomes a lynchpin linking the top management team to the division teams so that what evolves is a system of interlocking teams. If the program is large, like TAP's Head Start program, the staff will become part of subteams that carry out the core requirements of a first-class Head Start program.

INTERLOCKING TEAMS

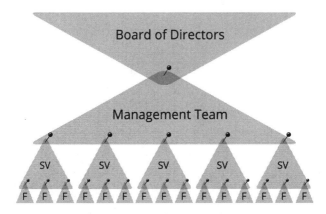

Interlocking items are held togher by link-pins. The CEO is the link-pin between the Board of Directors and the Management Team. The individual Directors who are on the Management team under the CEO become the link-pins with their Supervisory Teams (SV). The Supervisors become the link-pins with their Front Line Teams (F).

84

A necessary "family ritual" for each team is the planning retreat. When done properly, the planning retreat is where the team pays attention to evaluation of past efforts, focuses on planning what must be done in the future, and strengthens the relationships between members of the team through sharing and feedback.

At least once a year for the last thirty-nine years, TAP's executive team spends three days offsite in a team-building planning retreat to sketch out the year ahead. Part of the first day is devoted to sharing the highs and lows of the past year. Sometimes the vehicle for the sharing is a personal collage of the last year, made of bits of magazines, displayed and discussed by each person. At other times, each person writes a poem that describes the past year. Sometimes it is a recitation of the four personal lows and four personal highs of each person. By the time each person has shared, everyone is fully on board and able to focus on the here and now rather than other concerns. Everyone is

84 Likert, Rensis. *The Human Organization: Its Management and Value.* (New York: McGraw-Hill, 1967), p. 50.

more respectful to the others around the room, and we are able to see one another at a deeper-than-superficial level.

The next day and a half is dedicated to what needs to be accomplished in the upcoming year and how to make it happen. Usually we have discussed the agenda in a prior meeting, allowing everyone the opportunity to add their input and concerns to be addressed. This is where the blueprint involving mission, goals, benchmarks, and means of evaluation are fashioned. Before leaving on the last day, we devote three hours to personal feedback so that every member of the team hears from everyone else. We usually focus on positive feedback that is very specific and addresses something the other person has said or done that was helpful during our time together. We ask participants who have had difficulty with others to go to that person and set a time when they can meet and work toward a positive resolution. Often there is a temptation to skip the feedback session because staff members feel good about what we have already accomplished and people are anxious to get home and get to work. We always resist that temptation and are rewarded by even more energy coming from the genuine positive comments we have gotten from our teammates.

Every staff member who is head of another team is also asked to set up some time, offsite, to follow the same process with their team members. The offsite retreats are then reinforced by monthly meetings of the respective team to focus on carrying out the plans that were developed and to address new dynamics that have appeared since the team-building session.

Once a year, there is a total organization meeting, TAP Day, for all TAP employees. TAP Day includes welcomes by the board chair and local public officials, an inspirational address, a recitation of the outstanding accomplishments of each component, a lunch, the opportunity for interest groups to meet on subjects suggested by staff, and a drawing of prizes and gifts for those who have contributed to the United Way and the National Community Action Foundation. In 2014, the staff was divided into work teams and asked to come up with suggestions to improve the quality of TAP's operations. Staff contributed more than one hundred suggestions that were subsequently weighed and implemented as time and money permitted.

Shared Leadership, Not Designated Leadership

Central to the notion of teams is the notion of shared leadership. In "group training" dynamics, one learns that in order to make a group productive, one must rely on the leadership of all members of the team rather than a designated leader. Each team must rely on its members to contribute different skills to support the task or maintenance needs of the group. Task functions may be initiating ideas, seeking information, giving information, clarifying information, summarizing information, or deciding to move forward on ideas. Maintenance functions may be setting and testing standards, making sure no one is ignored, encouraging, relieving tension, or compromising. When members of the group perform these leadership skills, the result is far greater than when relying solely on a single, designated leader.

The same is true of the entire organization. When everyone is responsible for new ideas, contacts, or procedures, the organization will be far more dynamic. When our business development program was in danger because of failed leadership, it was Angela Penn, Vice President of Economic and Real Estate Development for TAP, who brought Curtis Thompson, now Vice President of Financial Services, into the fold. He has been a great addition to our team, bringing creativity and energy into the financial services component. A secretary in our This Valley Works branch referred us to information from the Urban Institute on how to measure outcomes with little additional money. Partnerships and collaborations with other organizations frequently depend on matching the right person in the organization with those with whom we are attempting to connect. Personal chemistry can be an important part of that initiative. The

TAP position is that if you're having problems with one of us, we have someone else that you're just going to love.

Furthermore, if an issue surfaces that requires an *ad hoc* team to manage it, whoever has the required leadership ability heads up the team. After the housing and commercial property crisis of 2009, Owen Schultz, the head of our Planning Department who also had a construction and IT knowledge base, headed up an internal team that prepared an eight-story building for sale and moved our entire operation into our current location, another four-story building. He asked for and received cooperation and support from everyone else on the team.

It has been my experience that organizations that invest in the development of teams at all levels of the organization, including a meeting once a year of the entire organizational team, create a high-trust, high-productivity work environment that elicits the very best of the people who work for the organization. These organizations will most likely fall in the Blake and Mouton (9,9) category of enterprises.

Creating a Learning Organization

The building of high-functioning teams with a high regard for both task and maintenance is the greatest hedge against a changing environment. The teams are geared to creativity and responding to unforeseen events—rather than carrying out the organization's duties in rote fashion. Peter Senge, in his book *The Fifth Discipline*, makes the case that the only organizations that stand a chance of surviving in a world that is constantly changing and shifting are ones that are constantly learning. Learning organizations are in tune with the changes in the environment, refuse to be blinded by presuppositions, and champion not only individual mastery but also "team learning" where the team IQ surpasses the average of the IQs of its individual members. Team learning can only be a product of team member interactions that presuppose a high degree of respect, the ability to listen and withhold judgment, and a commitment to set aside personal agendas and deal with the facts of the situation.[85]

A strong team-learning environment has enabled TAP to survive the changing priorities from government and private funding organizations, find ways to partner with organizations that started out as competitors, and find new avenues for program and resource development. It has been the leadership of many, rather than the leadership of a few, that has been our strength.

The encouragement of team retreats in which ideas are shared without criticism, the engagement of a planning department that is continually scouring ideas from other organizations across the country, attendance at conferences where new strategies are shared, visits to other organizations near and far, and the continued emphasis on excellence have made TAP an exciting place to be. The first action of Annette Lewis, upon being named acting CEO of the TAP organization was to put together an "Innovations Task Force" to further strengthen the agency's learning environment.

Managing for results has many parts that all have to work together to ensure success. Building trust, teams, and more takes time, but the payoff of a more motivated and highly successful organization is worth the investment of time and energy.

Managing for Results Take-Aways

- What are the results or outcomes toward which your organization is working?
- What data are you able to use that documents outcomes? Control group studies? Evidence-based best practices?
- In addition to service outcomes, what are the reform measures your organization advocates?
- How would you categorize your organization in terms of the Blake Mouton classification system (1,1; 9,1; 1,9; 5,5; or 9,9)

---

85 Senge, Peter M. *The Fifth Discipline: The Art and Practice of The Learning Organization.* (New York: Currency/ Doubleday, 1990), p. 233–269.

with regard to task and maintenance functions? Where do you need to spend more time, attention, and energy?

- If you were to recast your mission statement in terms of Ken Starr's eight-word formula (a verb, a target population, an outcome that implies something to measure), how would it read?
- On the way to the overall results and goals, what are the key objectives or measurable benchmarks toward which your organization is working?
- What data are you going to collect to measure your success in meeting your benchmarks, and how will you collect it?
- What is your organization's passion? What do you do better than anyone else? What are the economic engines available to your organization? What activities meet all three criteria? Which do not meet all three?
- What can you do to increase your relationship-building leadership?
- In terms of the Johari Window analysis, how would you measure the trust level in your organization? What opportunities do you create for genuine sharing and feedback?
- What is done on a consistent basis to recognize those who contribute to your mission? What can you do to increase the autonomy of those working for you on how to manage their work and the people under them?
- What are the critical teams that make things happen in your organization? What provision is made for annual planning sessions that incorporate sharing, task work, and feedback? What follow-up sessions take place on at least a monthly basis?

Profile in Excellence:
Cleo Sims

Bristow had once expressed frustration with TAP's Head Start program. He was not happy with its leadership, and he thought openly about spinning off the program. From 1975–1981, I hired a succession of four Head Start directors. Two sought other positions after one or two years. Two I terminated. What I needed was someone with leadership skills, knowledge of Head Start, and a long-term commitment to both the program and TAP. I found that in Cleo Sims, a mother whose daughters, Jeanie and Nicole, had been Head Start students. Years later, Nicole would graduate from the University of Virginia and Jeanie from Virginia Tech. Today, Nicole is a local prosecuting attorney, and Jeanie is an assistant principal working on her doctorate. Their achievement is a good example of quality early childhood education programs preparing children for future success.

Cleo had been hired in 1966 as a bookkeeper with Head Start and was promoted to coordinator of Purchasing and Planning. In 1980, I had promoted her again to personnel director for the entire agency because of her caring, communication skills, and directness. Cleo had a thorough understanding of Head Start, which had over two hundred employees, and she understood the program from the perspective of an educator and a Head Start parent. She had been through our three-phase human interaction, group development, and experiential education design skills training with the Mid-Atlantic Training Committee (MATC), and was open in her communication with others. She could listen and she could be firm. She had a cheerful demeanor and a great sense of humor. She smiled and punctuated conversation with laughter more often than not. While she had not completed her bachelor's degree, she had more than the equivalent in life and work experience, and worked on her formal education while on the job.

Under Cleo's leadership, from 1981 until her retirement in 2007,

TAP's Head Start program grew from five classrooms in one location to over thirty-five classrooms in seventeen locations. In addition, during this period TAP Head Start began a home visiting program for rural areas, was awarded TAP's first competitive grant for Early Head Start to serve infants and toddlers, and helped two other community action agencies establish Head Start programs. TAP's program also received a perfect score on more than one Health and Human Services annual review during Cleo's tenure. In addition, at the request of the regional Head Start Office, Cleo stabilized a failing Head Start program in Lebanon, Virginia, more than two hours away from Roanoke. Among her many distinctions, Cleo represented the Virginia Head Start programs in 1990 at a White House celebration of the program's 25th anniversary and received the key to the city from Roanoke's mayor.

Cleo transformed an ailing Head Start program that at best was a (5,5) organization division fluctuating between putting out performance fires and human interpersonal concerns into a (9,9) subset of the TAP organization. She accomplished this through her team-building skills that brought staff together to focus on the task at hand, interpersonal concerns that increased staff motivation, personal responsibility, and an attention to performance excellence in meeting the mission and objectives of the TAP Head Start program.

Chapter 8

ECONOMIC ENGINES AND ECONOMIC ACCOUNTABILITY

Rather than seeing the world as it is, those in charge would rather see it as they want it to be.

~ Jack Trout[86]

Every organization has to prepare for the abandonment of everything it does.

~ Peter Drucker[87]

In any nonprofit, the best teams and systems in the world will break down without resources to keep them going. This chapter will focus on the key components of attracting resources and managing them, including:

1. Protecting the core
2. Leveraging other financial resources
3. Making the markets work for you

---

86 Trout, Jack. *The Power of Simplicity: A Management Guide to Cutting Through the Nonsense and Doing Things Right.* (New York: McGraw Hill, 2001), p. 12.

87 Drucker, Peter. "The New Society of Organizations," *Harvard Business Review*, September-October 1992, https://hbr.org/1992/09/the-new-society-of-organizations (accessed May 10, 2015).

4. Ensuring economic accountability
5. Taking a financial snapshot
6. Hiring a first-class chief financial officer (CFO)
7. Using a financial decision-making grid

Protecting the Core

Every nonprofit organization has to find the resources (mainly volunteer labor and money) to support its mission. All nonprofits seek a combination of the two, though some rely more on volunteers and others depend more on money to support paid staff. For the last fifty years, the 1,100 community action agencies across the nation have survived and even flourished because of the Community Services Block Grant (CSBG), 90 percent of which according to federal law must go to the local community action agencies on the basis of formulae worked out at the federal and state levels. This is the "core funding" that each agency seeks to leverage by other means. TAP currently receives $561,000 in federal CSBG funds that we leverage into an $18 million budget.

Without CSBG, the network of local community action agencies would collapse. This money allows them to stand up and fight for the poor and crusade against poverty. Modest by federal standards, the national allocation for CSBG is $700 million, despite lacking presidential support since Lyndon Johnson. Every administration wants to build its own legacy and would rather launch new program initiatives that are distinctly theirs. Simply continuing a program of the past, no matter how effective, has little political "sex appeal." So year after year, it has been the Congress of the United States that has ensured the continuation of the Community Services Block Grant.

Community action agencies, which are mostly nongovernmental and nonprofit, are also distinctly local. These organizations discern local needs and find resources to help individuals and families develop the means of self-support. As such, community action agencies appeal to both Republican and Democratic sensibilities, but the Congress's continued support isn't automatic. It is up to agencies that earn a reputation for good work to inform Congress of their record of achievement. Extending agencies' reach, the National Community Action Foundation, a lobbying group based in Washington, DC, works on behalf of the nation's community action agencies, providing critical on-the-ground contact with federal representatives.

TAP takes all of this seriously. In support of NCAF, for the last forty years TAP staff members have voluntarily contributed approximately $6,000 per year and remain the largest contributor in Virginia. In one of the most politically polarized periods of American history, Executive Director of NCAF, David Bradley, has obtained bipartisan support in the House and Senate for full funding for CSBG and Head Start, a boost in funding for the weatherization program that was drastically reduced in the Obama budget, and the restoration of sequestration cuts, which were done in 2008 at the time of the financial crisis. These cuts to all government funding covered everything from domestic spending to the military.

Bristow Hardin, Jr. would often remind us to make sure that we didn't kill the goose that laid the golden eggs. To fail to support the National Community Action Foundation, which in turn supported community action core funding was essentially agreeing to "kill the goose." Every nonprofit has to have a stream of money that supports an essential infrastructure. Those foundational resources may come from one or more predictable, structured annual fund-raising events, earned income from social entrepreneurial projects, or government support from being part of a network. In each case, the nonprofit fails to give adequate support for those key dollars at its peril.

Leveraging Other Financial Resources

Where to spend that money and how to leverage more requires vision and a good plan. TAP committed to upgrading its grant development capacity in order to pursue every government or private foundation resource that we could "tap" to support our core interests of education and training, housing and community development, and business and economic development. The establishment of that grant-writing and reporting component has enabled TAP to be one of the two largest community action agencies in Virginia. It has allowed us to access public and private dollars at the local level, funding from multiple state agencies, and national grants from major federal agencies and national private foundations like those of Mott, W.L. Kellogg, and Ford.

All that said, there is an increasing need for discretionary income. Grant funding obligates the recipient to spend every dollar. It's impossible to accumulate reserves to support a line of credit to make payroll and pay for materials while you are waiting for outside money such as a federal reimbursement. And exclusively grant-funded agencies can't acquire the capital for innovation, experimentation, and the requisite predevelopment costs necessary to develop pilot programs or, in the case of housing initiatives, pay for architectural and engineering fees required for the building plans that are part of any application for government or foundation funding. Without discretionary income, a community action agency or other nonprofit organization may forgo meaningful opportunities.

Jim Olin, the local CEO of the General Electric plant in Salem, Virginia, and later congressman from the area, was an early friend of TAP's. I once asked him about his business model for the local GE plant, and he replied that 85 percent of their effort goes into doing what they do well and 15 percent of the effort is invested in experimenting with new product lines. For most of the last forty years, TAP has harnessed our future to the economic engine of grant development, performance, and reporting. At the same time, we have tried to, in the words of Crutchfield and Grant, "leverage free-market systems for social impact."[88]

---

88 Crutchfield and Grant, *Forces for Good*, p. 79.

Making the Markets Work for You

Forces for Good proposes two ways to get the markets to work for you. One is to start a business that will produce discretionary income. Another is to provide a service that will also benefit the private sector.[89] TAP experimented with starting a business that would generate discretionary income of $50,000 a year, with mixed results.

TAP saw the need to provide employment for the unemployed. Many companies make permanent hires out of temporary employees. It decided to create its own temporary employment agency to provide entry-level employment for participants coming from our various programs. The agency provided temporary employment for two hundred wage earners. Unfortunately, the rise in TAP's workman's compensation insurance premiums due to coverage of those temporary employees more than offset the income from the program.

TAP's catering business was awarded a one-year contract for one-fourth of the local Meals on Wheels program. While our meals were demonstrably the best tasting and the most nutritious, they also proved to be above the cost of the allotted per-meal expense. We did not reapply at the end of the contract.

Neither of these businesses had long-term success. Yet the intention of setting a goal and the experience of both these business ventures was valuable in later efforts. Most successful entrepreneurs do not make it on their first try. Often they start a number of businesses before developing one that is successful.

TAP currently has invested a great deal of staff time and overhead in supporting its economic development project, Business Seed Capital, Inc. (BSCI), which we believe has the promise of earning discretionary income for the entire agency. Founded in 1996, BSCI has helped to start eighty-one businesses, given technical assistance to 163 businesses, and created a loan fund that has loaned over $2

---

89 Ibid., p. 64–72.

million over the program's history. It qualifies as both a Community Development Entity and Community Development Financial Institution (CDFI), meaning it can apply for a substantial sum of New Market Tax Credits (NMTC). CDFIs raise capital in exchange for these tax credits from investors. The investor dollars then become equity in private or public projects that produce jobs in economically distressed areas, as defined by the US Treasury Department. Programs that receive an allocation of New Market Tax Credits are able to earn money by loaning those tax credits to eligible applicants, and managing those credits over a seven-year period. In 2013, Business Seed Capital, Inc., in partnership with TAP, applied for $25 million of New Market Tax Credits and was waiting for a decision by the Treasury within the first six months of 2015.

TAP has had more success in providing services that benefited investors. In 2007, TAP leveraged its four-story office building to purchase a 210-unit multifamily apartment complex in the heart of two strong Roanoke city neighborhoods. Our completion of the $27 million Terrace Apartments project had a steep learning curve because of Low Income Housing Tax Credit and Historic Tax Credit projects. These endeavors required a significant investment of time and capital, but ultimately positioned us to take advantage of other opportunities. We parlayed our development experience on the Terrace project into renovating and retrofitting two structures to house two Early Head Start facilities, managing two rural housing renovation projects, and serving as the general contractor for the construction of seven single-family homes being developed by the Roanoke Redevelopment and Housing Authority.

One of TAP's more recent ventures, still in development, is a Care Transitions program. With the passage of the Affordable Care Act, hospitals now face financial penalties if they readmit Medicare patients within thirty days after initially discharging them. Our Care Transitions program will provide coaches to assist Medicare patients in managing their health and preventing hospital readmission within thirty days of release. Medicare is willing to reimburse the cost of these coaches, whose job it is to help empower patients to connect with their primary care physician, home health service, and other services necessary to keep them out of the hospital. TAP had sought assistance from two other prominent Care Transitions programs in Virginia and had already trained four staff persons and planned to launch the program in 2015. What remained was getting the go-ahead from a major hospital in our area that we had contacted.

The building of affordable housing through the use of Low Income Tax Credits that leverage investor capital, New Market Tax Credits that engage private investment, and projects like Care Transitions, which create a partnership with a private hospital that leverages government resources, are current avenues that TAP is diligently pursuing to serve its mission and raise important discretionary income.

Ensuring Economic Accountability

An agency can do miraculous work, but failure to properly account for finances can close an agency's doors. In fact, in most organizational failures, overspending and misuse of funds are usually the culprits. While money is always tight in an increasingly competitive nonprofit environment, resources can be found if you work hard enough to deal with important issues. Money to fill problems resulting from fiscal mismanagement is almost always nonexistent. Over the past forty-nine years, TAP has had an excellent record of accounting for the funds we have received and their proper expenditure. The agency has been free from fraud and achieved the status of a low-risk auditee. It hasn't always been easy for TAP, though. We've weathered our fair share of storms along the way.

In 2009, TAP woke up to a financial crisis that was the result of an almost perfect storm. Congress slashed the CSBG funding in its appropriations, and state-level bureaucrats replaced precious and flexible general fund dollars with more restrictive Temporary Assistance for Needy Families (TANF) funds, which must be used to support families with children under eighteen. Eventually, even those dollars were eliminated. Our eight-story Crystal Tower office building, half of which was occupied by commercial businesses, was bleeding dollars due to an increase in utility costs. The collapse of the financial market resulted in loss of tenants who had helped to pay the Crystal Tower bills. The deterioration of the commercial real estate market reduced the value of the office building and made selling the building more difficult. In addition, TAP had other properties in the red.

To make matters worse, a delay in officially closing the Terrace Apartments project cost TAP an additional $10,000 per month, which dragged on for nearly two years. We were also sustaining programs that did not fully cover their expenses. A Housing Choice Voucher program for eighty subsidized apartments had run up expenses of $90,000. Reimbursements for that disappeared because of inadequate provision for those expenses by the US Department of Housing and Development (HUD). TAP had invested heavily in the renovation of the Dumas Center and was paying $7,000 a month on the interest of New Market Tax Credits without tenants to offset that cost. TAP's policy of allowing staff to save unused vacation time year to year added potential liability. In short, TAP was hemorrhaging money everywhere and, as a result, found itself living on a line of credit of which nearly three quarters of a million dollars was unreimbursable, instead of having the safety net of cash-in-hand.

Underlying these problems was the fact that TAP had moved from being a human service delivery system with a human service administrative infrastructure to an increasingly entrepreneurial format. We hadn't made sure we engaged the financial arm when we ventured into new businesses. The company had a finance director but not a chief financial officer to evaluate financial scenarios and recommend a course of action. My strength and experience has always been in program development. As the CEO, I realized that from time to time we were having cash flow problems but was under the illusion that our audits, which gave high ratings, told the whole story. The realization that the agency was facing severe difficulties was a humbling experience for one who prided himself on leading one of the best community action agencies in the country.

I immediately looked in the mirror and assumed the full responsibility and blame. I unilaterally took a 25 percent salary cut until we were on a path leading out of the financial crisis.

Taking a Financial Snapshot

I had taken responsibility, which was a good start. But that alone wouldn't solve the problem. I established an internal financial task force that would meet weekly, led by the director of resource development and planning, and assisted by the board treasurer. I instructed the task force to provide a full assessment of the issues and chart a path to solvency.

In addition, I instructed the finance director to provide a weekly "snapshot" of our financial position. The report would include:

- The current amount of the agency line of credit
- The current amount available on the line of credit
- How much of the line of credit was unrecoverable through current resources
- Changes from the last month's snapshot
- Total unpaid accounts payable
- Total unpaid accounts payable over thirty days
- Total unpaid accounts payable over sixty days
- Total unpaid accounts receivable over forty-five days
- Total unpaid accounts receivable over sixty days
- New financial problems that were forecast within the next one to three months
- Programs that were overspending
- The finance director's opinion on TAP's ability to meet payroll, taxes, and accounts receivable
- A rating for our entire financial situation (improving, unchanged, degrading, emergency)

- An assessment of current progress in meeting audit deadlines and any anticipated problems with the audit
- Recommended spending cuts

The board chair added members to the board finance and property committees, charging them to make a full evaluation of the situation and provide recommendations on all finance and property decisions. The finance committee asked for monthly expenditures by each program, even though there had been very few problems in this area.

Thanks in large part to the more powerful and engaged finance and property committees, as well as the weekly meetings of the financial task force, over the course of the next few years, the agency would:

- Resolve legal and financial issues with respect to the Terrace Apartments, eliminating the bleed of nearly $200,000 a year
- Sell the Crystal Tower building and pay off the debt on our line of credit, freeing the line of credit to pay bills that would be reimbursed by grant funds
- Sell a small rental complex and five single-family residential rental properties, all of which were losing money annually
- Work with HUD to transfer the Housing Choice Voucher program to the Roanoke Redevelopment and Housing Authority (eliminating overhead expenses for which we were not being reimbursed)
- Reevaluate all programs losing money
- Pay off the remaining interest on the Dumas Center
- Reduce the overall indebtedness of the agency by 50 percent
- Temporarily reduce TAP's 401(K) contribution from 8 percent to 4 percent (our strengthened financial position allowed an increase to 6 percent in 2014)
- Create a new vacation time policy in which all time must be taken in the year in which it is received, limiting the build-up of increased vacation pay liability

- Maximize the organization's grant making and program management capability to garner as much of the available stimulus money as possible and boost the total budget to over $20 million
- Utilize the 9 percent administrative fee on federal American Recovery and Reinvestment Act dollars to their full legal capacity, ensuring continued financial support for a strong administrative team necessary to oversee the organization's well-being and progress
- Upgrade the job description of the finance director to that of a CFO and hire someone with a strong business background for that position

For those of us who are in nonprofit leadership who desire to make a large positive impact, there is the temptation to let our organizational ambitions outstrip our resource capability and leave the entire organization in jeopardy. It is important to remember Jim Collins's insistence that an organization's passion and what they are good at be equally matched by the resources necessary to sustain that passion and work. As my friend, Jim Stamper, used to remind us, "The budget is the program!"

As we look toward the future, the TAP organization has set the following financial goals:

First, continue to sell off all properties that are bleeding resources.

Second, build minimum cash reserve that is greater than three months' worth of salary including fringe benefits and agency taxes.

Third, develop a cash reserve that can act as TAP's own line of credit, eliminating the cost of borrowing money until reimbursements are received.

Fourth, create maintenance and repair reserve to handle future costs on existing buildings.

Fifth, create a half-million-dollar endowment.

Hiring a First-Class Chief Financial Officer (CFO)

No nonprofit can do without a first-class CFO. The CFO has an obligation to accurately report the organization's financial position to the CEO and the finance committee of the board of directors. Keeping the financial records of a nonprofit organization is, in many ways, much more difficult than a larger for-profit enterprise. Because the sources of revenue are often so varied and highly regulated, accounting for their use is a complicated task. In many situations, if not most, revenue is acquired on a reimbursement basis that requires timely invoicing. Funding organizations frequently audit a program's finances, an occurrence separate and apart from the organization's annual audit performed by a third-party certified public accounting (CPA) firm. For these reasons, a first-class CFO will have both an accounting degree and preferably be a CPA. Since nonprofits frequently run small-business operations in addition to grant-funded operations, it is extremely helpful if the CFO has had prior experience in both the for-profit arena and nonprofit accounting. This is not the position for someone who is passive and hesitant to be vocal on matters critical to the financial health of the organization. It is also important that the CFO believe in the mission of the nonprofit organization and be able to build relationships with people as well as helping to keep the agency's balance sheet in the black.

Every nonprofit, especially one the size and complexity of TAP, needs a first-class CFO. TAP's financial books are far more complicated than a for-profit company five times our size. A CFO is more than a finance director. A CFO is a partner in every programmatic decision that involves financial resources. TAP's financial position was exacerbated by a number of bad financial decisions and fiscal problems with major development projects, in addition to the fallout of the 2009 financial crisis mentioned above. We needed someone who could help us work through it all.

Kimberly Butler filled this role for us. She graduated from the University of Mississippi with bachelor's and master's degrees in accounting and is a Certified Public Accountant. For seventeen years she was the owner, controller, and supervisor of a Sonic franchise, overseeing the finance and management of three restaurants. Kimberly has incredible financial skills, a tireless appetite for details, excellent staff management skills, the ability to say no to an ambitious and adventurous CEO, and the confidence of auditors and the board's finance committee. Kimberly has a deep belief in our mission and concern for the whole agency. She monitors all expenditures program by program, line item by line item, on a monthly basis. Thanks to her leadership, we have maintained our low-risk auditee status. Kimberly is also an upbeat individual and able to marshal energy to solve difficult problems. She has taken the lead in looking for ways TAP can involve itself in projects supported by the marketplace. She advises us in our efforts to acquire New Market Tax Credits to expand our economic development programs, and she plays a large role in our plans to create a start-up Care Transitions program to prevent early readmission of Medicare patients to hospitals supported by Medicare funding.

Using a Financial Decision-making Grid

With the right infrastructure, accountability, and a star CFO in place, all that was left was to set up a "repeatable" structure for our finances to keep TAP out of possible trouble. *Nonprofit Sustainability: Making Strategic Decisions for Financial Viability* by Bell, Masaoka, and Zimmerman, lays out a simple but instructive grid that measures mission impact and profitability. The grid has four quadrants along the two axes: The vertical axis, running from bottom to top, moves from low impact to high impact. The horizontal axis, running from left to right, moves from low profitability to high profitability. The lower left quadrant is low mission and low profitability and is represented by a *stop sign* and the message "close or give away." The upper left quadrant is high impact and low profitability and is represented by a *heart* with the caption "keep, contain costs." The upper right quadrant is high impact and high profitability and is represented by a *star* with the tag line "invest and grow." The lower right quadrant is low impact but high profitability and is represented by a *money tree* with the message "water and harvest, increase impact."[90]

Financial Returns

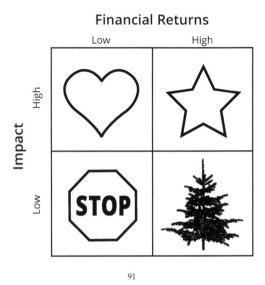

91

This is an excellent grid to measure projects and plan strategically. It is clear. It is easy to use. It is almost self-explanatory. Let's look at how we put these ideas in place at TAP. When the local area Agency on Aging declined to reapply for the foster grandparent program, TAP considered being the applicant, since foster grandparents have been a wonderful addition to our Head Start classrooms. This intergenerational program has high impact for low-income children and seniors. However, when we realized the grant would have required a match of $40,000 of discretionary income, we declined the opportunity. Even though it might have qualified as a *heart*, the cost made it a *stop sign*. TAP's Housing Choice Voucher program, with an

90 Bell, Jeanne, Jan Masaoka, and Steve Zimmerman. *Nonprofit Sustainability: Making Strategic Decisions for Financial Viability.* (San Francisco: Jossey-Bass, 2010), p. 25.

91 Ibid.

unreimbursed administrative cost of $90,000, was another program whose cost threw it into the *stop sign* category and forced us to give it away to another housing provider of vouchers.

Without the third ring of resource development and management in Collins's hedgehog three interlocking circles, an organization may have all the passion and expertise needed but fall short of fulfilling the mission for lack of resources. A "heart" can easily become a "stop sign." Here's an example of this that is very close to me. I sit on the board of a wonderful organization called Kimoyo, Ltd. This name in Swahili means "language of the heart." Kimoyo has built a hospital that sees one thousand patients a month in a remote part of northern Ghana where there was no modern medical care before. In addition, Kimoyo has built an Internet café, a soccer literacy program for girls, and a small business development loan program for women in that same area. Yet the program has no consistent economic engines and struggles each month to catch up on money owed to the hospital staff. In the long run, this is a challenge that must be met if the organization is to continue to function effectively.

In Summary

It takes all three of Jim Collins's "hedgehog" circles (passion, economic engine, what you're best at) to create a great and sustainable nonprofit. Passion and the ability to make a unique difference are not enough on their own. Resources are critical, but they need finances to continue. It is important for the nonprofit to support the sources of its key funding and to leverage those dollars. Wherever the nonprofit can make the market forces work for them in partnership with for-profit organizations, so much the better. The proper accounting and reporting of those dollars and expenditures is fundamental. Nonprofits are greatly aided in that endeavor by a first-rate audit firm, a competent CFO, and tools for making programmatic decisions like the "financial snapshot" and "financial decision-making grid."

Economic Engines and Economic Accountability
Take-Aways

- What currently are the major resources that allow your organization to be in business?
- What is it that you do well that you need to keep on doing? What additional areas might you add that would help to bring in resources?
- How does your balance sheet read? If you did a "financial snapshot" of your organization, how would it read? What needs to be done to improve the financial condition of your organization?
- What is suggested by your last agency audit?
- What is your organization engaged in that connects with market forces?
- Do you have the right CFO? What further training does your CFO need to meet the needs of the organization?
- In terms of the *Nonprofit Sustainability* criteria, what activities fall into the categories *stop sign, heart, star,* and *money tree*? What does that tell you about where to put your energy and where to stop putting your energy?
- Do you have enough cash reserves to carry three months' worth of salary, including fringe benefits and agency taxes?
- Can you handle your own line of credit through internal reserves or do you have to borrow it?
- What can be done over the next five years to develop an internal line of credit and raise a minimum of $500,000 for an endowment?

Profile in Excellence:
Owen Schultz

Owen Schultz is one of the smartest and most interesting persons with whom I have ever worked. No one at TAP has been more passionate about our mission, more creative in finding our niche, or contributed more to uncovering the necessary resources to further the agency's agenda. Owen grew up on Long Island, the product of a middle-class family. Against his father's advice, he left a Syracuse University scholarship in journalism after one year because he found the department out of touch with the revolutionary developments of the sixties. He enrolled in a newly formed international program, the Friends' World Institute. This "classroom without walls" used the world as its classroom. Over the next five years, Owen studied social change in the United States, Mexico, Sweden, Switzerland, Kenya, Japan, and India.

Owen is a devout Quaker. Under the Quaker leadership of Morris Mitchell, Owen registered southern African American voters during the civil rights voter registration campaign. He witnessed the violence against the voter registration drive organizers. He was arrested and spent time in a county jail. Owen acted in professional theater in California and worked as a lumberjack in West Virginia, where he also designed and built his own home that he still owns to this day. Owen joined the Southwest Virginia Community Development Fund, an early economic development project that TAP started in Roanoke. After a brief stint with TAP's weatherization program, he created his own company that designed and built the seasonal displays frequently seen in most large shopping malls. A fourteen-foot dinosaur was his masterpiece.

Owen was hired as a grant writer in TAP's Planning and Resource Development Department. When the director of the department left, I met with Owen to see if he might have an interest in the new opening. He spent more time interviewing me than I did him, to see if I was worth working for.

During Owen's seventeen-year leadership of the department, TAP more than tripled its funding from $6.5 million to $20 million and accessed more grant sources than any time in its history. In addition to being the king of grant writers, Owen became a magnet for young writers of talent and drew them into his department. Owen's mentorship helped to develop their skills and provided a collegial atmosphere of support for their work. In addition to writing grants for TAP, Owen was the lead writer for several grants for Roanoke City Public Schools, bringing in over $1 million of new funding.

Owen is TAP's Renaissance man. His vast knowledge encompassed the world of IT and building construction. Well versed in the language of "megabits" and "servers," Owen hired our in-house IT personnel and helped them design our web technology systems, as well as our first website. He also wrote, produced, and narrated TAP's annual video providing an introduction to TAP programs. When TAP moved its major offices from an eight-story building to our present location across the street, Owen took charge of the entire move, overseeing the renovations in the new facility and enabling TAP to maintain full IT service during the move. When the economy crashed in 2009, leaving TAP in a precarious financial state with property that had negative cash flow, I turned to Owen for leadership. With a cool head and meticulous attention to detail, he took charge of the assessment of our financial position and helped carve a path to solvency. In his spare time, Owen fully renovated his Southwest Roanoke home, built a peerless home stereo system, and wrote and published six novels.

Chapter 9

THE "RIGHT WHO"

The best executive is the one who has sense enough to pick good men to do what he wants done, and self-restraint enough to keep from meddling with them while they do it.[92]

~ Theodore Roosevelt

There are only three measurements that tell you nearly everything you need to know about your organization's overall performance: employee engagement, customer satisfaction, and cash flow. It goes without saying that no company, small or large, can win over the long run without energized employees who believe in the mission and understand how to achieve it.[93]

~ Jack Welch, former CEO of GE

In his book *Good to Great*, Jim Collins makes the point that great leaders begin by assembling the right people to lead and then let them help decide the organization's direction and priorities. All too often, heads of organizations decide on where they want the

92 "Theodore Roosevelt Quotes," GovLeaders.org, http://govleaders.org/quotes-leaders.htm (accessed May 8, 2015).

93 FrontStream Admin, "30 Inspirational Employee Engagement Quotes," *FrontStream* (blog), January 20, 2014, http://www.frontstream.com/30-inspirational-employee-engagement-quotes/ (accessed May 13, 2015).

organization to go and then attempt to assemble the right people to get them to their destination. Truly great organizations, however, begin by choosing the right people who then make the appropriate decisions about where to go and how to get there. It is about "getting the right people on the bus (and the wrong people off the bus) before you figure out where to drive it."[94] Having the right people on the bus gives you more opportunity to adapt and change direction in an ever-changing world. The right people are self-motivating, so you don't have to worry about creating extensive bureaucracy to manage them. The right people create a Level 5 management team that has sustainability beyond its current leader, as opposed to the "genius with a thousand helpers"[95] which may thrive as long as the genius stays around.[96]

The profiles in excellence contained in this book are good examples of the "right who." Jayne Thomas, Wilma Warren, Jeri Rogers, Annette Lewis, Alvin Nash, Lin Atkins, Betty Desper, Rick Sheets, Owen Schultz, Kimberly Caldwell, Angela Penn, and Curtis Thompson are people who have made things happen out of a deep sense of mission, unselfishness, excellence, and sacrifice. They never complained, and they expected the best of those who reported to them.

This chapter focuses on the essential aspects of the "right who," including:

1. Searching for the "right who"
2. Selecting the "right who"
3. Managing the "right who"
4. Keeping the "right who"
5. Helping the "wrong who" to move on

---

94 Collins, *Good to Great*, p. 44.

95 Ibid., p. 45–46.

96 Ibid., p. 40–46.

Searching for the "Right Who"

Choosing the right people has more to do with character traits than specific knowledge. Get the right people and they will learn as they go. The right people are those who score low on the Rotter Locus of Control inventory, a measure of self-motivation, indicating that they place the control over their lives on themselves, internally, rather than on external factors.[97] The right people are those who have "grit," defined as the ability to focus, set long-term goals, and persist in spite of challenges and setbacks.[98] These are people who are always thinking of better ways of doing the job rather than what is currently expected. They are people who are willing to take on additional tasks if it serves the mission, without complaint or request for immediate remuneration. They tend to see the bigger picture and are willing to make the requisite sacrifice. They do more than manage the tasks of others; they lead and create other leaders.

It makes sense to be concerned about the quality of service. You want the best teachers to teach, the best counselors to counsel, and the best community organizers to organize. At the same time, there is a tendency to associate the completion of an academic program with the ability to perform the required function.

From its inception, TAP has found that our very best community organizers, family advocates, case managers, and even Head Start teacher's assistants are those who have grown up in low-income communities and are intimate with the struggles of our clients. They have a knowledge base of experience and level of empathy difficult to produce in a classroom. While those whose training has been exclusively in a middle class educational institution resist visiting low-income homes in a poverty neighborhood, these folks

---

97 Mercer County Community College, "Rotter's Locus of Control Scale," http://www.mccc.edu/~jenningh/Courses/documents/Rotter-locusofcontrolhandout.pdf (accessed March 24, 2015).

98 Tough, Paul. *How Children Succeed.* (New York: Houghton Mifflin Harcourt, 2012), p. 74–75.

have little fear. That life experience is sometimes undervalued in the marketplace.

This is confirmed by Collins's study: "In determining 'the right people,' the good-to-great companies placed greater weight on character attributes than on specific educational background, practical skills, specialized knowledge, or work experience. Not that specific knowledge or skills are unimportant, but they viewed these traits as more teachable (or at least learnable), whereas they believed dimensions like character, work ethic, basic intelligence, dedication to fulfilling commitments, and values are more ingrained."[99]

Betty Desper was just such a person. Betty Desper was a woman of imposing physical stature with the drive, intelligence, and personality to match. Prior to coming to TAP, she worked as a short-order cook for a local diner. Betty was one of the original TAP outreach workers who had organized communities around water and wastewater issues. As she traveled our rural areas, she noted that there were hundreds of families living in substandard shacks on which they paid high rents. She was deeply bothered by the living conditions of these struggling families and was possessed with a passion to help them.

Betty became aware of a Farmers Home Administration (FmHA) subsidy program for new home construction for low-income families. She made it her personal mission to see how many of these low-income families she could put in new homes. Access to FmHA housing loans required filling out complicated application forms that often intimidated potential applicants. Betty met with family after family and sold them on the idea of a new home. She worked nights to personally help them fill out all the paperwork that stood in their way. As a result of her efforts, so many families completed applications that the FmHA had to open a special office in the neighboring town of Daleville to process them.

After attending a state workshop on how to stop energy loss in homes with wall cracks so large you could see through them,

---

99 Collins, *Good to Great*, p. 51.

Betty harnessed the volunteer power of the Roanoke chapter of the United States Junior Chamber of Commerce and started the first weatherization program in Virginia. Volunteers caulked holes and stapled plastic on the windows to prevent heat loss. When the federal government began its weatherization program, TAP became one of the first grant recipients in Virginia. Betty then hired a staff and helped more than one thousand residents substantially decrease their heating bills and stretch their budgets.

Betty was a taskmaster and would not tolerate less than optimal performance by her staff. As a result of her drive and commitment to decent and affordable housing for low-income families, I plucked Betty out from under a lackluster director of neighborhood services at TAP and installed her as TAP's first director of Housing Services. Later, she became one of the founders of the Virginia Housing Coalition, which has championed the housing cause throughout the state and helped to generate state dollars to the effort.

In 1975, Virginia social workers and counselors sought licensure. The proposed law included anyone who did any sort of counseling or performed a social work function, even community organizing. I organized a coalition of the Virginia nonprofit community, the peer counseling hotlines, and the personnel departments of businesses that were affected. I wrote a white paper called "Within Limits, Yes," arguing that community-based organizations with community boards, public entities such as Community Service Boards, and private businesses had accountability systems already built in to ensure quality performance. Licensure, which required a master's degree, more than two thousand hours of supervision, and a state examination, was only necessary for private practitioners for whom no such accountability system was present.

In the end, all of the exemptions that I proposed were included in the law. In the final meeting, when the exemptions that I had recommended were accepted, I indicated my pleasure at the outcome with the patron of the bill. He turned to me with a smile and said, "You should be. You got everything you wanted." Not everyone was pleased. After a hearing at which I spoke, a professor of counseling at a major Virginia university berated me, "If you get your exemptions how will my master's degree students be assured of jobs?" I had suspected that economic issues were behind the push for licensure. I was, however, surprised that the case would be made so blatantly. I suggested that I thought that there would still be plenty of jobs for his graduates.

What I had gotten was the right to select the best-qualified persons to do the jobs that TAP had to do. I had gotten the right to select people based on the essentials of "character, work ethic, basic intelligence, dedication to fulfilling commitments, and values." [100]

Selecting the "Right Who"

A key task of nonprofit leadership is to attract the type of leadership that is often smarter, more creative, and more daring than the CEO, and to create a framework in which they can work together and collaborate.

I have learned that I need the help of others on the staff in the selection of the "right who." I have been fooled many times. My first hiring faux pas was a secretary who had all the credentials and did very well on the interview. However, she did not have her heart in the job. She really wanted to be a community organizer instead of sitting behind a desk. I have hired development directors who were dazzling in the interview but could not write their parents for a loan. Now, I encourage panels of TAP staff to do the initial interviewing. While I retain veto power over all hiring, I rarely exercise it, leaving the hiring to those in charge of TAP's departments. They rarely disappoint me with their staff selection. The "right whos" are good at finding other "right whos."

I find that panels are most productive when they are not confined exclusively to a set of canned questions, particularly when those

---

100 Ibid.

questions are limited to present skills and ability or past professional experiences. I want to know what drives them, how they have handled tough decisions in their life, their vision for the future of our community, the kind of interactions that might reveal character and values. I concur fully with Collins when he urges "when in doubt, don't hire—keep looking!"[101]

There are times when it is the wise thing to hire from within. The person is a known entity. They have responded to the TAP culture. Promotions from within are good for the organization and they send a message that if you work hard, you have a future with growing responsibility in the agency.

However, there are also times when you need to look outside the organization. The TAP headquarters burned to the ground in 1989. We then purchased a downtown eight-story office building. At our old site, the personnel director had doubled as a manager of the facility. The new site, the Crystal Tower, would also house other businesses and nonprofits as commercial tenants. Enter Bill Skeen, a former mortgage lender, who became our first director of Business Affairs. Bill managed the Crystal Tower as a business and arranged for a $500,000 loan from four financial institutions to renovate a small shopping center that had been given to TAP by Kroger Foods. He then hired Dottie Avalon, a certified public accountant who had worked for a major hospital, as our new finance director. Dottie brought technology skills to transform an antiquated, handwritten ledger arrangement into a modern computerized financial system.

There are also times when the "right who" just appears out of nowhere. Jayne Thomas was on the run from an abusive husband. She called Bristow, TAP's Director. Bristow gave her a job over the phone. She went on to make TAP history. She made the dream of the Harrison Museum for African American Culture a reality, helped Pam Irvine create the Second Harvest Food Bank of Southwest Virginia,

---

101 Collins, *Good to Great*, p. 54.

and made a major contribution to Roanoke City Public Schools as a board member.

Managing the "Right Who"

Managing the "right who" begins with annual team retreats where goals are set for the agency and each division within the agency. Everyone is expected to have input, and everyone is expected to support the decisions that come out of those meetings. Team retreats help forge the norms and values of the agency and help build cooperative ventures that support the agency's work. Most importantly, team retreat participants develop trust in one another. Detailed notes of the goals, benchmarks, and responsibilities are prepared and distributed following the work of those sessions.

To ensure that we carry out the plans we set, we hold breakfast meetings twice a month in which everyone is expected to report on their progress. During these meetings, we are also able to address unanticipated opportunities and challenges. In between these meetings, on the intervening Mondays, I have breakfast with the vice presidents, CFO, and selected program directors to focus on financial issues, both revenue expansion opportunities and fiscal accountability.

I am a big fan of the *One Minute Manager* by Kenneth Blanchard and Spencer Johnson, which outlines three techniques of an effective manager: one-minute goal setting, one-minute commendations, and one-minute admonishments. Each of these takes only a minute but can have long-term effectiveness.

I make every effort to catch staff doing something right and praise them for excellent work. I also continue to catch folks in the parking lot, the elevator, or in the halls and tell them of concerns that must be addressed. I solicit their help in getting it right. If I have been to a lecture, read a book, or heard of an exemplary program elsewhere, I share the information and suggest that the appropriate person look into it to see if it might improve the work we are doing.

Frankly, for most of my tenure I have resisted formal annual evaluations of staff that report to me. I lead most effectively when I listen to staff and continually interact with praise, challenges, and suggestions. In recent years I tried a different approach. Annual evaluations can be productive if they begin with asking each staff person to do a written self-evaluation, documenting what they have done well and areas in need of improvement. I read over the self-evaluation in preparation for our meeting together. The self-evaluation often alerts me to many staff accomplishments of which I have been unaware. During the ensuing meeting, I am able to affirm accomplishments, share any concerns I might have, and make recommendations of actions that need to take place. I follow the meeting with a personal letter outlining what we discussed during the meeting.

Keeping the "Right Who"

Over the years, I have found that the best way to keep the "right who" is to employ the lessons from Frederick Herzberg's motivational theory. Herzberg differentiated between hygienic or maintenance factors (status, security, salary, work conditions, supervision, and company policy) and prime motivators (achievement, recognition, the work itself, responsibility, advancement, and personal growth).[102]

Problems in the hygienic area might cause dissatisfaction, but when it came to job satisfaction, even when hygienic factors were turned into motivation, prime motivators consistently trumped them. Let's look at some reasons why.

102 Herzberg, Frederick, Bernard Mausner, and Barbara Bloch Snyderman. *The Motivation to Work*. (New Brunswick, New Jersey: Transaction Publishers, 1993), p. 81.

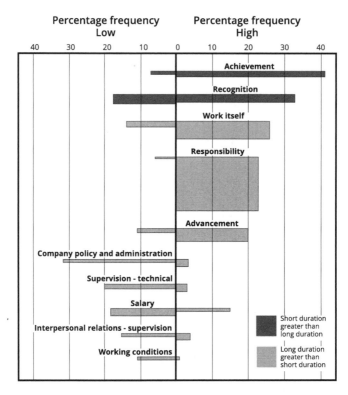

103

Nothing beats succeeding on the job. The use of clear goals and benchmarks by which achievement can be obtained constitutes a prerequisite to achievement—the first and most important prime motivator.

The next highest motivator, though it has to be repeated frequently, is recognition. Chief executive officers and managers need to remember that their greatest power lies in their recognition of their staff on a daily basis.

The third-highest motivator, with even more sustaining power, is the work itself. One of the reasons talented people come to work for nonprofits is because they love working for a company that strives to improve the lives of people, particularly in a high-trust environment.

103 Ibid.

The fourth-highest motivator with large sustaining power is the authority over how to do the job. In high-trust environments, greater and greater authority over hiring, supervision, and scheduling can be shared with the lowest levels of supervision. In fact, doing so produces trust.

The fifth prime motivator is personal growth. Opportunities for learning and skill training are a great reward in the nonprofit arena. They are key conditions that lead to another prime motivator, advancement.

Keeping the right people in the nonprofit arena is a matter of being part of an organization that makes a true impact and has rewarding work, recognizes people for the work done, provides people with the authority to do the job without constant micromanagement from above, and creates the opportunity to learn and grow.

The "right who" are not motivated primarily by monetary compensation. They are motivated by being part of an organization that makes a substantial difference and is organized in a manner in which they can freely contribute to that mission in partnership with others. Collins remarks, "The right people will do the right things and deliver the best results they are capable of, regardless of the incentive system."[104]

The hygienic issues are still important. Building high motivation also includes employees believing that the company provides employees with the best compensation that it can afford. That means at least providing a good, affordable health insurance program for the employee and their family and a 401(k) retirement plan. If the company produces less than that, it will have an impact on staff morale, which will in turn affect the end product of the organization. In TAP's case, that impact will be on lives of the consumers of the service who receive less than excellent service.

---

104 Collins, *Good to Great*, p. 50.

Helping the "Wrong Who" Move On

Jim Collins suggests that the role of middle management is most often to compensate for the lack of self-discipline and self-motivation of those who work under them.[105] He implies that there has to be a better solution to the problem than simply adding layers of bureaucracy. In any organization there are different levels of performance. "A" and "B" level employees are not a problem. They come self-disciplined and self-motivated. Additional layers of supervision will just stifle them. "D" and "F" performers are easy to deal with. Working within the agency personnel policies and system of discipline, they can be terminated. It is the "C" employee who presents the real difficulty.

I love the golf story of Tom and Sam. Tom leaves home for a few hours of golf. He returns home at 3 a.m. His wife is furious. "Why are you so late? I was worried to death."

"Well," said Tom, "we were on the tenth hole when Sam had a heart attack and died."

"Oh my God," his wife replied. "I understand now. You were at the hospital with Sam's wife?"

"No dear," said Tom, "it was hit the ball and drag Sam, hit the ball and drag Sam."[106]

Every "C" performer who never moves beyond that level is someone who takes management's time and energy to compensate for their lack of initiative and creates drag on the organization. Year after year, they do just enough to get by. They show motivation only when their job is threatened. Worst of all, they are taking the place of a potential "A" or "B" star performer. Too many "C" players and the disease of just-getting-by begins to spread and affect others. It is much better to replace them with those who will hit their own ball. Organizations must develop a set of personnel policies that are fair to staff, but allow managers to discipline and terminate staff that are

---

105 Ibid., p. 121.

106 Auclair, T.J. "Best Golf Jokes," a variation of Kevin Kinney's entry, *PGA.com*, http://www.pga.com/news/golf-buzz/best-golf-jokes (accessed March 29, 2015).

not performing at an "A" or "B" level. I recommend a probationary period of up to six months so that employees may be dismissed without cause during that time. This gives the organization time to make a decision on whether to invest more heavily in the individual or look elsewhere. Employee grievances that must be addressed at the board level should be limited to a committee of the board, with the option of having an agency attorney present. Some agencies will allow for a hearing before the full board of directors. This makes the already-difficult grievance process too time-consuming. Review by the full board should be at its discretion and limited to a review of the transcript of the board committee hearing the grievance unless the agency has violated the law. The court's main consideration will be whether the agency's personnel policies have been followed or violated in the dismissal of an employee. It is important that the organization retain the right to reorganize departments within the organization without employees having the right to grieve the process.

Local nonprofit organizations have a harder time than national nonprofits in changing program missions, goals, and benchmarks that require major staff changes. The closer to the community an organization is, the more likely the chance for bad press when terminations of long-term employees are mandated. Boards that hire new CEOs without investing them with the authority to make substantial staff changes doom them to dismal leadership prospects. Poorly performing organizations are usually staffed with many poor performers. There will be no possibility of change without getting rid of the "wrong whos" and getting the "right whos" on board to drive the bus in a new direction.

One of the lessons I learned during TAP's financial crisis in 2009 is that, as painful as they are, economic downturns also have their gift. They force an organization to choose which activities are most important to their mission and drop the least important. It is the opportunity to reorganize and keep the "right whos" while at the same time dismissing those who have never done better than a "C" job. Although this is not the ideal way to help the "wrong whos" move along, there's nothing like a financial crisis to force you to finally make staffing changes that you've been putting off.

Collins makes the strong point that it is not ruthlessness but rigor that drives helping the "wrong whos" move on.[107] Making these rigorous decisions assists the organization's outcomes, keeps the "right whos" free of dead weight, and often assists those who are misplaced in the organization. Very recently, I had a young man whom I had fired some time ago stop me on the street. He had found employment with a municipality that fully used his talents at a higher level of pay with better benefits than our agency could afford. He stopped to thank me for terminating his employment with TAP. Even though his termination had been painful at the time, it had forced him to look for something even better for himself and his family.

In Summary

There is no more important chapter in this book than this one. The organizations that can select the "right who," creatively manage teams of the "right whos," keep the "right whos," and rigorously help the "wrong whos" move on are the ones who will ultimately make the largest difference and achieve a level of greatness. A principal mark of Level 5 leadership is doing just that. An organization populated by the right whos has the best chance of becoming a Level 5 organization.

The "Right Who" Take-Aways

- What are you doing to ensure that you are the "right who" for your organization?
- Who are the "right whos" in the life of your organization?
- In what circumstances are the "right whos" brought together to work as a team?

---

107 Collins, *Good to Great*, p. 52.

- What use have interview panels been in the selection of staff?
- What can be done to enrich supervisory positions by providing more autonomy in the execution of their jobs?
- What can be done to increase the training opportunities for the "right whos"?
- What is being done to celebrate the work of the "right whos" in your organization?
- Have you tried using self-evaluations by staff as part of an annual evaluation process?
- Who are the "wrong whos" that need to leave so as not to block the progress of your organization?
- What kind of evaluation process are you using to help reward the "A" and "B" players on the team, and divest the organization of the "F," "D," and "C" producers who don't improve?
- Are your personnel policies adequate to protect the organization? Do you limit grievances that come to the board to a review of the transcript of the grievance committee hearing?

Profile in Excellence:
Rick Sheets

Rick Sheets is a tall, lanky West Virginian with a down-home manner. During the Vietnam War, he served as a helicopter crewman in Thailand, flying missions in Thailand, Cambodia, and Laos. Their job was to locate and extricate downed aircraft pilots while under enemy fire. Like many Americans, he entered the war gung ho for the battle to stem the Communist tide. Like many American servicemen, he left sickened by the sheer waste of human life and political miscalculation.

Rick grew up in a family where you hunted to put food on the table. If you couldn't find even a squirrel or rabbit, there was always digging for groundhogs. One day, he returned empty-handed from a day of sitting in a tree stand waiting for deer. His grandma asked, "Ricky, did you get anything?" Rick replied, "No, but I saw signs." His grandma replied, "Well, Ricky, we can't eat signs." Rick grew up with people who lived on the edge and pitched in with each other to keep their heads above water. Because of his upbringing, it was not surprising that after Vietnam when he relocated to Roanoke, Virginia, he turned to TAP to find a job assisting others who, like his family, were at best treading water.

In addition to a high degree of native intelligence and problem-solving ability, Rick has a high level of emotional intelligence that enables him to read people extremely well. On one mission in Laos after his helicopter had plucked out two downed pilots from a plane that made a forced landing on a highway, Rick was left to guard the plane with only a sidearm to defend himself. Soon he was surrounded by fifty civilians inching toward the plane, armed with homemade weapons and anxious to begin stripping the plane for parts that they could then sell or reuse. Recalling that the population had a fear of crazy people, Rick jumped on top of the plane and began furiously waving his arms and screaming like a deranged person. Forty-five minutes later, military back-up arrived. His emotional intelligence enables him to connect with people at the deepest level, too. Whether with someone coming to TAP for assistance, an employee, or the point person for a grantor agency, Rick was able to make a connection. He began his work in 1991 as the manager of the Transitional Living Center. In 1998, he was then asked to manage This Valley Works' growing number of education and training programs.

Finally, in 2004, Rick became director of TAP's growing Weatherization and Emergency Home Repair programs at a time of increasing certification requirements for those working in the field and more sophisticated criteria for weatherization measures. In his last year of service, the Virginia Department of Housing and Community Development was lagging in its number of weatherized housing units. The only way for Virginia to make its quota was to take on multifamily rental structures in which few local programs had any experience. TAP, under Rick's leadership, volunteered to tackle six apartment complexes with a total of seven hundred units over a six-month period, thereby establishing TAP as one of the lead local agencies in Virginia. In a twenty-one-year period, Rick Sheets had become an expert in working with the homeless, providing education and training to those seeking to improve their chances for employment, and weatherizing and rehabilitating homes.

Rick Sheets is the classic "right who." Self-disciplined, self-motivated, with high regard for others, able to place his ambition for the organization above his personal ambitions, he possessed the character traits that made him a successful leader in a variety of different positions. Again and again he was able to gain the training background, the practical skills, and the specialized knowledge to perform at an exceedingly high level. Whether working to help the homeless stabilize their lives, managing a high-level education and career component, or becoming an expert in home rehabilitation and weatherization, Rick's character traits made all the difference.

Chapter 10

THE ORGANIZATIONAL CULTURE

Culture does not change because we desire to change it. Culture changes when the organization is transformed; the culture reflects the realities of people working together every day.

~ Frances Hesselbein[108]

After getting the right people into an organization and the wrong people out, how do nonprofits move forward? Tony Hsieh is the CEO and founder of the Zappos Shoe Company, a dot-com industry breakthrough that, within ten years, was grossing $1 Billion. Under his leadership, the company built a culture that resulted in maximum happiness for customers, shoe vendors, and employees. The company culture, described in the *Zappos Culture Book*, combined an overriding commitment to creating the "WOW" response. Built into the equation was free expression of ideas and a good share of zany behavior among the staff. So important was the culture to Zappos' success that when Amazon bought out the company, the agreement allowed Tony to remain the Zappos CEO and operate the company under the norms

---

108 "Leading Thoughts: Quotes on Change," http://www.leadershipnow.com/changequotes.
html (accessed May 10, 2015).

and dynamics of the Zappos culture rather than folding it into the Amazon culture.[109]

At TAP, we also had to learn about organizational culture. Bristow, Wilma, Bill Hoffman, and I participated in a Mid-Atlantic Training Committee three-week residential training program for facilitators of organization development. The first two weeklong sessions provided the tools for connecting with an organization, understanding its goals and challenges, and working on the changes needed to move it in the direction to which it aspired. The third session involved finding a company on which to practice. Cabell offered the Stuart McGuire Company as the guinea pig corporation. Bristow and Wilma would meet with Cabell and his senior leadership, and Bill and I would do team-building sessions with members of the various order fulfillment departments.

Contracting with a professional mentor was part of the learning process. Bristow decided to go for the best and contacted Warner Burkhart, then the head of organization development for National Training Laboratories in Washington, DC. The major take-away lesson from our meeting with Warner was that if you are going to change an organization, you have to focus on its norms and values. The values of an organization shape its culture, which in turn shapes its future. He also gave us clues on how to discern the current values operating within a company. The clues to an organization's culture are everywhere. They display themselves in staff and volunteer body language, the organization's pace of activity, the organizational chart, the titles of address, the organization's publications and website, and stories people tell.

Even a nickname for the CEO might suggest something about the culture. Warner told us about a medical school with which he was working. The president was called "Big Daddy," suggesting his withering, authoritarian rule. Upon leaving Warner's office, Bristow,

---

109 Hsieh, Tony. *Delivering Happiness: A Path to Profits, Passion, and Purpose.* (New York: Grand Central Publishing, 2013), p. 130–200.

this burly giant of a man, turned to the three of us and said with a big grin, "I'm your mother." And indeed that was his nickname to those closest to him from then on.

An organization's culture drives and shapes an organization's present and future by attracting certain people and discouraging others. Culture and leadership have a symbiotic relationship—each shapes the other. TAP's distinct culture over the last five decades has differentiated it from many other organizations. The most important norms or values that are pillars of the TAP culture are:

- Remember who we work for
- Be the change you are working toward
- Never take "no" for an answer
- No shoddy performances
- Whatever it takes
- Real work is when "walls move"
- It's all personal
- No more organization than necessary
- It takes all of us
- Don't kill the goose

Remember Who We Work For

It is important for an organization to remember why it exists. Bristow's admonition, "the play's the thing," served to remind us never to forget TAP's purpose. The job of the theater company is to produce the very best stage play. TAP's job is to make a difference in the lives of the poor.

Wilma Warren and I toured community action agencies in Virginia, West Virginia, and Pennsylvania in an effort to document the types of projects undertaken. The Mingo County Community Action Agency, in the coalfields of West Virginia, was one of our most memorable stops. In its earliest days, the agency had taken the lead to remove substantial numbers of dead voters from the voting list who, despite their passing, continued to show up at the ballet box *in absentia.* The dead voters were known to tilt elections in favor of the establishment politicians. It was a West Virginia miracle!

The agency was also on the front line when flash floods ravaged the area. Their Head Start and senior citizen centers provided warm housing and hot meals for the flood refugees who had lost their homes and vehicles to flood waters inundating the narrow mountain passes. The Mingo County Community Action Agency was on the scene days before the Red Cross and the TV cameras could gain access to take credit for the rescue. When we asked the fellow who was head of planning for the agency what he saw the purpose of the agency to be, he replied in no uncertain terms, "We work for the poor."

TAP is answerable to the local, state, and federal agencies from which we receive much of our financial support. We are answerable to the United Way, foundations, and individual donors. We are answerable to the public on whose goodwill we depend. However, our mission is to increase the economic and personal independence of low-income individuals and families through education, employment, and promoting safe, healthy environments. The bottom line is that we work for the poor. We work for the infants, toddlers, and three- and four-year-old children whose parents struggle to give them a future of hope. We work for the first-time homebuyer mother and her two children whose home we just built. We work for the disabled veteran whose dwelling we weatherized and whose roof we repaired. We work for the mother who cannot find a medical home with a private physician or pediatrician for her children. We also work for the young high school dropout who was disruptive in class and was encouraged to leave. We work for the father who sold drugs, has just been released from prison, has nowhere to live, and needs help finding a job. We even work for the woman who has learned to use the system to find rent and fuel money from one agency after another. We work for the poor—all of them.

Another way of saying it is that we are mission driven. After fifty years, TAP remains serious about its mission to eliminate poverty through, in the words of the preamble to the Economic Opportunity Act of 1964, "education and training, the opportunity to work and the opportunity to live in decency and dignity."[110] We respect and recognize the dignity and talents of all who come through our doors, whether a single parent with small children struggling to survive, an unemployed dad looking for a job, an ex-offender trying to create a different future, a domestic violence victim battered on a regular basis, or a young person who has dropped out of school. We identify with their struggles. The strategy is always the same: Create opportunity. Applaud courageous decisions to change. Provide support and encouragement.

TAP is more than just a service organization. Working for the poor means advocating for reform when and where it needs to happen. It means making systemic reforms in favor of the disadvantaged. When Fluvanna County chose to exclude a small African American community from the benefits of its new water system, despite having included the community in its grant application to HUD for the project funds, the Virginia Water Project, led by TAP, and the Monticello Community Action Agency, which served Fluvanna County, sided with the community members. As a result of the protest by the offended community, HUD told Fluvanna County that it would never receive another dollar from the federal agency until the county served that community. The county wisely relented and the young Air Force veteran, Jerome Booker, who led that African American community, became the first African American elected to the Fluvanna Board of Supervisors. The breaking of the race barrier in a local election ensured that the African American community in Fluvanna County would have a voice on their behalf at the highest level of county power, preventing discriminatory actions like the misappropriation of HUD funds.

As a result of TAP's focus on high school dropouts, Superintendent Rita Bishop of Roanoke City Schools, supported by This Valley

---

110 Economic Opportunity Act of 1964, Pub. L. No. 88-452, 78 Stat. 508 (1964).

Works' Annette Lewis—who serves on the school board—has greatly improved Roanoke Public School's graduation rate. In addition to creating the first statewide pre- and post-incarceration reentry system in the Commonwealth, Virginia CARES has pressed for the automatic restoration of rights when a person has served their time and paid their financial obligations to the state. TAP's Virginia CARES project has urged the City of Roanoke to join other Virginia municipalities to "ban the box," the box at the end of most job applications for the purpose of indicating any prior convictions. A checked box discourages employers from interviewing ex-offenders and frequently discourages applicants from applying. Providing school board leadership unwilling to tolerate high dropout rates that predominantly affect low-income students and creating opportunities for employment for ex-offenders through the ban the box campaign are systemic changes that go beyond simply reaching out to school dropouts or counseling someone returning from prison.

Be the Change You Are Working Toward

"Be the change you wish to see in the world," is a famous quote by Mahatma Gandhi,[111] whose life inspired the end to British dominance of India and the American civil rights movement under the leadership of Dr. Martin Luther King, Jr.[112]

While I was still serving as minister to the Buchanan and Virginia churches in Botetourt County, I stopped by the Lindsey Robinson Building in the City of Roanoke, which was being transformed from a warehouse into TAP's center of operations. My Episcopalian colleague in Buchanan, the Rev. Dennett Slemp, suggested I meet Bristow Hardin, Jr., who was turning the world upside down at TAP.

---

111 "Quote by Mahatma Gandhi," Goodreads, http://www.goodreads.com/quotes/24499-be-the-change-that-you-wish-to-see-in-the (accessed April 3, 2015).

112 Gadahara Pandit Dasa, "Martin Luther King Jr. and Gandhi: The Liberating Power of Non-violence," *The Blog, The Huffington Post*, January 21, 2014 http://www.huffingtonpost.com/gadadhara-pandit-dasa/martin-luther-king-jr-and_3_b_4631610.html (accessed April 3, 2015).

In Buchanan, integrated prayer meetings were considered seditious. It was common to hear the illustration of the genetic separation of blue birds and black birds as a defense for segregation and against the cohabitation of whites and African Americans, the feared outcome of desegregation. Fear, suspicion, and anger permeated every conversation. When hostility was not spoken out loud, it was whispered. I invited Head Start Director Osborne Paine, who was an African American, to evaluate the church educational building as a potential Head Start center. An elder who lived across from the Presbyterian Church on Main Street witnessed his appearance. The next Sunday, only women exited the main door of the church after the service. I went to look for the men. The deacons and elders had decided to meet without notifying me because of their concern for what I was up to. To their credit, we had a good discussion and no adverse action was taken.

At the TAP headquarters on Shenandoah Avenue, I had entered an alternative universe. African Americans and whites, business suits and hippy attire, men and women, twenty-year-olds and senior citizens were working, arguing, and laughing side by side as if that was commonplace. There were Episcopalian and Catholic priests, African American Baptist ministers, white Methodist ministers, and lay people of all denominations setting up projects and discussion groups across the Roanoke Valley, working to end racial discrimination and open opportunity for the poor. There was a wonderful energy and joyful chaos about the place. I was reminded of the phrase in the Episcopal prayer book "all sorts and conditions of men." Here, nestled in a community controlled by racial and social economic stereotypes, I had found my home.

The change toward which TAP has been striving is a world with opportunity for all, a world that embraces diversity of race, gender, educational background, and economic status. Working at TAP is a different experience in terms of diversity from most private and public institutions in our community. No other organization, nonprofit or for-profit, in our area has as much diversity. African

Americans compose approximately 50 percent of our staff; women account for more than half. We consider life experience as important as educational degrees in many instances. Women and African Americans hold top positions of authority throughout the agency. Our insistence on diversity in senior positions is in stark contrast to most Fortune 500 companies as well as the majority of nonprofits.

The gifts of diversity are many. In a diverse setting, we all learn to recognize our stereotypes and to work through them on a day-to-day basis. A diverse work environment contributes to "cultural intelligence." We benefit from exposure to each other's cultural institutions and a greater understanding of how the history of a people, like the experience of slavery, is reflected in individual consciousness and our culture. Diversity brings the different leadership styles of men and women together. The inclusion of women leaders tends to promote a culture that contributes to teamwork and disparages self-serving ego needs. Diversity increases an organization's outreach and ability to communicate more effectively to wider groups of people. Staff diversity is an asset that enables us to work more effectively with different populations and create strong levels of support from other organizations and their leaders. In order to realize the benefits of diversity in the workplace, an organization must be intentional about the creation of a diverse workplace. If it isn't, the company will inevitably fall prey to stereotypes and fail to get the very best talent.

Never Take "No" for an Answer

There is always a bias for the status quo. There are always excuses as to why something cannot be done. TAP found a cluster of forty houses at the east end of Botetourt County with feces standing in the front yards because the septic systems refused to percolate. We approached the health department on the community's behalf and were told that the situation did not rate as a health hazard because it did not get enough points on the health hazard assessment grid. This was because, although there was feces in the yard, the homes had potable water from the water system in the nearby town of Iron Gate. We were appalled. Who in their right mind could deny that children playing in a yard contaminated with human waste was a health hazard? TAP staff refused to be put off by bureaucratic nonsense. TAP applied for a Small Town Emphasis grant and hired Virginia Tech to do an epidemiological study linking the bacteria in the feces in the soil with the poor health records of the residents. The study demonstrated the obvious. Voilà! The points now added up on the health hazard tally sheet indicating a health hazard. The community now qualified for a HUD grant, which was submitted by Botetourt County on its behalf. The result of not taking "no" for an answer: New septic systems, renovated housing, improved lives.

Frequently the "known" is the enemy of knowledge. I love the story that Joe Hyams tells in his book, *Zen in the Martial Arts*. He tells of meeting Bruce Lee with the hope of training under him. Bruce told him that he would take him on as a student, but the one requirement was that he forget everything he knew about the martial arts. Already proficient at karate, Hyams balked. Bruce then told him the story of the Zen master who, frustrated with his prospective student's know-it-all attitude, sat him down at tea. The master continued pouring the fellow's tea until it ran over the student's cup. When the student questioned what was happening, the master explained, "How can I show you Zen unless you first empty your cup?"[113]

Often it is better to approach a situation or problem from the stance of Peter Faulk's Columbo in the detective series of the same name who always had one more question to ask, the position of not knowing until the right answer appeared. The day I joined TAP, I knew that I was in an environment for which I was unprepared. It was an environment for which there was no academic program and in which the body of knowledge was scattered or yet to be discovered. This sense of "unknowing" was reinforced by Bristow's honesty that we had initially had no idea about the problems faced by the poor,

113 Hyams, Joe. *Zen in the Martial Arts*. (New York: Bantam Books, 1982), p. 9–11.

let alone how to solve them. We found ourselves very much in a laboratory. It helped us question pat answers and past explanations and refuse to take "no" for an answer. That sense of unknowing has fostered in me a desire to learn and explore better ways of operating and solving problems and build on a growing body of knowledge in the fields of education, psychology, and community and economic development. It has helped me to ask questions about why the mainline structures of our society fall short when they fail to connect with the lives of low-income people.

No Shoddy Performances

As Bristow would say, "The play is the thing!" Opening night is when the production either holds together or falls apart, determining whether there will be another evening performance or the show closes down. Excellence is the only acceptable standard.

From the beginning, TAP has been conscious that it was a significant part of the American drama and that it was making history. In the early days, Bristow even hired a historian to document what was taking place. In fact, during the last five decades, TAP has had two published accounts of its extraordinary work.[114] Thus, the standard of excellence, "no shoddy performances," is something to which the organization continues to aspire. That is not always the case with organizations. Thirty years ago I was with a group of Virginia's nonprofit leaders. Over lunch, one executive actually said, "I think that mediocrity is the highest that we can shoot for." Over the years, I have known people who have acted as if that was their goal, but he was the only one I ever heard claim it. His agency demonstrated his words. Within twenty years, the agency lost over 50 percent of its programs and has been left in the dust by newer agencies.

---

114 Cobb, Edwin L. *No Cease Fires: The War on Poverty In Roanoke Valley.* (Cabin John, MD: Seven Locks Press, 1984), p. 176; Brand, Elizabeth. *Community Action at Work: TAP's Thirty-Year War on Poverty.* (Roanoke, Virginia: Total Action Against Poverty in Roanoke Valley in conjunction with Pocahontas Press and R.R. Donnelly, 2000), p. 158.

When Ronald Reagan came to office in 1980, he empowered Budget Director David Stockman to "starve the beast"—meaning to cut taxes that supported the federal social and economic support system for those at the bottom of American society, in the form of expenditure on education, welfare, community action, Social Security, Medicare, and Medicaid. The prevailing wisdom was that tough times were coming and that everyone, including nonprofit agencies, would have to do more with less. This meant proverbial belt tightening. My calculation was that if one extrapolated this position to its extreme and nonsensical conclusion, it would mean that we could do everything with virtually nothing. I decided that TAP would expand its horizons of potential impact and redouble our search for the necessary resources. The truth is that money is always available to those who are the most aggressive in their quest. The staff rose to the challenge and, as a result, TAP expanded its programs and more than doubled its budget, going from $7 million to more than $18 million.

"No shoddy performances" refers to quality as well as quantity. Hence TAP is increasingly a data-driven organization. For instance, the decision to ensure the "bundling" of services so that TAP clients are enrolled in two or more programs that meet their needs will be measured accordingly:

- One hundred percent of TAP clients will be referred to applicable internal components and outside agencies.
- Seventy-five percent of referred clients will follow through on referrals or recommendations made to them.
- Seventy percent of referred clients will receive other services through TAP and/or other agencies, including financial education.
- Forty-five percent of clients will access benefits through online submission or referral to Public Access Benefits programs.
- Forty-five percent of clients will receive financial literacy education.

Quality is being enhanced with our Tools of the Mind curriculum pilots in Head Start, a two-generation program model addressing parents and children, and a feedback system that allows Head Start teachers to see on a weekly basis where the children in their classroom stand with all the other Head Start classrooms in the agency. The motto of the Reformed Church, in which I was trained, was "reformed and always reforming." It might also be TAP's motto as well.

Whatever It Takes

Excellence is maintained by a "can-do" and "whatever it takes to get the job done" mentality. Only one other community action agency in Virginia has tackled as many issues faced by low-income families and individuals. Whether it is a matter of education, health care, housing, small business development, or community and economic development, we believe that if someone else can do it, we can do it, too. It is just a matter of learning, planning, executing the plan, and reflecting on what does and does not work. We always presume that there is someone else out there who is doing it better. We then find out who they are and frequently get free technical assistance. Here are other examples of TAP's commitment to "whatever it takes":

In most of the statewide organizations TAP has built, the staffer in charge of the demonstration has done double duty as the leader of the demonstration and as the unpaid acting executive of the new organization until funding permits a full-time executive director and administrative team.

If we have to work all weekend or nights to get a grant proposal out or to ensure that program enrollment is met, staff committed to TAP's mission sacrifice without hesitation.

When the federal funding was eliminated for Virginia CARES, we started all over again with a $125,000 grant from the Virginia General Assembly, building up the program a year at a time.

We twice applied for a nationally competitive Early Head Start grant. After we were turned down a second time, we employed a national grant writer who had specialized in Early Head Start grant applications. After two more tries, we got our award. In addition, when the American Recovery and Reinvestment Act money was available, we were a successful applicant for $3 million, to expand our program and retrofit a vacant Roanoke City elementary school and an office building in Buena Vista. We consider every grant application denial another step before the next submission is approved.

When we needed to create a video to help the Virginia General Assembly meet Project Discovery's college graduates, TAP IT Director James Lane built our capacity to shoot video footage and produce a documentary that changed the Virginia Secretary of Education's perception of the program.

Real Work is When "Walls Move"

There is a difference between looking like you're working and actually working. Bristow once gave the example of the fellow who so wanted to appear to be working that he carried his briefcase to the restroom. Bristow said, "Work is not pushing against a wall. Work is when the wall moves!" Too often, people come to a job and sit at a desk, looking like they are working rather than actually accomplishing something. Better to take a break, take a walk, do something crazy, and then get back to the business of "making walls move."

To be sure, the work itself is a great source of joy. There is nothing like making a huge difference in someone's life. Hearing an entire family tell of the joy they feel after moving into a brand new home that TAP built and financed is the greatest "drug" in the world. Seeing an ex-offender that you have hired perform better than anyone else you have previously had in that job is an unbelievable high. Seeing a Head Start mother get her GED and graduate with both bachelor's and master's degrees in social work is enough to put a smile on your face for months.

However, the environment you work in can kill that joy and even keep you from performing at your very best. I have friends who work in community colleges, local school systems, and hospitals under the tyranny of small-minded supervisors who care only if people look like they are working and think that the way to produce more work is to harass their employees with requirements and threats. There are many jobs that require that staff be there at a certain time and in a certain place. There is little time flexibility for a Head Start teacher or assistant teacher who must be in the classroom in time for the children's arrival. Even here, though, the teachers and assistants can make arrangements each day to share duties and provide time for planning for the next day. There are some jobs, like those of grant writers, for which we can make accommodations. A person with a sick child may work from home on a computer linked with the office computer. Ironically, a grant writer working from home, away from the onslaught of office phones and email, can concentrate more fully and very often produce a superior product.

Everyone has a work style that brings out the best in them. Simply chaining people to a desk does not mean something will happen. I remember when I started work at TAP. Deputy Director John Sabean advised me, "Just remember: Keep your feet firmly planted, your nose to the grindstone, your eye on the ball, and your shoulder to the wheel. Then try to work in that position." One of my favorite scenes from *Butch Cassidy and the Sundance Kid* is when the Kid and Butch decide to give up bank robbing and go straight. They try to hire on as security guards to a delivery of silver ore from the mine to the town bank. The mine boss asks, "Can you shoot?" He then takes the Kid's gun from his holster, hands it to him, and says, "Hit that rock over there." Painstakingly, Sundance takes aim and misses the rock by a mile. The mine boss shakes his head. Sundance then asks, "This time can I move?" He places the gun in his holster and in less than a second the Kid has drawn his revolver and hit the stone on the ground and then twice more in the air. He twirls the gun and replaces it in his holster.[115] To do your best work, you have to be able to move!

---

115 *Butch Cassidy and the Sundance Kid,* directed by George Roy Hill (1969; Los Angeles, CA: Twentieth Century Fox, 2011), DVD.

TAP is also a place where staff is encouraged to eat together. Celebrations of birthdays and milestone accomplishments are frequent. In addition, we have avoided time clocks, which ostensibly force people to work a full forty hours a week. Instead, we found employees often voluntarily stay longer to finish an assignment that benefits the company.

Too often a workplace is geared to create the atmosphere of the appearance of work, pushing against walls, rather than be a place where "the walls move." You can usually tell those places because there is so little laughter and warm human interaction. The staff can't wait to get the hell out of there and go home.

It's All Personal

Feelings always play a part in our interactions no matter how we try to disguise them. Many years ago, I was doing some teambuilding with a group of social workers in the local Department of Social Services at the request of the superintendent. We had just participated in a session in which the team members had been very animated. I suggested that we stop for a moment and share our feelings. One member of the team responded, "I'm a professional; I don't share feelings!" as if it is possible just like that to remove what is personal from a heated discussion. I remember Alvin Nash, Director of Housing, telling me about a confrontation he had just had with a city official. The person had leveled a barrage of outlandish criticism on him and then concluded, "I want you to know it's not personal." Alvin responded, "It's all personal!"

In his Harvard Business Review article on "What Makes A Leader" Daniel Goleman writes: "I have found, however, that the most effective leaders are alike in one crucial way: They all have a high degree of what has come to be known as *emotional intelligence.* It's not that IQ and technical skills are irrelevant. They do matter, but mainly as 'threshold capabilities'; that is, they are the entry-level requirements for executive positions. But my research, along with other recent studies, clearly shows that emotional intelligence is the sine qua non of leadership. Without it, a person can have the best training in the world, an incisive, analytical mind, and an endless supply of smart ideas, but he still won't make a great leader."[116]

In his study of competency in 188 companies, the skills that separated star performers from average ones were:

1. Self-awareness, "the ability to recognize your moods, emotions, and drives, as well as their effect on others."
2. Self-regulation, "the ability to control or redirect disruptive impulses and moods."
3. Motivation, "a passion for work that goes beyond money or status."
4. Empathy, "the ability to understand the emotional makeup of other people."
5. Social skill, "proficiency in managing relationships and building networks."

Goleman concludes that emotional intelligence is twice as important as IQ and technical skills "for jobs at all levels."[117]

TAP staff goes through the "Pickle Training," led by a series of instructional videos created by a successful restaurateur because he never hesitated to give customers something extra and build relationships. When a waitress refused to give a customer an extra free pickle with a sandwich, a longtime customer complained to the owner and indicated they would never be returning. From then on, he instructed his staff always to give customers a free pickle and to provide that little extra that would bring them back again and again.[118]

While it is tempting to try to remove the personal aspect from our interactions, we in the nonprofit world are in the people business.

---

116 Goleman, Daniel. "What Makes A Leader?" *Harvard Business Review*, January 2004, vol, 82, no. 1.

117 Ibid.

118 Media Partners Corporation, "The Pickle Principle," http://www.giveemthepickle.com/pickle_principle.htm (accessed March 31, 2015).

Our customers are people. Too often, both public and private agencies treat the public as the potential enemy. For instance, visitors are screened from behind glass barriers by staff—who wear badges to distinguish themselves from those that don't belong—and have to wait for someone to escort them to the appropriate office. There ought to be a penalty for architects and their clients who build Departments of Social Services offices like cold, stark prisons where the customer is treated like an inmate. I have never forgotten the words of Paul Lehmann, who wrote in his *Ethics in a Christian Context*, that the Christian path is to comply with the work of God "to make and to keep human life human."[119] At TAP, every effort is made to treat strangers coming for help with appreciation and respect. It is about making human life more human. It is about being personal!

One of the first things a visitor to TAP notices is the warmth and friendliness of staff toward each other and those we serve. We are a first-name culture, and no effort is made to put a distance between staff, or between staff and customers, by the formality of titles, degrees, or even last names. Cabell was Cabell. Bristow was Bristow. I am Ted. Annette is Annette.

A first-name, non-title culture makes appreciating everybody in the organization easier. Everyone is important because everyone has a role to play. They all have input that can benefit the organization or can offer an idea that can make a big difference. I have never seen a public agency or a nonprofit organization fall in love with academic or position titles and not have its culture affected. Invariably it creates an atmosphere where those without titles are looked down on as less intelligent or at the very least less important.

A high-performance culture has to take into account the skill set that contributes to emotional intelligence. It is absolutely necessary to look at the brutal facts, to manage on the basis of hard evidence of output performance, and to make mid-course corrections in light of a changing environment. This can only be done by taking the personal

---

119 Lehmann, *Ethics*, p. 99.

into account and operating in a culture of high respect, deep listening, and emotional self-regulation.

No More Organization than Necessary

A few years ago, I had to laugh. One of the firms that rented space in our Crystal Tower building was a major engineering firm that sold manufacturing equipment. The rented space was for a staff of three engineers who sold and serviced the company's products to manufacturing firms within a large region of Virginia. The firm's lease extended beyond the sale of the property, so we had to compensate the firm or provide comparable space. We worked with the engineers involved—who were well acquainted with the area and the available space options—and found a space that met their specifications. Actually, it was better than the one they had previously occupied. However, final approval could not be obtained until three corporate executives from three different states had flown in to personally sign off on the new location.

My experience, echoed by an article I read a long time ago, is that the greater the distance between someone delivering a service and the chief executive officer, the greater the chance for ineffectiveness. The reverse is also true: the fewer management levels between the boss and the front-line worker, the more productive the organization. In all my years, I have never found an organization in which people at the lower levels are happier than the people at the top. Therefore, it stands to reason that the greater the difference between the two, the greater the unhappiness of those on the front line.

The maximum that I shoot for is two levels of management between myself and those on the front line. Bristow added another layer, hiring a deputy director on whom he depended to manage his top directors. I wanted contact with the top-level staff and, as often as possible, those on the front line. In recent years, I have relied on Annette Lewis, Director of This Valley Works, to also be Senior Vice President of Program Coordination. At the same time, all director-level personnel are responsible to me. That immediate contact with director-level staff has decreased my distance from front-line operations, eliminated a layer of middle management bureaucracy, and facilitated my engagement to the highest possible degree in the work that is taking place to ensure quality.

It Takes All of Us

At TAP, the norm is shared leadership, so leadership is ostensibly in everyone's hands. Everyone is a leader in the role for which they are responsible. Everyone's performance reflects on the agency. Anyone can come up with a breakthrough idea, and everyone's thoughts are considered. For years, we had been struggling with the agency's name, Total Action Against Poverty. We wanted to keep the acronym, TAP, but wanted a name that would emphasize the positive. For TAP's name change, it was Pete Clark, who had been Director of Property Management and Maintenance for a few months, who blurted out "What about Total Action for Progress?"

At any moment on a particular task, one person takes the lead and the others support them. A moment that has stuck with me was when I was at the University of North Carolina. UNC won the National AAU Basketball Championship against Wilt Chamberlain's team. In the last second of the game, it was the smallest man on the squad, Billy Cunningham, who hit the two-point jump shot that defeated the best team in the nation.

The notion of shared leadership does not mean that TAP is a democracy. When I was Head Start Director, I experimented with rotating staff between lead teacher and center director. It was an abysmal failure. There can only be one director of the agency and one leader of a project component. That person consults with the rest of the team, considers opinions, and ultimately makes a decision; the rest of the team falls in behind to implement it to the best of their ability.

Generally, responsibility for leadership of a team or department is given to a single person who then draws out the support and talent of team members. Of course, there are exceptions to nearly every rule. When Owen Schultz, Vice President of Planning and Resource Development, retired after an unprecedented seventeen-year run of grant submissions and awards, I put an ad in the paper for a successor. Two veteran members of the staff, Kristen Moses and Amy Hatheway, came to my office and suggested that I appoint them as co-directors of the department. Ordinarily that would be a bad idea, but the two of them blend different skills and work together seamlessly. Any other decision would have been a shortsighted one.

The advantage of shared leadership is one of simple math. Since everyone pitches in, many more creative ideas are generated, more eyes are focused on improvements that can be made, and more hands are quickly employed to solve problems. That is so much better than the designated leader model, where everyone suspends thought and action until the word comes down from on high. A bunch of folks sitting at a table staring at one another doesn't solve anything.

Don't Kill the Goose

Bristow's number one admonition was, "Don't kill the goose." Essentially, never forget the bottom line. Nonprofits in the "red" are not nonprofits for long. The worst days of my four-decade career were the result of not paying enough heed to that admonition. The CHIP project mentioned in earlier chapters is the envy of every nonprofit in the Roanoke Valley. CHIP has an established endowment of $1,000,000 and have their sights set on a $5,000,000 goal. In addition, People, Inc., which serves a large section of Southwest and Northern Virginia, has just been awarded their third major allocation of New Market Tax Credits. The goal of their agency is to build a $5,000,000 endowment through the money that they make on the sale of the $30,000,000 of tax credits they have received to invest in projects that produce employment in economically distressed areas.

TAP has emerged from the last three years of difficult financial times with a strong balance sheet. Plans to strengthen that balance sheet include a signature event to raise $100,000 of local resources, and projects that are geared to produce discretionary income.

In Summary

Nothing is more important than the culture of an organization. The culture is determined by the operational values of the organization that are set and promoted by leadership. The organization's culture determines the people who are attracted to the organization, the way they work together, and the impact the organization has in carrying out its mission. At TAP, always remembering why we are in business and who we work for, being the change we are seeking to make in a more diverse world, refusing to take no for an answer, constantly striving for excellence, making walls move rather than simply pushing against them, doing whatever it takes, honoring the personal, working in teams, and always being concerned with the bottom line are the norms that make up the TAP culture.

The Organizational Culture Take-Aways

- How would you describe the culture of the organization that you work for?
- Who is it that defines the culture of your organization?
- How does the culture of your organization differ from the TAP culture as described in this chapter (remember who we work for, never take "no" for an answer, no shoddy performances, real work is when "walls move," whatever it takes, it's all personal, no more organization than necessary, it takes all of us, don't kill the goose)?
- What is it about your organizational meetings, important events in the life of your organization, the space your organization occupies, how offices are connected, the written material that you produce, your organization chart, the interaction of staff,

and the agency's connection with those on the outside that best defines the culture of the organization?

- What plans have you made for attracting discretionary income that can be used to fund important positions or activities and attract other dollars to support your organization?
- What, if anything, would you like to change about your organization's culture? How would you go about making that change?

Profile in Excellence:
Angela Penn

Angela Penn, Vice President of Economic and Real Estate Development at TAP, is an impeccably dressed, petite, soft-spoken young woman. She holds a business administration degree from James Madison University and an MBA from Radford University. She has had extensive experience in the area of communications and affordable housing, having served as the Roanoke Redevelopment and Housing Authority's Public Information Officer and Communications and Grants coordinator, as well as their vice president of Real Estate Development. Her experience at TAP spans twelve years and multiple positions: before serving as vice president for Economic and Real Estate Development, she managed the affordable housing and community development component.

Her easy manner belies an incredible mind for details, and her diminutive appearance cloaks a tenacious spirit. Her day starts at five in the morning when she rises to complete a P90X hour-long workout program in her home before waking her husband and three children for breakfast. She is a conspicuous note taker and is a master of organization. Everything is planned down to the last detail. It is not enough just to have birthday parties for each of her three children. Each birthday also has a special, unique theme.

Angela is an expert at facilitating community meetings, allowing stakeholders maximum participation in the project design and development process. She is flawless in estimating construction costs and bringing in projects on time and under budget. She manages complex housing construction programs in the urban center of Roanoke, the small town of Clifton Forge, and rural Bath County. Angela has a thorough grasp of the facts of any situation she works with, making it extremely difficult to put one over on her.

Angela provided the key leadership in managing the second phase of construction of the $27 million Low Income and Historic

Tax Credit renovations of the Terrace Apartments, the renovation of thirty-four structures in two rural communities in Bath County, and the construction of affordable housing for first-time homebuyers in the City of Roanoke and the town of Clifton Forge. When TAP won a $3 million Early Head Start expansion grant, her department managed construction on two major Head Start facilities in Roanoke and Buena Vista. Angela is instantly recognizable on any construction site because of her pink hard hat.

In addition, she leads TAP's development team, which meets to plan and discuss projects she is directly managing as well as those of our weatherization, property management, and financial services components. Angela is so dedicated she insists on managing property closings, even when out of town on vacation. Angela lets nothing get in the way of her job. No one was surprised when the new mother showed up at a three-day senior staff retreat with her two-week-old daughter, Gracie, in tow.

In addition to leading the TAP Development Team, Angela has directly assisted the thirty members of the TAP Board during the last four years, providing them with the agenda and supporting documentation for each monthly board meeting.

Her leadership extends beyond TAP to the community at large, where she has been a member of the Roanoke Neighborhood Revitalization Partnership, and has served as chair of the Planning Committee for the City of Roanoke.

Angela Penn embodies all of the values of the TAP culture at its best. She will do whatever it takes to make the walls move to improve housing for low-income families. Her personal regard for others and exceedingly high emotional intelligence enable her to work through differences with others. She is master at finding a way around challenges that would discourage others and is never satisfied unless the work she oversees is of the highest standard. Her entrepreneurial drive has attracted additional resources to help the organization further its mission.

Chapter 11

NETWORKS, PARTNERSHIPS, COLLABORATIONS, AND COLLECTIVE ACTION

If everyone is moving forward together, success takes care of itself.

~ Henry Ford[120]

It is the long history of humankind (and animal kind, too) those who learned to collaborate and improvise most effectively have prevailed.

~ Charles Darwin[121]

Great organizations work well on their own, but they can also work with one another. At this writing, TAP has a total of 121 public and private partners for its more than thirty programs; twenty of the partnerships are for our Head Start program alone. We developed these to build education, housing, business loan, community

120 Stephanie Sarkis, "25 Quotes on Collaboration: Learn from Successful People About the Importance of Working with Others," *Here, There, and Everywhere* (blog), *Psychology Today*, May 7, 2012, https://www.psychologytoday.com/blog/here-there-and-everywhere/201205/25-quotes-collaboration (accessed May 10, 2015).

121 Douglas Satterfield, "The Origin of Species—Charles Darwin," *The Leader Maker* (blog), November 24, 2013, http://www.theleadermaker.com/the-origin-of-species-charles-darwin/ (accessed May 15, 2015).

development, and health care initiatives throughout Virginia. Partnerships are essential in today's environment in order to make a substantial difference and are considered a prerequisite to serious funding from outside sources.

Historically, four agencies had competed for local Community Development Block Grant (CDBG) funds in the City of Roanoke: TAP, Habitat for Humanity, the Roanoke Redevelopment and Housing Authority, and Blue Ridge Housing and Development Corporation. TAP's Vice President of Real Estate Development, Angela Penn, brought all of the groups together. The City of Roanoke targeted its CDBG dollars to one of the poorest neighborhoods in the community, Hurt Park. Angela worked to submit a joint application to build and renovate homes there that worked on the strengths of the individual organizations to provide a greater overall impact. Together, the coalition of agencies transformed housing in one of the poorest neighborhoods in the City of Roanoke with a total of sixty-four homes that were either new construction or total renovations, now in the hands of low-income homeowners. The four agencies had a greater impact working together than they would have had separately.

While the establishment of partnerships is an entry-level requirement in today's community development world, state-of-the-art social change frequently requires collective action.

The Stanford Social Innovation Review listed five key conditions for achieving social change through collective impact:

1. Looking at the same plan
2. Making sure everyone knows how factors like progress and performance will be tracked
3. Having tasks that support one another
4. Communicating often
5. Making sure part of the organization exists to direct all other parts

The National Demonstration Water Project

The development of the Demonstration Water Project into the Virginia Water Project, the National Demonstration Water Project, and the national Rural Capacity Assistance Program is a prime example of collective impact.

TAP's outreach into low-income rural communities had resulted in the identified need for potable water, sanitary waste disposal, and indoor plumbing as high priority items. A coalition of five hundred families from five counties surrounding Roanoke was formed. Representatives from the coalition, accompanied by TAP staff, went to Washington, DC, to ask Office of Economic Opportunity (OEO) officials for $150,000 to drill the wells that would serve clusters of homes, and $111,000 in grants and loans to finance the remaining cost of the water systems and training residents to manage those systems.

Subsequently, TAP helped form a separate corporation, the Demonstration Water Project. Low-income residents from areas without water and wastewater comprised the majority of its board. DWP staff applied for $350,000 from OEO and finally received an award of $166,000 to begin operation. With additional loan dollars from the Farmers Home Administration (FmHA) for construction and operations training, the project gained traction. Within three years, more than fourteen community water systems were operational, serving more than one thousand families.

While the Farmers' Home Administration was active in developing rural water systems based on applications and contributions from eligible communities, poorer communities were not able to make the cut because they did not have the local leadership and financial resources to make successful applications. Moreover, at the county level, existing water authorities, new housing developers, and local business leaders were more interested in supporting projects that had a direct financial return based on new residents that could support the increased taxes, project fees, and profits. Consequently, the needy communities could not move up the FmHA list for eligible water projects. The lack of potable water prevented these communities from qualifying for other federal or state assistance programs for economic or community development projects.

TAP's development of the Demonstration Water Project caught the eye of Gersten Green, appointed Director of Research and Demonstration for the Office of Economic Opportunity (OEO). OEO envisioned the network of community action agencies as laboratories for the creation of strategies to end poverty in the United States. Gersten envisioned an expansion of DWP's grassroots effort throughout the country, since rural access to water and sanitary waste disposal was a national problem.

When Bristow and Margo Kiely contacted Gersten Green, he turned to Stan Zimmerman, Associate Professor of Public Law at NYU Law School and Deputy Director of the Center for Social Welfare Law, to ascertain his interest in providing assistance and oversight to the project. Stanley had assisted the US Department of the Interior in the development of economic opportunity programs. He also worked in the OEO General Counsel's Office. Upon returning to NYU Law School, Stanley obtained and administered OEO funding for the school to pay professors to develop and add sections on legal rights of the poor to the more traditional courses they taught. Stanley had also worked with the Southwest Alabama Federation of Southern Cooperatives and the Ford Foundation, providing recommendations concerning its national Minority Business Development Program.

It soon became obvious that the problems shared in the rural areas of Southwest Virginia were also shared by other OEO projects (community action programs, community health centers, and housing projects). Stanley began monthly meetings with Bristow and TAP staff. Battle hungry, Stanley wanted out of central command and into the field where the action was. That attitude and passion would lead him to become the CEO of the National Demonstration Water Project.

With a technical assistance grant from OEO, Stanley began

working with Bristow and Wilma to develop the national effort. Later, Wilma and I helped to expand the Demonstration Water Project from a local organization into the Virginia Water Project (VWP), using the network of Virginia community action agencies as the field system throughout the Commonwealth. The National Demonstration Water Project (NDWP) began in 1972 as a coalition of community-based organizations in Virginia, including VWP, PRIDE (a community action agency in Logan, West Virginia), two health centers, one in Arkansas and one in South Carolina, a rural electrical cooperative in Florida, and a Chicano uplift/empowerment organization in New Mexico.

By 1973 NDWP was fully incorporated, and by 1976 two additional projects had joined NDWP, a Chicano-controlled nonprofit water company in Texas with an ethnic uplift agenda, and a self-help housing program in California. CONSET, the company established by Zimmerman and his partners, John Foster and Edwin Cobb, provided staff leadership, supervised by the NDWP Board of Directors. John, an African American graduate of Ohio State in civil engineering, had worked for the Farmers Home Administration and had broken in to a profession dominated by white individuals. He created a milestone system that identified the progress of NDWP projects. The milestones included neighborhood eligibility surveys, predevelopment engineering studies, funding, construction, and completion. For the next five years, John lived out of his car and suitcase as he traveled from state to state, overseeing the development of low-income community water and wastewater systems. Edwin Cobb, a former professor of Political Science and published writer, handled all of the funding applications, reports, and publications.

In a 1979 article in *New Spirit Magazine*, I discussed the core features of a reform network and the results of collective action. Below, in parentheses, I reference how each concept applied to the National Demonstration Water Project. These features are:

- *It must not lose its reform orientation, since those services that serve the majority of Americans did not function to equally serve low-income families.* (NDWP did an extensive report that raised questions about the Farmers Home Administration's [FmHA] performance and challenged the agency to focus on their mandate to serve the low-income rural population.)

- *It must have the appropriate legal structure and an effective fiscal and management accountability system.* (NDWP had an impeccable programmatic and fiscal record. This was due in part to Stanley's foresight when setting up the CONSET corporation. He structured it so that he would need the support of at least one of the owners in any decision, to protect both CONSET and NDWP from the potential of his leading the organization down the wrong path.)

- *Its board must be made up of the executives of the member projects.* (In NDWP, no substitutes were allowed. There also was high involvement of all personnel in the work plan of the organization. Nationally, workshops were continually held to train field staff and ascertain frontline information.)

- *There must be a competent central staff with adequate authority to manage the network program.* (The board of directors closely reviewed CONSET's performance and work plan and approved the final document. During the year, each project was subject to both a staff evaluation and peer review. In all of these meetings, nothing was held back. Everyone was respectful but brutally honest.)

- *It must fulfill its mission.* (By 1977, NDWP facilitated the building of fifty thousand water and wastewater connections across the country.)

- *It is important to make local, state, and federal public officials aware of the need and the work of the network in each locality.* (NDWP affiliates excelled at unceasing communication with all elected officials.)[122]

---

122 Edlich, Ted. "Networking: An Overview," *New Spirit Magazine: The Magazine of Human Service,* June 1979, p. 22.4–22.7.

In my new role as executive director of TAP, I became the chairman of the board for the VWP and a member of the board of the NDWP. At one of the NDWP board meetings in my first year, it came time for a staff and peer review of the VWP. Central to our contract was to fully utilize the Virginia community action agencies in the delivery of local water and wastewater services. During the review, the VWP was chastised for its failure to involve these agencies and our consequential failure in the production of water and sewer connections. Upon our return to Roanoke, I called the executive director of VWP into my office and told him that I would never go through such a blistering and humiliating experience again. If he could not find a way to involve the community action agencies in the project, I would find someone who could. Within a month, he had resigned and Wilma Warren took the position. By the end of her tenure in 1995, two hundred thousand low-income Virginians would be connected to water and wastewater services.

In 1976, NDWP's three-year contract with OEO was up for review. It was time for renewal. None of us had doubts about renewal. The need was there. NDWP had an incredible track record. President Carter came from the rural South, the location of most of the nation's substandard housing. Our previous grant officer in OEO, Pat Stoffer, had warned that her replacement might not be as committed.

Six months ahead of the new contract year, I met with Bob Landman, head of planning and development for the Community Service Administration (CSA, the federal successor to OEO) to talk about a contract renewal. I was so confident in the work that NDWP had done that I suggested that CSA do a third-party evaluation. If the project received a good report, I expected the contract to be renewed. If the project failed to pass muster, I urged him to defund the program. For four months, we did not hear anything about our renewal. Two months before our contract expired, I visited Bob in DC and asked if CSA had decided to refund NDWP. Landman answered that the agency decided not to. They also had not commissioned a third-party evaluation on which to base their decision.

I asked why, on both counts. I will never forget Bob's reply. "Well," he said, "NDWP was a Nixon demonstration. We're looking for a Carter demonstration." I told Bob Landman that this was a terrible mistake for the agency as well as for a successful program that had produced incredible results. I warned him that the program had a wealth of congressional support and there would be repercussions for CSA. He had no idea what was to come. Within days, NDWP had over one hundred congressmen and senators of both parties calling the White House daily, urging the refunding of NDWP. At the ends of the political spectrum of support were segregationist senator Strom Thurmond and the "liberal lion" of the Senate, Ted Kennedy. CSA extended the contract for NDWP but came out the loser in political prestige with the administration. At Carter's White House conference to lay out his rural initiatives program, the director of CSA was the only invited department head not asked to speak.

When Bob told me his "reasons," I understood the fickleness of political regimes. Mayors, governors, and presidents want to have a program to put their name on. Anything with a history, even a successful one, has an uphill battle in the transition from one administration to another. No wonder funding for community action has been zeroed out or received minimal support by all presidents, Republican and Democrat, since Lyndon Johnson. (In 1978, an evaluation of the National Demonstration Water Project was completed by Louis Berger & Associates for the Community Service Administration. The study, which was highly favorable to NDWP, was never released! A copy was accidentally discovered in an agency trash can.)

While supporting the development of water and wastewater systems, bureaucrats in the CSA and FmHA disliked NDWP's political clout. Used to deferential treatment, they felt threatened by NDWP's leadership that came to the negotiating table as equals. Local projects had too much political support, so they took aim at Stanley Zimmerman and CONSET, making successive grants dependent on NDWP hiring its own internal staff rather than contracting with

CONSET for leadership services. Under Stanley's lead, CONSET poured its small profits back into NDWP during transition years just to maintain the program.

In 1977, the CSA awarded a planning grant to NDWP to extend the reach of the program through the use of community action agencies in other states. In 1979, it funded expansion through the Midwest Assistance Program, which covered the Dakotas and Nebraska, and Rural Housing Improvement, Inc. located in New England. Over the next two years, NDWP would add four more affiliates, ensuring coverage of the entire United States, and NDWP would morph into the National Rural Community Assistance Program, overseeing work of the six regional RCAPs. I would serve as the first chairman of the board of the national RCAP organization, assisting in the transfer of responsibilities from NDWP to RCAP. Edwin Cobb would be RCAP's first Executive Director, ensuring experienced leadership.

In his capacity as RCAP CEO, Edwin Cobb wrote:

Although the 1980s was a difficult decade for social programs, both NDWP and most of its affiliates were able to weather the changes. By the late 80s, NDWP had achieved many of its goals. The NDWP's trial efforts had been successful not only at widening and improving service delivery but also at achieving policy reform at state and federal agency and legislative levels. In the field, NDWP pioneered the use of cluster well systems, fostered the involvement of rural electric cooperatives in water supply and sanitation facilities development, developed the concept of regional support companies for small rural systems, and was instrumental in obtaining state funding for rural water programs.

At the policy level, NDWP was able to achieve significant changes in key funding and regulatory agencies (including a new method of figuring loan-to-grant ratios by the Farmers Home Administration), bring about the first technical assistance program in that agency's history, support innovative and alternative technology set-asides in the Environmental Protection Agency, and engender an increased emphasis on appropriate technology, operations and maintenance, and affordability in both agencies.[123]

In Retrospect

The reality is that a local issue is often an issue shared by other communities, and a solution necessary to tackle an issue in one locality requires scaling up to get the resources necessary to address the issue in many localities. Collaborative networks of many nonprofit agencies working across communities often grow from this up-scaling. Collaborative networks are most effective when the core features of a reformed network are adhered to (as demonstrated by the National Demonstration Water Project). The development of one collaborative effort can lead to working partnerships that transfer to other issues of importance. The networking approach of VWP in the Commonwealth of Virginia developed the connections between the more than twenty community action agencies in the state and enabled TAP to build similar collaborative networks, addressing the issues of prisoner reentry, primary health care for children, and college access for low-income minority and rural young people.

Networks, Partnerships, Collaborations, and Collective Action Take-Aways

- What are the current strategic partnerships with which your organization is involved?
- Are there organizations with which your agency competes that can be changed into partnerships?
- Are there particular projects you have undertaken that could

---

123 "RCAP's history," RCAP.org, January 28, 2010, http://www.rcap.org/rcaphistory (accessed April 2, 2015).

be scaled up to address similar needs elsewhere and strengthen the resources base for a larger network including your own?

- Which of your partnerships could be turned into collaborations that involve more than one or two partners? And what collaborations can be turned into a network that meet all or many of the criteria that I have suggested for a reform network (an agenda that includes reform as well as service, the involvement of the executive leadership of the membership, a strong planning and financial system that ensures that the mission, goals, objectives, and data gathering will serve the network purpose beyond support for the local members, and training for all of the staff and volunteers who are part of the network agenda)?

- What partnerships and collaborations might be expanded into collective action?

- What issues in your community cry out for new or revitalized partnerships, collaborations, and network development?

Profile in Excellence:
Lin Atkins

Lin grew up in a middle-income family. She never knew her father, who had deserted the family while she was a baby. Her mother— described by her sister as someone without the capacity of love—beat Lin, yet lavished praise on her much younger daughter by a second marriage who could do no wrong. Lin, who bore a resemblance to Bette Midler, spent her best years with her grandfather, a local fire chief, and her grandmother. After graduating high school, she married a man who was very jealous. Every morning she would tell her husband that she wanted to leave with her son. Each morning he would point to his shotgun and tell her he would kill her if she tried to leave. After more than a year, he relented.

A child of the sixties, she began to dabble in uppers and downers and then LSD and heroin. She was smart and streetwise but out of kindness gave some prescription drugs to an undercover agent who begged her for a fix to get over his feigned shakes. Lin was finally busted on passing bad checks and given the option of going to prison or to Rubicon, a residential drug treatment program in Richmond, Virginia, fashioned after the early residential treatment programs like Daytop in New Jersey, which used a military-style regime to break residents from their past destructive self-images and behavior and rebuild them into responsible citizens. Lin graduated from Rubicon and earned a staff position. She then came back to Roanoke as Director of Women's Programs in a new residential treatment program, Hegira House.

Upon leaving Hegira House, Lin joined my training staff and participated in the Mid-Atlantic Training Committee's personal growth and group development experiential education program. When I was appointed Executive Director of TAP, I promoted Lin to lead TAP's new Prisoner and Ex-Prisoner Rehabilitation Program. Immediately, Lin developed Stop-Gap Jobs for ex-offenders and expanded the self-awareness groups in local jails and prisons. Lin was a rehabilitation success, a natural leader who knew all the games that addicts and ex-offenders played. She was passionate, confrontational, and could speak to ex-offenders from experience. Lin was the personification of tough love. In one minute, she could put you through a drill sergeant dress down and the next minute give you a hug that left you knowing she valued you.

Lin scaled a local ex-offender demonstration reentry program at TAP into a statewide collaboration with collective impact. Involving more than twenty local community action agencies, this effort became the first statewide reentry program for inmates in the nation. She was respected throughout the state for her passion, her genuineness, her ability to relate to people at all levels and garner their support to help those who attracted the least public sympathy. Virginia CARES was the first organization in the Commonwealth to advocate for the automatic restoration of rights to ex-offenders who had served their time and paid their fines by having a constitutional amendment placed on the ballot.

A single mother and former heroin addict, Lin became a well-respected expert on ex-offender and criminal justice issues at the Virginia General Assembly, which supported the Virginia CARES initiative. Lin, whose favorite childhood story was *Peter Pan*, in which Peter saved and captained all the Lost Boys, would positively affect the lives of more than thirty thousand Virginia felons attempting a successful reentry into society.

Lin received special recognition from the Rubicon drug treatment program and the National Association of Blacks in Criminal Justice for her leadership in creating opportunity for ex-offenders through Virginia CARES. Governor Mark Warner appointed her to a Virginia state commission dealing with criminal justice issues. At her death in 2002, the Virginia General Assembly recognized her leadership to the Commonwealth of Virginia through a joint resolution of both houses.

Chapter 12

Marketing: Getting the Story Out

*A brand for a company is like a reputation for a person. You
earn reputation by trying to do hard things well.*[124]
~ Jeff Bezos, founder of Amazon.com

Jim Collins in his work on good to great organizations uses the idea of
a flywheel, which builds up increased momentum from a continued
series of pushes in a consistent direction to describe building a brand
through decision after decision in the right direction. The thrust
comes from the ability of an organization to produce results through
the application of disciplined thinking and action.[125] While nothing
can make up for a lack of disciplined thinking and action, it has been
my experience that brand identification and loyalty also have to do
with intentional marketing, the ability to communicate to others what
needs are being addressed, and the organization's mission, success,
and future. Good marketing becomes a megaphone for great works.

On rare occasions, we at TAP have even had national visibility. In
the early years, through Cabell Brand's contacts, TAP had a spread in
the March 1976 issue of *Ebony Magazine*. The feature was titled, "TAP:

---

124 "Online Extra: Jeff Bezos on Word-of-Mouth Power," *Bloomberg Business*, August 1, 2004,
http://www.bloomberg.com/bw/stories/2004-08-01/online-extra-jeff-bezos-on-word-of-mouth-
power (accessed May 10, 2015).

125 Collins, "The Flywheel and the Doom Loop," Chap. 8 in *Good to Great*.

The Little Poverty Organization That Could."[126] TAP was also a focus of the *Charles Kuralt CBS Sunday Morning Show* in a piece called "A Small War Against Poverty."[127] Two books have been written about TAP: *No Cease Fires* by Edwin Cobb and *Community Action at Work: TAP's Thirty-Year War on Poverty* by Beth Brand.

But all of these triumphs utilized more traditional media and marketing strategies. In an increasingly crowded nonprofit arena and an ever-changing media landscape where new platforms have made it easier and faster to connect with people, it became painfully clear to me that our good works would no longer speak for themselves. In fact, they wouldn't speak at all if we weren't intentional in communicating them. Thirty years ago, we commissioned a local internal marketing study by Martin Research Inc. to determine the share of people who were aware of TAP and its work compared with other charitable organizations. We came in third behind The Rescue Mission and The Salvation Army.

A number of local nonprofits, including The Salvation Army, Feeding America, Habitat for Humanity, the Red Cross, Goodwill, and the Girls and Boys Club have national organizations whose marketing campaigns assist their local organizations. Their advertisements are frequently seen on local and national TV.

Until 2013, TAP had not focused a great deal of energy, money, or time on marketing. This was in part because of a four-decades-long holdover from Bristow's philosophy. During a trip we took together, we stopped for lunch at a restaurant whose menu boasted that it served the best food in Virginia. Bristow commented, "If you have to say it that means it probably isn't true." He believed that TAP's work could, and should, speak for itself.

In this regard, TAP is not unique among community action agencies

---

126 Ebony Magazine: vol. XXXI No. 5, March 1976, pp.72-84 "TAP The Little Poverty Organization That Could" Publisher: Johnson Publishing Co., Inc. Chicago, Illinois.

127 Bahorich, Susan. "Then and Now: TAP: CBS Sunday Morning Featured TAP Nearly 30 Years Ago," *WDBJ7 News*, April 7, 2014, http://www.wdbj7.com/news/local/then-and-now-tap/25364296 (accessed March 19, 2015).

and local nonprofits across the country. Very few do any marketing beyond developing a website and publishing an annual report. Virtual CAP (http://www.virtualcap.org) is the national community action best practices website. If you enter "marketing" into the search area, you discover a remarkable absence of examples of focused marketing efforts. Even our national association has trouble with marketing—some years ago, the National Association of Community Action Agencies spent more than $100,000 on its rebranding effort. The best it came up with was the National Community Action Partnership, which hardly set aside the movement as distinctive. All agencies involve the community, are engaged in action, and develop partnerships. We just can't compete with agencies whose national organizations effectively assist their local chapters with marketing efforts.

Other factors have also discouraged community action agencies' marketing activities. Grant dollars, on which we rely for most of our funding, allow little for marketing expenditures. Additionally, over the years, corporations have become increasingly interested in directing their contributions to specific program activities rather than agency support and tend to champion projects supported by their employees.

There are, of course, some exceptions. Years ago, under the leadership of Ken Ackerman, the Monticello Community Action Agency developed a way of telling the success stories of some of their remarkable program participants as part of the agency's 30th anniversary celebration. After picking thirty individuals to be highlighted, the agency recruited professional photographers who volunteered to do portraits of the participants. Local professional writers volunteered to write their stories. Each story, with an accompanying photograph, was featured in the local paper in successive issues.[128] The stories and photographs were then bound

---

128 Loevinger, Nancy. "The Writer and the Community," *University of Virginia Archive*, April 5th, 1996, http://www.virginia.edu/insideuva/textonlyarchive/96-04-05/1.txt (accessed March 19, 2015).

in a coffee table book and widely distributed. Photographs of the participants were put on a rotating display in the agency's lobby. The organization also developed a major annual fundraiser, "Men Who Cook."[129]

TAP's own business plan of developing local components that operated on an entrepreneurial model also created a number of brands that were better known than the parent organization. Head Start, This Valley Works, Energy Conservation and Home Repair, The Transitional Living Center, Sabrina's Place, and even Business Seed Capital Inc. developed their own advisory boards, logos, and lists of financial contributors. What money TAP did raise from a variety of sources was often easier to attract if targeted to specific programs rather than an agency that ran more than thirty different programs at one time. The work of a single-purpose agency with a single mission and single clientele is easier for the public to comprehend—and therefore support—than a large and diverse organization like TAP.

Over the years, TAP has sought to communicate to the public through a number of ways. The most frequent tool used is half-morning tours of our programs for interested parties. Rarely do we have someone who visits TAP programs who does not come away impressed with what we do. The comment that we hear again and again is, "I had no idea that TAP did so much good in our community!" Through these tours we are able to introduce them to participants who are currently involved in or who have graduated from our programs. In addition, we show them the water systems, apartment complexes, and single family homes that we built, and the small businesses that we have helped to launch. Those who volunteer to help with the programs or participate on the board of directors or board committees also join the force of those who can tell our story to others.

When Republican Bob Goodlatte ran for his first term of the House

---

129 VirtualCAP.org, "Men Who Cook! Fundraising Event," http://www.macaa.org/NewsandEvents/MenWhoCook.aspx (accessed March 17, 2015).

of Representatives, his Democratic opponent was Steve Musselwhite, a local businessman. We arranged to take them both on a tour of TAP. The tour launched a two-decade supportive relationship with Congressman Bob Goodlatte. Goodlatte led the Republican delegation that met with House Speaker Gingrich to encourage support for community action. As a result, Gingrich initiated the largest single increase in the Community Services Block Grant since the presidency of Lyndon Johnson. Goodlatte has since joined as a cosigner of HB 3854, the new Community Services Block Grant reauthorization legislation.[130] His opponent, Steve Musselwhite, became one of the most important board chairs of the TAP organization.

Since TAP's inception, our chief publicity has been through developing good relations with the media, who are quick to print stories about our organization, programs, and successful participants, or to air them on TV. Every year, *The Roanoke Times* and *The Roanoke Tribune* have printed op-eds penned by a TAP staffer or board member. In 2013, board member Carter Turner took pains to rebut a negative op-ed disparaging the work of Head Start. One year, we paid for a multipage Sunday supplement in *The Roanoke Times*, written by several local reporters, covering the work of the entire agency. So successful have we been with the *Times*, that a sister agency called it "the TAP newsletter."

Unfortunately, our best coverage came when our renovated forty-thousand-square-foot warehouse, housing most of our programs and administrative offices, burned to the ground on Christmas Eve, 1989. Over the next twelve months, TAP received incredible local media coverage as the community volunteered space, telephone systems, furnishings, and volunteer labor to help the agency get back on its feet.

By 1990, TAP had taken the proceeds of the insurance claim and purchased an eight-story building in the heart of downtown Roanoke, across from the offices of *The Roanoke Times* and cattycorner to the

---

130 Community and Economic Opportunity Act of 2014, H.R. 3854, 113th Cong. (2013–2014).

Noel C. Taylor Municipal Building, the headquarters for Roanoke's city government. Just the move from across the Norfolk and Southern train tracks to the heart of the business and commercial center of Roanoke itself made TAP a mainstream organization. The move to and occupancy of an eight-story office building whose staff ate lunch and shopped in local stores had an impact that helped to market the agency to the broader community.

It has always interested me how physical development projects help to sell an organization. When we started building water systems, TAP gained a new respect. The same applied to our completion of the Terrace Apartments, Dumas Center auditorium complex, and our single-family home developments. Even though it is a much more complicated task to help turn an individual life around from despair to hope and help them reinvent themselves, there is something about a water system or building that markets itself.

During the last decade, TAP has created a number of avenues to market the organization. We have continued to publish an annual report every two years with an update insert on the off year. We have also developed the capacity to film and edit our own videos, telling the story of people whose lives have been turned around through various programs. In 2013, we produced a video telling the stories of six Project Discovery students to help sell the program to Virginia's secretary of education and superintendent of public education. We also produced a series of informational talks on a variety of subjects that will be available to Virginia CARES participants across the state directly through the Virginia CARES website.

While TAP's legal name remains Total Action Against Poverty, TAP is doing business, and will hence be known as Total Action for Progress. The new name denotes a positive rather than a negative, similar to being for mental health rather than against mental illness. Furthermore, brand names such as Virginia CARES (Community Action Reentry Services) and This Valley Works allow for a discussion to continue rather than turning off the audience before you get to tell the story. Think of what a turn-off our statewide pre- and post-release reentry program would have been if it had been branded "Ex-felon Reentry" rather than Virginia CARES. Likewise, This Valley Works has attracted a great deal more attention than the previous title, "TAP Employment and Training Services." It is clear that a strong brand requires that the organization do good work and be able to demonstrate it. However, the brand name should not be an obstacle to communicating the work.

Clearly, our marketing efforts have been better than many, if not most, nonprofits. An occasional national media spotlight on a major network or publication in a national magazine has little shelf life in the public's attention span. Book publications, tours for those who will take the time, even a name that evokes a positive emotional response are helpful but not adequate to create the public awareness that can lead to sustained support and increased resources. One does not want to count on the benefits of a fire to highlight an organization's mission and importance. What was needed was a more concentrated effort with the right people on board. Thus begins the story of TAP's marketing committee.

The Marketing Committee

In 2013, sensing the need for a focused and sustained marketing initiative in an increasingly competitive environment, the TAP board sought the help of Joe Jones, the Director of External Affairs for Appalachian Electric Power (AEP) utility company, in setting up a marketing committee that would direct the venture. It would be a first in the agency's history. Joe was a recent newcomer to Roanoke from Charleston, West Virginia, who was looking for a community venture in which to invest his time away from work. Most important was that he had a marketing background. Consisting of two additional board members, the CEO, senior vice president of programs, the co-vice presidents of Resource Development and Planning, the CFO, and the recently hired communication specialist, the committee has made a number of crucial decisions under Joe's firm leadership.

Until Joe arrived on the scene, the most we had done was hold a press conference to change our name from Total Action Against Poverty to Total Action for Progress and make the requisite changes to our website. While retaining the TAP acronym, which has become well-known, the new name replaces a positive for a negative and takes the organization out of the intellectual debate on poverty. The notion of progress implies confidence in the future, which aims at the heart as well as the head.

The first issue that the committee addressed was written standards for all printed material. It was decided that the TAP logo, pictured below, remains "TAP into hope", which creates a positive emotional response.

To build on the "TAP into hope" slogan, we have changed our central phone number to 777-HOPE, which helps to reinforce our brand.

Other problems remained. At the top of the list was lack of brand cohesion. Over four decades, TAP and its components have produced an incredible number of documents, newsletters, and publications with many different looks, toying with different colors and typefaces. Their commonality was that few looked as if they came from the same company. Over the course of two months, the marketing committee produced a marketing and publications guide that covered identity standards (logo size, placement, and colors), use of other division logos in subservient position to the TAP logo, uniformity of typeface, a review process for all documents including press releases and business cards, and uniform stationery for all TAP business.

Under Joe Jones' leadership, one of the first items the committee produced using the new standards was a one-pager (shown at the end of the chapter) that tells the reader the story of what TAP is, what it does, and describes our community impact. It is our written "thirty-second elevator speech,"[131] the time of an audience's attention span before you lose them.[132]

As committee discussions proceeded, it became clear that there was a need for a dedicated staff person, a communications specialist with the requisite skills to push the marketing effort forward.

Communications Specialist

Before TAP began its new marketing initiative, its This Valley Works component lost a contract to an out-of-state organization with very polished materials. It was a stark lesson that our visual material lacked the polish of our competition. Though they lacked our performance record, their slick, classier-looking material made them appear more competent for the task, even if that wasn't true. We explored outsourcing the work but found that the cost easily outstripped our budget. Our CFO, after reviewing a quote for collateral pieces, including an annual report, program brochures, and new agency marketing materials, exclaimed, "We could hire someone to do the work in-house for this price!" So we did, and it's been one of the best decisions we've made in recent years. Had we simply added the duties of the communication specialist to an existing staff member, the progress we have made never would have happened.

The time taken for a careful selection process by Moses and Hatheway, Vice Presidents of Planning, paid off. They waited until they got the "right who." In the first six months of her employment, TAP's Communication Specialist, Sarah Gatrell, produced a greatly improved annual report with pictures of the people impacted, their

---

131 Giang, Vivian. "How to Sell Yourself in 30 Seconds and Leave People Wanting More," *Business Insider*, November 14, 2013, http://www.businessinsider.com/how-to-tell-your-story-in-30-seconds-2013-11 (accessed March 18, 2015).

132 Salisbury University, "How to Craft a Killer 60 Second Elevator Pitch That Will Land You Big Business," http://www.salisbury.edu/careerservices/students/Interviews/60secondElevator.html (accessed March 18, 2015).

stories, and key statistics that present the bigger picture of agency accomplishments. In addition, she produced a three-page economic impact document that demonstrates both the economic impact of tax dollars spent in our community ($29,000,000) and the cost savings TAP's programs help realize in SNAP and unemployment benefits, TANF benefits, incarceration, special education, and preventable illnesses.[133] The information is provided in a readable format with graphics that help to drive the point home. The professionalism of the presentation gives further credibility to the report. Her presence has contributed to TAP's adherence to publication standards and greatly unified the brand.

Sarah Gatrell has also enlarged our media net through social media. The public can stay in touch with TAP through our Facebook page, *Total Action for Progress,* and Twitter, @TAPin2Hope. The number of "likes" on TAP's social media sites grows week after week. At the end of March 2015, Sarah reported to me: "Since I began at TAP in October 2013 our Facebook fan base has grown from 152 likes to over 1500. Additionally our 'reach' (the number of people who were served [by] any activity from our page including posts, posts to our page by other people, page ads, mentions, and check-ins) on Facebook has gone from between nine and eighty to between two thousand and twenty thousand depending on the post content and if any posts were 'boosted' with marketing funds."

Sarah has closely overseen all marketing efforts. When contracts for programs like Youth Build and Fathers First allow for marketing expenses, we take full advantage, underwriting videos and creating advertisements that are shown on prime viewing sites like the local planetarium, the sides of buses, and billboards. A separate domestic violence awareness campaign, "Paint the Town Purple," involved local restaurants that donated a portion of their proceeds on a given day to our domestic violence program. In addition, the TAP blog,

---

133 Total Action for Progress, "2013 Economic Impact Statement," http://www.tapintohope. org/downloads/EIS_Jan_2014_FINAL_12914.pdf (accessed March 19, 2015).

which can be accessed on our website, also draws attention. A recent blog post, "Desperate for Reform: Mental Health Care and the Criminal Justice System," by grant writer Emily Pielocik, drew four hundred persons to our webpage in one day.[134]

Looking Toward the Future

As the marketing committee turned toward the future, major items were the new website, the 2014 Annual Report, and the celebration of the 50th anniversary of TAP in 2015. Also receiving top billing was the development of an annual "signature event" promoting the work of the TAP organization that would raise discretionary funds for the organization. The local community school had their strawberry festival, the Northwest Child Development Center had their peach festival, and the Brain Injury Center had their Wings Fest. All raised tens of thousands of dollars annually to support their organizations. TAP's This Valley Works had raised over a quarter of a million dollars for dropout recovery in Roanoke City Public Schools. Yet, though the whole agency supported the Western Virginia Education Football Classic, its proceeds could only support one part of TAP.

At its July 2014 meeting, the TAP Board of Directors unanimously voted to approve the recommendation by Joe Jones, on behalf of the marketing committee, to endorse a contract with Big Lick Entertainment to host the 2015 July 4th celebration in Elmwood Park, in downtown Roanoke. The Revolution of Hope event was a full-day celebration with live entertainment and a myriad of events ending with a fireworks display. The theme: The Hope Revolution would place Total Action for Progress in its proper context, the American Revolution, the Civil Rights Movement, the Women's Movement, and the War Against Poverty, all of the efforts to bring hope and

---

134 Emily Pielocik, "Desperate for Reform: Mental Health Care and the Criminal Justice System," TAP blog, June 11, 2014, https://www.tapintohope.org/Blog.aspx, (accessed May 7, 2015).

opportunity to those who had been marginalized and left out. The message was clear: supporting TAP is the patriotic thing to do. It remains to be seen, but it appears that TAP has finally found its key annual signature event, which added to our expanded marketing efforts to reach the broader public and raised vitally needed discretionary income.

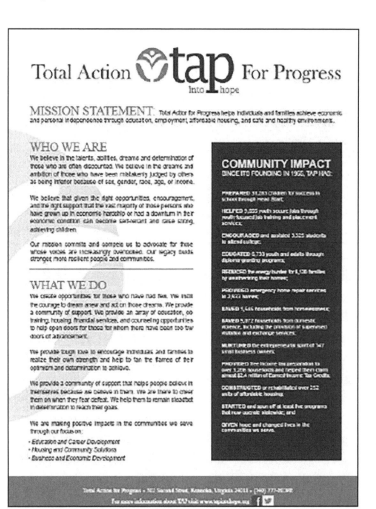

In Summary

An organization's brand is driven by its accomplishments. Nothing replaces the end product and outcomes produced by the organization's work. Nevertheless, intentional marketing can become a megaphone announcing those results and connecting the work of the organization with the values of those who support its endeavors. This best occurs when marketing is done intentionally and not on the fly. A hardworking marketing committee, committed chair, and creative communications specialist are core features of a first-class marketing campaign. The tasks of the marketing committee may include standardization of all print media, development of an attractive and communicative website, strong print and TV media connections, the use of social media, the development of video productions featuring the organization's impact, and even signature events that communicate the work of the organization and generate income at the same time.

Marketing: Getting the Story Out Take-Aways

- What nonprofits in your area are the best at marketing their agency? What makes them so good? What steps can you take to improve your market share of support in your community?
- Is there a board committee in your organization that meets regularly to communicate the importance of the need that your organization addresses, your mission, and accomplishments to the public?
- Have you reviewed the material that you are currently sending out to ensure that there is consistency of style, color, and format, including the agency logo?
- Is it time to reevaluate your agency's name, slogan, and/or logo to ensure that it is connecting with the deepest values of the people whose support you need?

- Who on the staff is in charge of connecting with the media?
- What signature events do you have annually that garner support and further the branding and the work of your organization?

Profile in Excellence:
Joe Jones

Joe Jones is Director of External Affairs for Appalachian Power Company (AEP) in Virginia. At sixty-three years of age he is in trim condition. Intense and cordial, Joe is a study in optimism and a serious student of human psychology and top performance. He has also been Chair of TAP's Marketing Committee for the last eighteen months in addition to being Vice Chair of the United Way and active in the Chamber of Commerce.

Joe grew up in Huntington, West Virginia. He was raised by his grandparents in their later years. They were working-class people who raised Joe in an atmosphere of unconditional love despite having to scrape by with minimal financial resources. They knew hardships. His grandfather had a bad heart, and his grandmother contracted a disease that left her deaf. It was a family that loved music. His granddad played the mandolin and harmonica. They listened to bluegrass music on the Grand Ole Opry. Joe learned at an early age that "there is no shame in being poor. The only shame was if you didn't make the most of your life and if you conducted yourself without honor." Even though the family had minimal resources, they were taught the value of giving and being able to receive help. As a kid, Joe identified with TV figures of stature and used them as role models for how to speak and carry himself.

Joe developed a love of music, began performing as a singer, and later became a bassist and guitarist. He came close to a recording deal with the Apple record label and shared a stage with famous musicians.

Joe married his high school sweetheart in 1970, just a year after graduation, and they soon started a family. He worked at a wholesaler in Huntington and played music. Encouraged by his wife, Joe entered college and began his journey of self-development, which continues to this day. He graduated summa cum laude from Marshall University with a major in marketing and a minor in economics.

Joe found employment with American Electric Power Company. He has served in leadership capacity in both West Virginia and Virginia. Once the state manager for marketing in West Virginia, he now is AEP's Director of External Affairs for Virginia and Tennessee. He has been vitally engaged in the communities in which he worked. In Charleston, West Virginia, he helped to fashion an alliance that included the Chamber of Commerce, the Charleston Renaissance organization, and BIDCO, an economic development group. He served as the chair of the Alliance's Community Affairs Team and spearheaded a think-tank series of forums that created important dialogue, which moved the area forward. He was honored with an award for his leadership by the Charleston City Council.

Joe's motto is that "leadership is the igniter of great outcomes." He is incredibly well organized. Every marketing committee meeting begins with an agenda and a summary of what has been done and what is left to be done on the strategic plan the committee has created. He personally takes notes and sends them out to all members of the committee, board members, and staff. Rarely does a month go by when he does not also email a printed article of inspiration and insight that he has read or written himself.

At the outset of his agreement to head the marketing committee, Joe was sure of three things: The committee would have to set standards on all material leaving the agency and on our electronic media as well; the job would require a full-time staff person dedicated to the process and work plan; and we had to develop an eighteen-month plan to increase our marketing impact. In each thing he undertakes, Joe asks the question "Why?" before proceeding to "What?" and "How?"

He is persistent in getting things done. A favorite comment of his is that "you cannot control the wind, but if you know where you are going you can control the set of the sails to get to your destination." At the same time he is a fanatic about details, he exudes a generous regard and respect for all with whom he works and is held in very high esteem by both the board and staff. Joe Jones' leadership of the

TAP marketing committee has made a decided difference and greatly heightened public appreciation and support for the TAP organization and its mission.

Chapter 13

SOCIAL CAPITAL: IT IS WHO YOU KNOW

Get someone else to blow your horn and the sound will carry twice as far.

~ Will Rogers[135]

There are all kinds of capital that a first-rate nonprofit needs to acquire to fulfill its mission. Equally important to resources (financial capital) and people (human capital) is social capital, the network of supporters who champion your cause and advocate for your organization.

Thirty years ago, Cabell and I were walking to the capitol building in Richmond, Virginia, to make a presentation on behalf of one of our network organizations to a group of state delegates and senators. Reflecting on my own fortunate upbringing and life, and the many people with whom I had become acquainted who grew up in poverty or were still in poverty, I remember saying to Cabell, "The major difference between you and me and people who were born into poverty is that you and I are connected. The poor are disconnected." Without missing a beat, Cabell replied, "That is why we are here. We're here to help connect them."

135 "Will Rogers Quotes," *World of Quotes*, http://www.worldofquotes.com/author/Will+Rogers/3/index.html (accessed May 10, 2015).

In their book *The Charismatic Organization*, Shirley Sagawa and Deborah Jospin emphasize how essential building social capital is for the nonprofit. It is an area that separates the successful nonprofit from the hundreds that spring up every day and die within a year. The authors distinguish two types of social capital, *bonding* and *bridging*. *Bonding capital* refers to the degree of connection between those involved in the organization and their level of commitment. *Bridging capital* refers to connections with others and their circle of influence.[136] When a bridge is made to an important person in a new circle, they become a connector to others in their circle of friends and colleagues, who in turn become connectors to yet others in additional circles. Sagawa and Jospin conclude: "In short, *social capital is the key to unlocking all other essential forms of capital that nonprofits need: financial, human, and political.*"[137] The authors then comment, "Each staff person, board member, volunteer, and client is the hub of a potentially vast network of other contacts."[138]

So, the strength of any single individual or organization is its connectedness to others at the highest levels of influence. For the first three decades of TAP's history, Cabell Brand was TAP's super-evangelist. As a prominent businessman in the Roanoke Valley of Southwest Virginia, Cabell linked TAP with the business community in our region, as well as across the country through his membership in the Young Presidents Organization, National Direct Selling Association, and National Chamber of Commerce. His contacts led to articles on TAP in *Ebony*,[139] a mention of the Virginia Water Project in *National Geographic*,[140] and inclusion of the TAP story on Charles Kuralt's

---

136 Sagawa and Jospin, *Charismatic Organization*, p. 18–19.

137 Ibid., p. 21.

138 Ibid.

139 "TAP: The Little Poverty Organization That Could," *Ebony Magazine*, March 1976.

140 Canby, Thomas. "Water: Our Most Precious Resource," *National Geographic*, August 1980, page 156.

Sunday Morning on CBS.[141] His involvement in politics led to connections with local public officials, state senators and delegates, and members of the United States Congress. Those connections translated into considerable government support for TAP and our community action networks. Cabell's involvement made it attractive for other business leaders to become a part of the TAP organization's board and boards of commissioners.

At the state level, The Virginia Water Project and Virginia CARES became vehicles that helped TAP connect to powerful political leaders throughout the Commonwealth of Virginia. TAP's connection to Delegates Chip Woodrum and Vic Thomas, powerful members of the House Appropriations Committee, helped to bring millions of dollars of funding to those two projects, and over $6 million a year of state money to all thirty of the community action agencies in the state. When Dick Cranwell became Democratic Majority Leader of the House of Delegates, using his office as a meeting place was itself a powerful connector to others of importance. One particular Dick Cranwell meeting with an obstructive commissioner of the Virginia Department of Social Services convinced the commissioner that his full cooperation with the community action network in Virginia might well be in his own self-interest.

TAP has been blessed with extremely supportive relationships with three of the congressmen representing the city of Roanoke and surroundings: Congressman M. Caldwell Butler, Congressman Jim Olin, and Congressman Bob Goodlatte. Caldwell Butler became a strong supporter of the Virginia Water Project (VWP) and the National Demonstration Water Project (NDWP) and made personal calls to the Carter White House when the Office of Economic Opportunity refused to continue funding for NDWP. Congressman Butler also supported funding the Virginia CARES program with the admonition that we see to it that the program was a success.

---

141 Bahorich, Susan. "Then and Now: TAP: CBS Sunday Morning Featured TAP Nearly 30 Years Ago," *WDBJ7 News*, April 7, 2014, http://www.wdbj7.com/news/local/then-and-now-tap/25364296 (accessed March 19, 2015).

Many years later, after Congressman Butler retired from office, I met him at St. John's Episcopal Church where both of us were members. We exchanged pleasantries. When he asked me how things were going, I shared with him that Governor Warner had just eliminated all pre- and post-incarceration funding from his budget and that without those dollars Virginia CARES might very well go out of business. He asked if he could help. I told him that Congressman Wolfe, who served a section of northern Virginia, was chairman of a House committee dealing with criminal justice issues. The congressman was in a position to put in a $1 million earmark for the Commonwealth to continue ex-offender reentry funding for one year until the state money could be restored. Caldwell replied that Congressman Wolfe was a good friend of his. Shortly after our chance meeting, Congressman Wolfe placed a $1 million line item in the federal appropriations budget. The next year, Governor Warner replaced the dollars to the Department of Criminal Justice Services, continuing funding for Virginia CARES.

I mention these instances to illustrate how crucial maximizing social capital is to nonprofit agencies. "Moving walls" becomes much more possible when you have strong supporters adding their shoulders to the effort.

Each board member, employee, volunteer, donor, and client is a potential connector to others of influence. The other day, I wondered about TAP's potential for expanding our social capital. A quick calculation revealed that among the potential connectors were: 360 employees, fifty board members and members of TAP boards of commissioners, 1,899 volunteers contributing a total 125,110 hours of work, thirty-two individual donors, and sixty-five corporate donors.

But to what extent had we capitalized on the potential social capital of all these connections? The answer is pretty poorly—we've left much of the social capital at our fingertips on the table. We have capitalized on a small percentage of the social capital available to us but have left too much of it unmined. As TAP looks toward the future, it needs to (and can) do better.

So, going forward, what would constitute a strong plan of action for enlarging TAP's social capital through bonding and bridging? Attention to these social-capital-building initiatives (six in all) can only increase TAP's support base in the future (and can be adapted to the situation of other nonprofit organizations). Here they are:

First, develop a strong historical database of TAP supporters as far back as we have records. One would have thought that a $20 million organization would have kept a database of its supporters over the years. We have board minutes going back to 1989 that list every board member from that time forward. We have names and addresses of current and past employees spanning the last two decades. We have scraps of previous lists of donors and contributors. However, until now we have had no single database of all TAP supporters.

It is not that we didn't recognize the importance of this task. Rather, we never deemed it important enough to dedicate at least part of a staff position to the function. Instead, we dumped this assignment onto the workload of an existing employee. We now understand that while it is important to keep overhead low, it is also important to make it possible to develop social capital by making adequate resources for that task available.

Second, fully utilize the network of relationships of TAP's strongest supporters, especially those in the business community. These are at the forefront of TAP's best evangelists. To that end, TAP continues to reach out to new leadership for the board of directors and our boards of commissioners. We reinstated annual meetings of past and present board chairs to garner their thoughts and ideas on how to strengthen and promote the mission of TAP, and we will continue to invite other leaders to a special annual luncheon. This meeting will also be used to discover ideas to build bridges to others in the community.

Third, continue new marketing to increase the public's awareness of TAP's activities through additional TV and newspaper exposure, and continued social media linkage with Facebook and Twitter. The increased media exposure validates the interest of key supporters and helps them in their effort to attract others to the TAP cause.

Fourth, spend the time creating personal, front-row volunteer experiences that allow folks to "get their hands dirty" and experience making a difference in the lives of others. It is often the case with nonprofit organizations that deal with complicated situations and complicated solutions that there are things that volunteers with little professional training are either reluctant to do or unable to do. I remember a Junior League volunteer group that wanted to work with homeless persons in our Transitional Living Center. However, they made the stipulation that their volunteers did not want to work with persons who had been involved with substance use or had been convicted of a crime. The problem was that nearly the entire group of TLC residents fell in one of those two categories—sometimes both. However, activities suitable to volunteers were found. While the volunteers were not equipped to deal with clients suffering from high levels of dysfunction, they were able to lend their efforts to remodeling, decorating, and furnishing the rooms. As a result, most of the rooms at the TLC were remodeled and furnished by local churches and service organizations.

Fifth, create frequent communications to our network of supporters that tell stories of the difference that, together, we are making in the lives of others. When we had to worry about printing and mailing costs, these costs were often sacrificed to getting the job done, which appeared more necessary. The development of online newsletters and the use of social media have changed that situation to nonprofits' advantage.

Sixth, intentionally find ways to recognize the work of volunteers at every turn, through newsletters, the news media, annual luncheons, signature events, and annual reports.

In Summary

The importance of building social capital is often understated or ignored. It cannot be taken for granted. Every effort should be made to increase both bonding and bridging types of capital. Bonding happens best when people have some form of direct volunteer experience with the people whom the agency is impacting. Frequent communication about that impact through videos and mailings enhance the bond. The more those direct contacts by those bonded evangelists bridge to other people of influence with whom they are connected, the stronger the social capital for the organization. This does not happen without the infrastructure to create meaningful volunteer activities, maintaining a contact list, and communicating on a regular basis.

Social Capital Take-Aways

- Describe the present level of social capital for your nonprofit.
- How far is your reach into private businesses, service organizations, government officials, and local decision-makers?
- Does your organization have endorsements by important persons and organizations?
- Who are your champions, evangelists, and super-evangelists?
- Do you have a database of supporters? How well is it maintained?
- What are you doing to communicate with your supporters?
- What events are you holding to create bridges to other potential supporters?
- How strong is your media presence, and what can be done to increase it?
- What can you do to increase hands-on volunteer activities to attract new supporters?
- What are you doing to recognize your supporters?

Profile in Excellence:
Curtis Thompson

TAP created Business Seed Capital, Inc. (BSCI) in 1996 to provide assistance to low- and moderate-income residents in the Roanoke Valley who sought to improve their economic situation by starting or expanding a small business. In the first few years of the twenty-first century, the program floundered under the leadership of two former commercial bankers. In 2007, Curtis Thompson, a small business owner himself, joined the staff. The word on Curtis is that he can sell snow to Eskimos. He is the quintessential entrepreneur. He works nonstop and is a magnet for opportunities. Curtis is all grit. He delayed a bone spur operation (on both feet) to oversee the collection of outstanding loan payments, and came into work with kidney stones to make sure a grant was submitted on time.

Curtis is one of only two of the six children in his family to obtain a college education. Son of two devoted working-class parents, he won a scholarship to Seattle University, a Jesuit School in a totally different environment than he was used to, and traveled across the country to pursue his education. His daughter, a nationally ranked track star, has just received her MBA from Virginia's Darden School of Business. His son, Drey, is enrolled in Roanoke's prestigious North Cross School.

Curtis is an incredible connector with others. He is well known in Roanoke but even better known across the country. In our second application for New Market Tax Credits, he has developed a pipeline of projects throughout Virginia extending into neighboring states. His connections are so far-flung, he's talking to a small-town Mississippi mayor about an economic development role that TAP can play in a section of the town with six hundred dilapidated structures.

Under Curtis's guidance, BSCI operates a loan fund in excess of $2.5 million that has catalyzed more than one hundred businesses. The program received the Community and Economic Development Healthy Food Financing award of $800,000, aimed at financing food-related businesses in low-income communities that are host to "food deserts," areas without local access to grocery stores. A planning grant of $7,500 from the Virginia Enterprise Initiative leveraged an additional $60,000 in capital for cottage industries in low-income neighborhoods.

Curtis also oversees a free tax clinic operated with the help of volunteers every year, which has filed 5,100 returns and helped local taxpayers receive over $5 million in refunds. Seventy-five low-income participants have participated in a matched savings program (Individual Development Account), which has led to $154,005 in savings by participants and $180,000 in matching funds from public and private resources. Curtis piloted the first local public/private partnership in which TAP is a facilitator between clients needing loans for dental services and dental providers.

Since 2007, BSCI has earned Community Development Financial Institution (CDFI) and Community Development Entity (CDE) designations. BSCI has also seen its service area expand under the Small Business Administration program to include Pulaski County and the City of Lynchburg.

Although TAP was denied funding in its first application for $25 million of New Market Tax Credits to develop employment in high unemployment areas, it is only a matter of time before a future grant is funded. The first application received a score of ninety out of one hundred points. To assist in preparation of the next application, Curtis has assembled a high-level New Market Tax Credit Committee, and is working with external consultants out of Detroit that he had met at an economic development conference.

Through his tireless work with volunteers at the free tax clinic and on the BSCI and New Market Tax Credit Advisory boards of directors, as well as important leaders in the financial community, locally and across the country, Curtis is an expert at increasing the bonding and bridging social capital of the TAP organization.

Chapter 14

KEEPING IT TOGETHER: MANAGING STRESS

Your mind will answer most questions if you learn to relax and wait for the answer.

~ William S. Burroughs[142]

To experience peace does not mean that your life is always blissful. It means that you are capable of tapping into a blissful state of mind amidst the normal chaos of a hectic life.

~ Jill Bolte Taylor[143]

This chapter is about maintaining balance and equilibrium for those of us who aspire to be Level 5 leaders. Whatever the cause, a life completely dedicated to the mission will kill you, physically and emotionally. It can often involve the sacrifice of one's closest relationships. I know it's true. I've served four decades leading an excellent nonprofit that survived radical economic and political changes, and our own missteps. Not to mention my own highly

142 "13 Quotes to Help You De-Stress After a Long Day," *O: The Oprah Magazine*, post published January 1, 2014, http://www.oprah.com/spirit/Quotes-to-Destress-Stress-Quotes-Relaxation-Sayings/4 (accessed May 13, 2015).

143 "13 Quotes to Help You De-Stress After a Long Day," *O: The Oprah Magazine*, post published January 1, 2014, http://www.oprah.com/spirit/Quotes-to-Destress-Stress-Quotes-Relaxation-Sayings/6 (accessed May 13, 2015).

personal issues. In 2000, I was diagnosed with prostate cancer. The treatment was only partially successful and never fully killed the cancer. Unregulated stress makes cancer more likely to spread faster.[144] Stress can be an issue both of organizational effectiveness, and a matter of life and death. What follows are the strategies I've used to maintain balance and equilibrium in life and work.

Dealing with the Stress of Nonprofit Leadership

One of the major issues in both the nonprofit and for-profit sectors is burnout. Frankly, we at TAP were pretty naïve fifty years ago. We really thought that we could eliminate poverty in our lifetime. We really believed that the momentum to reach out to the millions of Americans who had been left back, left out, and pushed aside would be sustained because people would recognize that it was in America's self-interest to help everyone lead productive lives. We believed that we would live to see a race- and gender-blind America where children would no longer be the largest group in poverty and people would no longer be at risk of homelessness. As I look back at the past, I do not disparage our lack of worldliness. I think, "God bless our naiveté!" Otherwise, we might not have given ourselves to the mission as we did.

Nevertheless, the issue of poverty is more stubborn than it appears. The remarkable consistency with which prejudice is transmitted from one generation to another is a major obstacle. The need for quick fixes and the preference to cast blame on the victim, rather than building fairness and equal opportunity, reinforces it. A constantly changing battlefield in which new forces impede the mission creates difficulty. We cannot underestimate the impact of globalization and the loss of manufacturing jobs as major factors in reducing opportunity for much of America's middle class and for those seeking to improve their lives.

---

144 Rosch, Paul J., MD, FACP. "Stress and Cancer," *The American Institute of Stress*, http://www.stress.org/stress-and-cancer/ (accessed March 20, 2015).

In this ever-evolving battle against poverty, burnout is a major debilitating factor for those who were once gung ho about the cause. How do you sustain a high level of passion, hope, and hard work in the face of greater and greater difficulties? As I write this book, TAP's core funding has dropped from $1,154,323 in the 2007–2008 fiscal year, to $487,656 in the 2013–2014 fiscal year. As a result, we are maintaining an $18 million organization on a narrower and narrower financial base. From the vantage point of human infrastructure, it means fewer than thirty administrative people supporting an organization of 350 employees. When, suddenly, over forty years of achievement is compromised by financial issues that have converged to threaten the entire agency, how do you come to work with excitement and hope and not allow despair to envelop you?

Facing the bare-bones odds common in the nonprofit world is also demanding on one's physical and spiritual resources. Hans Selye, the father of stress research, has noted that the greatest stressors in life are frustration and failure. Facing down the ogres of frustration, fear, and despair with courageous hope requires an effort of mind, body, and willpower. According to Selye, while we have a well of adaptation energy, that well is not unlimited. Each time we draw from that well, there is a little bit less to draw on in the future.[145]

The choice is pretty clear: Either you give up your ambition for your work and the agency you lead, or you find a way to renew and refresh yourself. I know too many nonprofit leaders who have simply settled for mediocrity rather than invest the energy and will to make their organization more effective. The worst of them settle down on the job as if they were already in retirement, doing as little as possible, showing up at the office simply to draw a paycheck. The downward trajectory of their organizations reflect that decision.

The search for balance requires taking care of yourself physically, having non-work activities in which to engage, places to retreat to, and finding a source of support and meaning for your life.

---

145 Selye, Hans. *The Stress of Life, revised edition.* (New York: McGraw Hill, 1976), p. 82.

My Personal Journey

Knowing burnout needs to be avoided is fine, but how is it actually done? Creating balance is paramount. I have personally sought activities that have helped me find relief and refreshment. Some years ago, I found diversion playing competitive chess and dabbled as an artist with watercolor paintings. In both activities, one focuses on one thing and shuts out the rest of the world. There is nothing quite like being under sail in my twenty-five-foot Catalina, *No Problem*, letting the wind propel her, and watching sunlight dance off the waves like a sea full of diamonds. A few days of camping focusing on building a fire, fixing a meal, and taking a walk in the woods is always a grounding experience. Meeting each week with my Universal Chinese Kempo Karate school, concentrating on defense and attack moves, is both physically and psychologically invigorating. Not many seventy-six-year-olds can do seventy-six pushups on their birthday. A full-body workout with my trainer at the gym and a steam bath afterward are also things I look forward to. Two years ago, I took up hiking in the mountains surrounding my area of the country. In 2013, I spent a week hiking in the Moab area of Southeast Utah. In May 2014, I tackled six days of hiking in the Havasupai area of the Grand Canyon.

Nevertheless, I have found I need more to deal with the anxiety, fears, sense of responsibility, and uncertainty that are part of being a nonprofit leader. Many of my friends and colleagues have a spiritual well of hope and energy that they draw on from their community of faith. It's wonderful to believe that all is in the hands of a good God, that everything happens for a purpose, and that God gives us even more strength than what is needed to handle any situation. I must confess that I have a hard time believing that the Holocaust, the lynching of African American men, or the death of a child from cancer have a purpose. Nevertheless, the Judeo-Christian belief that we are, despite evidence to the contrary, in the hands of Providence that is moving history in a direction consistent with the work TAP has been sustaining at many points in my life. I have also been strengthened by the conviction that we are on the right side of history. If we as a nation, indeed a community of nations, are to prevail, the requirements of justice and equal opportunity for all people must be achieved.

For years I looked for some kind of grounding or spiritual practice besides attending church that would help me deal with anxiety, fear, foreboding, and self-criticism and empower me with the energy, optimism, compassion, and drive necessary for my work and life. Working with many people of different religious convictions, I have considered myself an inclusive rather than exclusive person of faith, refusing to be trapped in a "my way or the highway" attitude in religious matters. Having given up leadership in a particular faith, I have been freer than I would have been as a proponent of a single-faith alternative. So, for more than two decades I read widely in Buddhism, Islam, and Hinduism, and studied different forms of meditation. One of my heroes is Huston Smith, the MIT professor of religion who wrote about the major world religions after having practiced each one for a considerable period of time.[146]

Like many people, I would meditate for extended periods of time but without long-term consistency. That was until I read *The Heart of the Buddha's Teaching* by Thich Nhat Hanh. It was Thich Nhat Hanh's clarity, gentleness, and simplicity that struck me as the real deal. The fact that he was a leader of an engaged Buddhism that worked for peace during the Vietnam War and was nominated by Dr. Martin Luther King, Jr. for the Nobel Peace Prize attracted me as well.

Providentially, in 2008 I happened to be eating lunch downtown and spied a poster advertising a Sangha that was part of Thich Nhat Hanh's Order of Interbeing. The group practiced every Sunday morning in a room at the Universalist Unitarian Church of Roanoke. This was perhaps a place where I could learn how to meditate.

---

146 Dana Sawyer, "Huston Smith, the man who took religion seriously," http://www.gemstone-av.com/HuDan.htm (accessed March 16, 2015).

The Heart of the Blue Ridge Sangha was founded by Laurie Seidel, nurse educator for the Department of Psychiatry and Behavioral Health Medicine at Carilion Clinic. She had met Thich Nhat Hanh during his visit to the States and had asked him what advice he could offer her to help her meditation practice. "Thay" responded, "Start a Sangha." He directed her to lay practitioners for help. The hour-and-forty-minute session at the Heart of the Blue Ridge Sangha is a simple one. It combines sitting meditation (sometimes guided) with slow walking meditation, reading a chapter in a book together, a period of sharing from the heart about the problems or benefits with one's practice, and a closing. From the first visit, I knew I was home and that there was something here that filled my soul.

There are some very simple principles of the Order of Interbeing to which I respond:

1. The only time you are alive is in the present moment. The past is history. It does little good beating oneself over "could've, would've, should've." Furthermore, the future is yet to come and is out of our hands. All we have is the present moment to decide how we want to think, act, and interact with others. It is just another version of the AA motto, "one day at a time,"[147] or Jesus' admonition "tomorrow shall take thought for the things of itself," (Matthew 6:34).

2. In order to deal with the whirlwind of thoughts, perceptions, anticipations, and feelings that sap our energy and distress us, we need to get in touch with what is going on in our bodies by focusing on our breath and sensing what is happening inside us.

3. We are more than our disturbing thoughts and difficult feelings. Our thoughts are not truths or reality, but simply thoughts. Our feelings are merely physical phenomena that we can either just watch or get carried away by.

4. Life is impermanent. Nothing remains the same. Everything is changing. The greatest stressor is trying to resist change

---

147 Alcoholics Anonymous, "Frequently Asked Questions About A.A. History," http://www. aa.org/pages/en_US/frequently-asked-questions-about-aa-history (accessed March 16, 2015).

and force life into a certain mold. Impermanence means those good times will probably be followed by bad times and that bad times can yield to good times.

5. Everyone has challenges and hardships. Everyone will lose something or someone dear. Everyone will experience illness. Everyone will die. One newspaper article recently predicted that 75 percent of Americans will experience poverty at some point in their lives.[148]

6. We can be happy. We can choose to recognize the wonders of life in the midst of the most awful circumstances. We can choose to water the seeds of hope, love, compassion, and peace by choosing to practice those behaviors. We can deal with the seeds of anger, hate, anxiety, jealousy, and despair by simply recognizing them as old friends and embracing them like small babies, with understanding and love, until they pass from our present consciousness.

7. Everything and everyone is connected. We are not distinct, isolated individuals. We inter-are. We all depend on others for our welfare. As Noel C. Taylor, distinguished pastor and past mayor of the City of Roanoke said, "If you walk through the woods and find a toad on a high stump, you know he didn't get there by himself; someone put him there." We have all been the benefit of assistance—if not public assistance then family assistance.

After I had been meditating with the Sangha for less than a year, I attended a retreat at "Thay's" Blue Cliff Monastery in Pine Bush, New York. I went principally because he was one of the great leaders of our time. I had previously been in the presence of theologian Karl Barth, considered by many to be the key Christian theologian of the twentieth century; Dr. Martin Luther King, Jr., the tremendous civil

---

148 Rank, Mark R. "Toward a New Understanding of American Poverty," Washington University Journal of Law & Policy 20 (2006): 28, http://openscholarship.wustl.edu/cgi/viewcontent.cgi?article=1241&context=law_journal_law_policy (accessed March 16, 2015).

rights leader; and the Dalai Lama, the great Tibetan Buddhist leader. This was too good an opportunity to miss.

In one of his first talks, Thay led us in a breathing meditation: "Breathing in, I know that I am breathing in. Breathing out, I know that I am breathing out." He instructed us to take deep breaths that filled our abdomens and chests and to slowly let them out. Then, with a big smile he looked at all of us and said, "You are alive!"

Oh my God, I said to myself. *This is what it is all about, being wondrously alive!* Not just the thought, "I am alive," but the *experience* of being alive! Life was not about meeting a list of my own or others' expectations. It was about honoring the miracle of life. I stayed to the end of the five days, but in that one day had gotten a great message. I could return to my family, work, and all my roles back home with an appreciation for the incredible miracle of being alive, no matter what the future might hold. It was truly an epiphany moment.

In 2010, I attended a conference in mindfulness and education at Omega Institute in Newburgh, New York. Among the presenters were Jon Kabat-Zinn, Dan Siegel, and Linda Lantieri. Jon Kabat-Zinn is a pivotal voice in the mindfulness movement. He has taken the practices of mindful sitting, mindful walking, and mindful movement (yoga), and made them more accessible, creating a base of scientific research for their effectiveness in reducing stress and promoting health and well-being.[149] His work began at the University of Massachusetts Hospital. Kabat-Zinn noted that stress aggravated the conditions of some high-risk patients who were in danger of heart attack or stroke, suffering from chronic pain, or dying of a terminal illness. In response to this, Kabat-Zinn and his colleagues developed an eight-day program that taught patients how to reduce that stress through a concentrated program of deep relaxation, yoga, and mindful sitting meditation. Their program, which is called *Mindfulness-Based*

149 Center for Mindfulness in Medicine, Health Care, and Society, "Jon Kabat-Zinn," http://www.umassmed.edu/cfm/about-us/people/2-meet-our-faculty/kabat-zinn-profile/ (accessed March 29, 2015).

Stress Reduction program described in *Full Catastrophe Living*,[150] was so successful that it is now part of the treatment plan in 250 hospitals around the globe.[151] Reams of studies have been done to document that success. Kabat-Zinn described the basics of the MBSR program in his book, *Full Catastrophe Living*.

Mindfulness has other benefits outside of stress reduction. A growing cadre of evidence has been found to support the effect of these practices on brain development. Some of the findings are:

1. Our brains are wired with a *negativity bias*. Evolution has geared us to watch for threats to our survival. Often, the drive to ward off threats is greater than the drive to find opportunities for food, shelter, and the necessities of life. In addition, humans may be even more geared to negativity because we have the capacity to look into the future and envision threats that may or may not be there.[152]

2. The human brain is connected to both a "heat-up" (sympathetic) neurological system and a "cool-down" (parasympathetic) neurological system. When the alarm system (amygdala) in the brain spies a threat, the heat-up system sends hormones throughout the entire body through the blood system. As a result, the breath shortens, muscles tighten, heartbeat increases, and the body sweats in preparation for action.[153] When the body is at rest, the cool-down system stops the flow of hormones. The breath lengthens, the heartbeat slows, the muscles relax, and the body heat drops.[154]

150 Kabat-Zinn, Jon. *Full Catastrophe Living: Using the Wisdom of Your Body and Mind to Face Stress, Pain, and Illness, The Program of the Stress Reduction Clinic at the University of Massachusetts Medical Center.* (New York: A Delta Book Published by Dell Publishing a division of Bantam Doubleday Dell Publishing Group, Inc.,1991), p. 467.

151 U.S. Department of Veterans Affairs, "Mindfulness Based Stress Reduction," http://www. pugetsound.va.gov/services/mindfulness.asp (accessed March 17, 2015).

152 Rick Hanson, "Confronting the Negativity Bias," *Your Wise Brain* (blog), Psychology Today, October 26, 2010, https://www.psychologytoday.com/blog/your-wise-brain/201010/confronting-the-negativity-bias (accessed March 30, 2015).

153 Harvard Medical School, "Understanding the Stress Response," March 1, 2011, http://www.health.harvard.edu/staying-healthy/understanding-the-stress-response (accessed March 30, 2015).

154 GoodTherapy.org, "Parasympathetic Nervous System," Psychpedia (blog), last updated

3. The problem for modern folks is that our lives are moving so fast that we stay in the heat-up mode and the hormones, especially cortisol, begin to damage our bodies and shrink the prefrontal cortex, the center of our brain's executive function.[155] It is through meditation that we are able to engage the cool-down neurological system and allow our bodies and minds to repair from the constant onslaught of stress. This practice, done for a few minutes each day, can change our brains and experience of life, improve our decision making, and help us to be physically and mentally healthier.[156]

4. We are creatures of routine and habit. The stress cycle involves recurring patterns of thoughts, feelings, sensations, and behavior. When our thoughts are fearful and self-critical, our feelings are anxious and fearful, our sensations are distressing and our behavior is often fight, freeze, or flight. Unless we interrupt the patterns of thoughts, feelings, and behavior, the outcome is increased stress. As Elisha Goldstein put it at a recent conference in Roanoke, "What we practice and repeat in life is what we get." [157]

5. Mindfulness meditation enables us to step back from the whirlwind of thoughts, feelings, and habitual behavior and to look at them from outside. It gives us a window of choice and provides the freedom to react differently. To create a more balanced view of the world, you can choose to purposefully center your attention on those people, opportunities, and

---

May 13, 2013, http://www.goodtherapy.org/blog/psychpedia/parasympathetic-nervous-system (accessed March 30, 2015); Hanson, Rick and Richard Mendius. Buddha's Brain: The Practical Neuroscience of Happiness, Love & Wisdom. (Oakland California: New Harbinger Publications, Inc., 2009), p. 58–59.

155 Melanie Greenberg, "How to Prevent Stress from Shrinking Your Brain," *The Mindful Self-Express* (blog), *Psychology Today*, August 12, 2012, https://www.psychologytoday.com/blog/the-mindful-self-express/201208/how-prevent-stress-shrinking-your-brain (accessed March 30, 2015).

156 Hanson and Medius, *Buddha's Brain*, p. 51–60.

157 Elisha Goldstein, "Mindfulness Conference: Strategies, Practice, and Application, Roanoke, Virginia, September 17, 2014," unlisted Youtube video uploaded October 13, 2014 by William Sellari, http://youtu.be/nqdYIS2w53U, (accessed April 23, 2015).

blessings that enrich your life. It is no surprise that those who are the happiest are those who practice gratitude.[158]

6. Our brains are capable of change and growth just like our bodies. The term for that is *neuroplasticity*.[159] Each time we do something, an unbelievable number of neurons begin to fire and make new connections. Hence, the saying "What fires together wires together."[160] We connect new pathways to our heat-up or cool-down system, enlarge or decrease the size of amygdala, and strengthen or shrink the size of our prefrontal cortex. That is the part of the brain that houses our control over our impulses and problem solving. Mindfulness practices strengthen those areas for thought and problem solving and decrease connections for the automatic reactions of flight, fight, or freeze.[161] Today these changes in the brain are observable through the use of MRI technology. Each decision to change what we focus on physically changes the brain.

Most of us in the human-service business are aware of cognitive psychology. How we think largely affects what we feel and how we act. It is not what happens to us, but what we believe about what happens that determines how we are going to feel and respond. The task, then, is to get in touch with our thoughts and expectations and evaluate how they are determining our reactions to the present and driving our future. Simple enough? In fact, it's often more difficult than

---

158 Emmons, Robert. "Why Gratitude is Good," *The Greater Good Science Center*, November 16, 2010, http://greatergood.berkeley.edu/article/item/why_gratitude_is_good/ (accessed April 3, 2015).

159 Gary Stix, "Neuroplasticity: New Clues to Just How Much the Adult Brain Can Change," *Talking back* (blog), *Scientific American*, July 14, 2014, http://blogs.scientificamerican.com/talking-back/2014/07/14/neuroplasticity-new-clues-to-just-how-much-the-adult-brain-can-change/ (accessed March 30, 2015).

160 Gregoire, Carolyn. "How to Wire Your Brain For Happiness," *The Huffington Post*, October 2013, http://www.huffingtonpost.com/2013/10/17/how-tiny-joyful-moments-c_n_4108363.html (accessed March 17, 2015).

161 Rebecca Gladding, "This is Your Brain on Meditation," *Use Your Mind to Change Your Brain* (blog), *Psychology Today*, May 22, 2013, https://www.psychologytoday.com/blog/use-your-mind-change-your-brain/201305/is-your-brain-meditation (accessed March 30, 2015).

it sounds. So much of the time we are caught in a cyclone of thoughts and feelings that whirl through our mind and body, and we're not able to focus on them. To really take notice of what is happening in us, we need to slow down. Therein lies the gift of meditation. In slowing down our mental and bodily processes, we become more aware of what goes on in our minds and bodies. Awareness allows us space in which we perceive options and choice. In those choices is freedom, and that freedom can be used to be more compassionate to ourselves and others.

Mindfulness is about the practice of stopping the automatic pilot, the habitual pattern of thoughts, feelings, and behaviors that contribute to stress, and paying attention in a particular way to what is happening in the here and now inside us and around us without judgment or criticism. In its simplest form it is about applying the acronym, STOP (Stop, Take a breath, Observe, then Proceed) to daily life.[162]

Sharing the Practice of Mindfulness with Others

I began to think about the people who come to TAP and who of them might benefit from learning the simple techniques that Jon Kabat-Zinn was using to improve the lives of patients at the University of Massachusetts Hospital. The first group I thought of was prisoners in our local jails. Beyond the fact that they were a captive audience with little else to do, these were folks who needed the benefit of these practices to get a grip on their lives, make the best use of their time in jail, and develop practices that would benefit them in the very difficult transition from prison to freedom. Upon release, they would be confronted with a barrage of stressful decisions: Finding housing and a job, making positive friends, dealing with family, paying fines and child support, and carrying the stigma of being a felon.

---

162 Elisha Goldstein, PhD, "Stress Got You Down? Try This Tip to Balance Throughout the Day," (blog), *PsychCentral*, January 2009, http://blogs.psychcentral.com/mindfulness/2009/01/stress-got-you-down-try-this-tip-to-balance-throughout-the-day/ (accessed March 20, 2015).

Since September 2010, a group of men and women facilitators have helped me adapt the MBSR program to the inmates of the Western Virginia Regional Jail. Over the course of ten weeks, we introduce them to techniques for deep relaxation, the practices of mindful sitting, mindful walking and movement, and mindful eating. In addition, we utilize both chi gong and yoga as movement exercises. Each Monday's evening session goes from to 7:00 to 8:30, except for the last Monday session, which lasts the better part of a full day. Attendance is always high and inmates are always asking the officials when the next ten-week session will begin. At first, staff members were a little apprehensive of this new program. However, after three years they too have bought in. Not only are the men and women calmer when they return to their "pods" (group housing units), but the pods as a whole are calmer and there is an ease of tension throughout the jail.

The second group at TAP to which I have exposed mindfulness practices is our top staff. Each annual staff retreat begins with personal sharing, moves to the discussion of business, and concludes with feedback so each person on the team gets to hear how they are coming across to each of their teammates. In recent years, we have also included exercises in deep relaxation, short periods of mindful silence, and yoga. At most meetings, we will take ten full breaths to look around the room and savor how good it is to be able to do the work that we do and work with the folks in the room. A number of the staff have used what they have learned to deal with the pressures of work and family. One member, who was given an opportunity at the pulpit of her church, introduced the practice of focusing on the breath to the entire congregation.

In 2013, I worked with two classes in our Head Start program to introduce teachers and children to the mind/body stress reduction practices. Our Head Start staff is made up of truly talented professionals who structure activities that help the children develop their minds, bodies, and abilities to positively interact with other children and adults. Head Start children are bright, talented, and resilient. However, in order to succeed, these children have to develop the ability to control impulses, express their feelings verbally, and deal with the many pressures of life to which they are exposed. There is considerable evidence that long-term success in school, in the family, and on the job is the result of having a well-developed executive function of the brain, the prefrontal cortex.[163] Since mindfulness practices use the STOP technique (Stop, Take a Breath, Observe, Proceed),[164] they help build the brain's executive function, which can help children resist thoughtless, automatic pilot responses.

A study by Robert Whitaker, professor of public health and pediatrics at Temple University, found that women working in Head Start programs reported higher-than-expected levels of physical and mental health problems. A subsequent study of 2,160 adults working in sixty-six Pennsylvania Head Start programs found that:

> . . . nearly one fourth of those surveyed reported three or more types of adverse childhood experiences, and almost 30 percent reported having stress-related health conditions like, depression, headache, or back pain . . . However, the risk of having multiple health conditions was nearly 50 percent lower among those with the highest level of mindfulness compared to those with the lowest. This was true even for those who had multiple types of childhood adversity.[165]

Whitaker noted that mindfulness exercises might cut down on

163 Alex Korb, "Shaping Your Kid's Brain for Success," *Prefrontal Nudity* (blog), *Psychology Today*, April 30, 2012, https://www.psychologytoday.com/blog/prefrontal-nudity/201204/shaping-your-kids-brain-success (accessed March 17, 2015).

164 Elisha Goldstein, PhD, "Stress Got You Down? Try This Tip to Balance Throughout the Day," (blog), *PsychCentral*, January 2009, http://blogs.psychcentral.com/mindfulness/2009/01/stress-got-you-down-try-this-tip-to-balance-throughout-the-day/ (accessed March 20, 2015).

165 Robert C. Whitaker, Tracy Dearth-Wesley, Rachel A. Gooze, Brandon D. Becker, Kathleen C. Gallagher, Bruce S. McEwen, "Adverse Childhood Experiences, Dispositional Mindfulness, and Adult Health," *Preventive Medicine* 67 (October 2014): 147–153, http://www.sciencedaily.com/releases/2014/09/140913141308.htm (accessed April 1, 2015).

the expense to society generated by adults who have gone through hard childhood experiences.[166] The study reinforces our effort to provide mindfulness training to TAP staff, especially those in Head Start classrooms.

Outside of TAP, I continue to work a couple of hours a month counseling individuals at the free mental health clinic supported by Mental Health America in Roanoke Valley. I have found that my clients who suffer from anxiety and depression respond well to deep relaxation and mindful breathing. They often experience a calm and peace that, most of the time, eludes them. Psychologists Mark Williams, John Teasdale, and Zindel Segal have taken Jon Kabat-Zinn's program and adapted it to persons suffering from depression. The program has demonstrated that "it reduces the likelihood of relapse by about 40 to 50 percent in people who have suffered three or more previous episodes of depression."[167]

To further promote awareness of the use of mindfulness practice in a variety of occupations, I took leadership in bringing together a coalition of leaders to attract national leaders on the subject to the Roanoke Valley community. On September 17th, 2014, in coordination with Radford University, Mental Health America in the Roanoke Valley, Family Services of the Roanoke Valley, Virginia Western Community College, Jefferson College of Health Science, and Roanoke City Public Schools, TAP held a full-day conference titled *Mindfulness: Strategies, Practices and Applications in Education, Health Care/Mental Health, Human Services, Business, and Law Enforcement*. The conference introduced 250 professionals in the area of nursing, human services, counseling, and business to psychologist Elisha Goldstein, PhD and Patricia Jennings, PhD. Elisha Goldstein is a prolific writer in the practice of mind, body, and stress reduction. Tish Jennings is an expert on mindfulness and education. She has done considerable research in the use of mindfulness with teachers to improve their

---

166 Ibid.

167 Williams, Mark and Danny Penman. *Mindfulness: An Eight-Week Plan for Finding Peace in a Frantic World*. (New York: Rodale Books, 2011), p. 52.

classroom performance. In addition, Congressman Tim Ryan of Ohio, the author of *A Mindful Nation*, was gracious enough to produce a welcoming video for the conference, highlighting the growing role that the practice of mindfulness is playing in our communities. The conference received high marks from the participants, who requested a follow-up conference in 2015. On October 16, 2015 a second Mindfulness Conference was conducted featuring Ron Siegel, Psy.D, from Harvard University, and international expert in the field. Siegel is Assistant Professor of Psychology at Harvard Medical School and serves on the Board of Directors of Meditation and Psychotherapy.

In Summary

Aspiring to be a Level 5 leader of a nonprofit involves a great deal of stress that has to be skillfully managed if we are to continue having the required level of energy and intensity that our mission requires. Each of us will find a different mix of ways of keeping ourselves physically healthy and mentally grounded. We ignore the issue of finding balance and equilibrium at our own peril and rob our organizations of what we potentially have to offer. My adventure into the arena of mindfulness shows one method of achieving that balance and fostering the thrill of being alive, no matter what happens. It has further offered strategies that are valuable to those who I have worked with, and for low-income individuals and families whose circumstances magnify the stresses of life. It represents a whole new frontier in the area of human development.

Keeping it Together: Managing Stress Take-Aways

- What are the steps that you have taken to deal with the daily stress of the job and other areas of life?
- How have you preserved your equilibrium and balance?
- What workout and healthy living practices have you incorporated into your lifestyle to keep you at your best?

- What diversions from the job have you engaged in that help to refresh you on a continuing basis?
- What opportunities have you created for healthy living education for your staff and volunteers?
- What experience do you have with the many "mindfulness" experiences, including yoga, tai chi, qui gong, deep relaxation, and sitting meditation?
- What conferences might you go to that would help you connect with some of these stress-reducing, life-enhancing practices?
- What are the steps you have taken to make these evidence-based approaches to reducing stress available to others?
- What client groups do you serve that could benefit from what you have learned about mindfulness techniques?

Chapter 15

CONCLUSION

You would not have picked up this book if you didn't want to make a positive difference in the lives of others. You may be a member of a nonprofit board of directors. You may be a college student thinking of working at a nonprofit. You may have an exciting idea and are interested in founding a nonprofit corporation to implement that idea. You may be a staff person serving in a nonprofit, providing important leadership for that organization. You may be a person just hired as CEO, looking for information to help build a great organization. What follows is a summary of all the sections and techniques in this book for doing just that, organized by chapter.

A Calling in a Growing Industry: The nonprofit community represents a growing industry that produces jobs, economic activity, and improved quality of life in ways that are not addressed by market forces of supply and demand. Nonprofit leadership is both an art and a science. While each leader, depending on their personality, will leave a different imprint, there is a growing "science" of best leadership practices that will determine their impact on the organization they serve. Those who have served with distinction in this arena know that it is more than a job. It is a "sacred" calling.

The Quest to Make a Difference: Launching a Project: The nonprofit experience, if done well, is all about making a difference in the lives of people and the life of a community. Done well, the nonprofit experience is also an adventure. The major steps of that adventure are defining an unmet need that affects a number of people, developing a solution, creating a leadership team, packaging the solution to solicit support for its implementation, securing of institutional commitments to support the solution, implementing the solution, evaluating and refining the solution, and adapting to a changing environment. Not everything has to be started from scratch. Nonprofits can learn from others and implement programs that were successful in other communities. Events often take place that will lead to opportunities if a nonprofit is already engaged with the community. In this business, a successful project will invariably lead to another opportunity.

Making a Larger Difference: Scaling Up and Collective Action: In order to make a more decisive difference, it is often important to build collaborations that frequently involve other nonprofits, the private sector, and government. Such was the case in TAP's initiatives to bring water and wastewater services to those without indoor plumbing, create a pre- and post-incarceration program for ex-offenders, and quality primary health care for poor children. In the case of the Virginia Water Project, Virginia CARES, and CHIP of Virginia, it also required the scaling up of these projects beyond a region within a state to the entire state in order to make a more dramatic difference on the larger problem and to garner the necessary resources for the efforts.

Creating a Vision: Nonprofit leadership begins with a vision. Visionaries dream of things that never were and ask "Why not?" Then they give their all to make that dream come true. Just like Cabell Brand did. Visionaries refuse to give up, even when their vision does not instantly become a full reality. Visionaries take a longer view of things, realizing that some of the great cathedrals of Europe took hundreds of years to complete,[168] each workman contributing his part to the finished product that he would never live to see. John Rawls' thought experiment in his *A Theory of Justice* is a good place to

---

168 "Q&A: Ancient Megastructures," *National Geographic*, http://www.natgeotv.com/ca/ancient-megastructures/q-and-a (accessed April 2, 2015).

start. Of course, you can always adopt a future that someone else has envisioned and make it yours.

Executive Leadership: If we aspire to leadership capable of leading a great organization as opposed to a mediocre or even good organization, it is a matter of adopting Level 5 character traits: an unrelenting ambition for our organization, personal humility, and palpable conviction that the organization will prevail whatever challenges present themselves. We learn from others and have our models and mentors. Bristow Hardin, Jr. was mine. I learned from him key lessons of leadership that have served me well for thirty-nine years. He taught me "The play's the thing!" "No shoddy performances!" "No prima donnas!" "There can only be one director!" "We would not only survive but survive gloriously." Through his actions, he emphasized that nothing was more important than our mission, to be honest about what you don't know, to learn from others, to stand up for what is important, to not let anyone threaten you, and to tell the truth. He taught me to work hard, have fun, and celebrate the successes of others.

Boards of Directors: No organization achieves greatness without a strong board of directors and strong executive leadership that work hand in hand to get the work done and "make walls move." Strong boards hire strong executives. Strong executives build strong boards. The reverse is also true. Weak boards and weak executives attract each other like flies to flypaper. The board creates the policy and approves the work program and the budget. The board hires and evaluates the executive. There are ways to facilitate the work of building a strong board. These include use of focus groups for board training, the development of strong board committees, and recruitment of talented members especially from the business community, strategic planning sessions, and the use of boards of commissioners for additional involvement. Monthly meetings and well-organized meetings lasting no more than ninety minutes build involvement. Strong boards are made of people who become knowledgeable about the work of the organization through engagement. Nonprofit boards are wise to protect themselves from legal issues by engaging a committed corporate attorney and a contractual relation with the executive, which allows the board to walk away at the end of the contract period if necessary.

Managing for Results: A results-oriented organization needs to evaluate its impact with the best measures available. The gold standard is studies based on control groups. When that level of certainty is not available, the use of evidence-based approaches is important. The objective of providing a service should never replace advocacy and meaningful organizational change. Strong results stem from a combined focus on the task to be done and the people doing the work. Great leaders lead in defining outcomes and measuring their achievement. They assess the fit between the organization's passion, what it does best, and the resources that can be marshalled to support the work. At the same time, great leaders fashion a high-trust environment by creating opportunities for sharing and feedback among staff. Maximizing a focus on both task and maintenance takes place best in teams through retreats that foster shared leadership. In work teams where there is optimal respect and honesty, and the free give-and-take of ideas without defensiveness, maximum learning takes place. The desired goal is an organization that is constantly learning, where the group IQ is greater than the aggregate of the individuals.

Economic Engine and Economic Accountability: It all comes down to resources. In most cases that means money. Great leaders find ways to increase those dollars to support the agency mission. Core dollars must be protected as those dollars can be used to leverage other monies. Nothing is more precious than discretionary dollars. Agencies that are able to develop businesses that generate income or work with the for-profit sector are able to create a pool of important capital. The CEO is responsible for the financial health of the organization. A strong CFO is an important partner. The use of simple "financial snapshots" provides an up-to-date measure of the organization's financial health. A financial grid is a good template for deciding on what ventures will most benefit the agency. Three months of salary, including fringe benefits and taxes, in reserve, is the bare minimum of what is necessary to keep an organization out of financial trouble. Working toward an endowment of substantial capital is optimal.

The Right Who: Great organizations populate themselves with the "right whos." These are individuals who are self-motivated and self-disciplined. They locate the center of control over their lives in themselves rather than external people or forces. They have the "grit" factor that allows them to focus and persist in spite of obstacles that inevitably confront them. They do whatever it takes and work until the job is done. The "right whos" are good at finding other "right whos" and are encouraged chiefly by achievement, recognition, the work itself, the authority to do the job in front of them, and the opportunity to learn and develop their skills. It is more important in managing the "right whos" to engage them with approval, concerns, and ideas on a regular basis instead of waiting for formal annual review time. Annual reviews can become valuable if preceded by self-evaluations by those under review. It is important to make sure that the agency personnel policies enable the organization to help the "wrong whos" move on. An organization should also ensure that agency reorganizations due to reduction in funds or changes in strategic plans do not allow for employee grievance. Organizations should also limit the number of persons who perform below an "A" or "B" level. Limit grievances above the level of a board grievance committee to review of the committee transcript at the board level.

The Organizational Culture: Organizations are more than a collection of individuals. They are cultures that are built on values that mold individual behavior and the relationships between people. Organizational change is about understanding the current norms of an organization's culture and promoting those which will make the organization more dynamic and effective. TAP's cultural norms often distinguish it from other, less dynamic organizations: Remember why we're here, never take "no" for an answer, nothing less than excellence, real work is when things happen, do whatever it takes to succeed, remember the people who make up the organization, limit bureaucracy, promote teamwork and shared leadership, and, above all, protect the financial bottom line.

Networks, Partnerships, Collaborations, and Collective Action: Making a significant difference can rarely be done without the help of others. Solving an important community problem means reaching out to other organizations. At the very least it means fostering partnerships with organizations that otherwise are competitors, as in the case of the Hurt Park housing partnership. Coalitions are built of many partnerships aimed at a broader impact. Networks can be the result of scaling up a program in order for the project to have a wider impact. Partnerships, coalitions, networks, and collective action will have the greatest impact when the top leaders of the individual organizations are involved, goals and benchmarks are set, and there is a high degree of mutual accountability. Through partnerships and networks, a local organization can scale up a project and have a statewide or national impact. Building one network that addresses an important issue can lead to relationships. Those relationships can more easily lead to the formation of networks to address other issues.

Marketing - Getting the Story Out: You have to have a story to tell. It all begins with the quality of work performed. Nevertheless, you can't assume that because your organization does good work that people will know about it and support it. Brands are built on a record of accomplishments and a strong marketing plan. Marketing will include the name of the organization, its slogan, quality of its printed materials, its website and social media, annual reports, media coverage, and signature events to promote the work of your organization. A strong marketing committee is a must in the competitive nonprofit environment. The talents of a communications specialist, with graphic design capability and expertise in the use of social media, are extremely helpful. A strong marketing committee may lead to the creation of a signature event that not only promotes the work of the organization but raises discretionary income to support its future.

Social Capital: It is Who You Know: An organization is only as strong as its social capital. Social capital comes in two forms: bonding and bridging. Bonding is the strength of the organization's connection with its friends. Bridging is the reach of that influence through connections with others and their networks. An organization's clients, staff, board members, and volunteers are all potential connectors to persons and networks of influence that create support, credibility, and opportunity for the organization. Amassing social capital begins with a strong database of all those who have supported the organization. It involves creating volunteer experiences that build tighter bonds with supporters. Continued communication of impact stories and recognition of supporters is essential. Organization evangelists and super-evangelists create greater connections that garner important resources for the organization. Strong marketing and media exposure validate those who support the organization.

Keeping it Together: Managing Stress: We live in stressful times. Nonprofit leadership is a stressful undertaking. Our world is constantly changing. We are confronted with new challenges every day in addition to the challenges of the day before. Stress affects our mental and physical health and, unattended, will affect the quality of the work we do and the relationships we build with others. Strong leaders have to find ways of taking care of themselves so that they can be fully there for the organization. There is significant scientific evidence that the practice of mindfulness can reduce the impact of that stress as well as increase focus, persistence, and job performance. It can also improve physical health, psychological adjustment, and overall well-being. Mindfulness can be useful to leaders in reducing anxiety and improving relationships with others. It can be useful for staff in dealing with the pressures on and off the job. It can be useful to various client populations as they seek to build their lives in very difficult and challenging circumstances.

AFTERWORD

Ted Edlich's book distills so clearly his 40+ years of not-for-profit organizational and managerial experience in the evolution of TAP. What the thoughtful reader will soon grasp is that the greatest threat to the strength of our Country is NOT external – it is INTERNAL. The strongest defense of our free market economy, the fundamental source of our national strength, is found in the effort to create a continuous universe of opportunities for those who have not, or cannot, or are otherwise unable to participate in it. Over the long span of recorded history, great countries have inevitably collapsed from the internal corrosion of their core values and uneven-handed governance. In the absence of genuine opportunities for those who exist at the margins of our society, we blindly weaken our own comfortable status quo. TAP's artful combination of public (tax revenues) resources with those of resources from the private sector is the ONLY value-added approach to genuine creation of the opportunities for participation. The alternative is dependence on the public sector, a zero-sum game where no societal value is created – only generational hopelessness. *Navigating the Nonprofit Rapids* makes clear that there must be disturbers of the established order in the effort to create opportunity for all. Cabell Brand, Bristow Hardin, Jr. and Ted Edlich have all understood this fact. Now, Edlich has produced an exquisite roadmap with national application. TAP's mission is oddly Adam Smith in disguise: we must follow our own self-interest, but we must realize that the absence of opportunity for our less fortunate fellow citizens is completely contrary to our own self-interest. Even-handed governance has been the secret to the great success of TAP. This even-handedness is no different from governance in the private sector: the latter has shareholders to whom it must answer. The former is a perfect example of the mission of a 501©(3) – it is a public trust, owned by the public for the benefit of all citizens. TAP is a splendid example of responsible public leadership, at times painful and discomforting, but its underlying values are universally ethical and the fruits of its labors benefit every citizen across society.

I simply could not put Ted's manuscript down. I was completely enthralled – and I still am!

~ George W. Logan

George W. Logan has been a Provost-appointed Lecturer at the University of Virginia's Darden School of Business since 1997. He has co-authored the definitive text "Corporate Governance", published by McGraw-Hill in 2003, and translated into six languages. He also co-authored "Principles of General Management" published by the Yale Press in 2007. A native of Salem, VA, he and Cabell Brand had a vigorous 40 year friendship, characterized by endless debate about the **HOW**, not the **WHY**. Cabell often called him " his favorite serial capitalist." Logan has lived in Charlottesville with his wife, Harmon, a music therapist specializing in Guided Imagery, since 2006.

ABOUT THE AUTHOR

You do not have to be a small particle physicist to know that the observer has an impact on what is observed.

I grew up a child of privilege in Greenwich Village, Manhattan, New York City. That position of privilege meant a childhood of wonderful options, great educational opportunity, and a belief that anything was possible. It was additionally a buffer against class intimidation the rest of my life.

We lived at No. 1 Fifth Avenue, one block away from Washington Square Park with its landmark arch commemorating George Washington. My father was a family practice physician who made house calls and served everyone who came through his doors, regardless of income. He would become a favorite physician of painter Franz Kline and counted among his patients celebrated artists Willem and Elaine de Kooning, playwright Leroi Jones, and actor Robert De Niro. Kline, who painted portraits of my mother, two brothers, and me, would often give or sell Dad a painting in exchange for medical care for his ailing wife. As a result, my father would end up with the largest collection of Kline's pre-abstract work in the country before his international breakthrough as a member of New York's Abstract Expressionist movement in the 1950s.

My mother and father were hardworking, upper-middle-class parents. My dad, Theodore J. Edlich, Jr. was a second-generation New York City physician who had grown up during the Depression in which his father had lost over a half-million dollars in the stock market. He ran his own practice, supervised his nursing and lab staff, kept his own books, handwrote his own bills to patients, made house calls, and provided for his three children. My mother had migrated from the small town of New Martinsville, West Virginia, where her father was a carpenter. She graduated from nursing school in New York City and married my father, a doctor. She was beautiful, intelligent, artistic, tough, the oldest of two sisters and a brother, a consummate hostess, and a woman of great energy. When my father joined the Coast Guard as a lieutenant commander during World War II, my mother worked full time with another doctor to hold his practice together until he returned after the war.

My father's social position in lower Manhattan provided every financial opportunity a child could wish for, including connections that would assist us in college preparation and admissions. My mother's ferocity on behalf of her children would ensure that my brother, Dick, would not be held back in the third grade because he could not read at grade level. Dick would later enter college at fifteen, enter medical school at eighteen, and become a doctor at twenty-two. He would go on to earn his PhD in Biomedical Engineering in addition to his MD and become a full professor in three years at the University of Virginia Medical School. He would become a leader in burn care and emergency medicine in spite of heroically living with MS during the last thirty years of his tenure.

As with many families of means, there was a certain WASP (white Anglo-Saxon Protestant) bias and prejudice that shaped our family preferences. Nevertheless, as children with busy parents living in multiethnic New York City, we had great freedom to meet different people from different stations and walks of life and form our own opinions. At Stuyvesant High School, a premier public math and science school, we found ourselves in an environment where 70 percent of our classmates were highly competitive Jewish kids at a time when there were limits on Jewish admission to college. I found time to shoot pool on Fourteenth Street with tough Eastside Puerto Rican kids with lots of street smarts. The president of the student council was a handsome and distinguished young African American whose last name was Carpenter.

Prior to high school, we played Little League baseball on Long Island. Our team came in second in the league to the winners, who were members of an all-African American team with whom we became friends. We spent one of the best summers of our lives with my mother's parents, Ora and French Bargerhuff, in small-town New Martinsville, West Virginia, where we played ball with kids who could run on gravel with no shoes, smoked our first corn-silk cigarettes, and learned from our grandfather how to put soap on the threads of screws to ease their way into wood.

In addition to my father's friends—General Hildring, who served under General Dwight D. Eisenhower; "Brock," the cigar-smoking head architect of Gulf Oil; and bestselling author Thomas B. Costain—my mother attracted an eclectic crowd of devotees that included her cousin, *Chicago Times* sportswriter Jim Fair, who spent his early childhood in a West Virginia brothel and dedicated his book on fighter Harry Greb (*Give Him to the Angels*) to his wife, Francis, and my mother. Frequent visitors to our Greenwich Village home included local prizefighters from Whitey Bimstein's gym; Morty and Sam, a commercially successful gay couple who served as her hair stylist and interior decorator; and Ed Olson, Professor of American History at NYU who became the constant movie-going companion to my brother, Dick, and me. The breadth of diversity in my early years left me questioning the cultural prejudices of the time regarding ethnicity, economic class, and even sexual orientation. These stereotypes fell short of the reality that I observed. I was determined early on to form my own opinions.

Professor of Psychology Harold Greenwald, a friend in later years, suggests that early on we all make one of four decisions that shape our lives: To be different, to be perfect, to be loved, or to suffer. To those who said that none of these fit, he would say, "Oh, you're just trying to get it perfectly. You're a perfectionist." Each decision has both advantages and drawbacks. I, clearly, to the regret of my father who wanted his namesake to be a physician, chose to be different. In my case that meant refusing to believe that I was by nature smarter, more able, and more deserving than those who were less privileged or held in less high esteem. It meant seeking my own path, with its own pitfalls and wrong turns, rather than the one that had been laid out for me. It meant questioning practically everything.

With my brother, Dick, I left Stuyvesant High School in Manhattan in 1954 to enter Lafayette College in Easton, Pennsylvania, on a Ford Foundation Early Admissions Scholarship. After a less-than-stellar freshman year, I transferred to the University of North Carolina where I earned a Bachelor of Arts in American History and a minor in philosophy. During my college years at UNC, I became active in the Westminster Fellowship of the Presbyterian Church just off campus. Membership in the group, whose initial attraction was a Sunday night meal, was not focused on having the right answers but raising the right questions such as "Why am I here?" "What does it mean to be a member of a community?" "What does it mean to be a citizen in a democracy?" "What does it mean to be a sexual being and live responsibly?" "Toward what end is history moving?" We became acquainted with the writings of Jean-Paul Sartre, Albert Camus, Reinhold Niebuhr, Paul Tillich, Dietrich Bonhoeffer, and Karl Barth by reading the works, writing papers explaining their relevance, and presenting those papers to others in the group for discussion.

I was deeply moved by Tillich's "You Are Accepted" in his book of sermons, *The Shaking of the Foundations*,[169] and for weeks I felt like the weight of the world had been lifted from my shoulders and that I could walk on air. Old Testament scholar John Bright's *The Kingdom of God* presented me with a history that I could be a part of, one going in a direction that amounted to more than earning a living, buying a house in the suburbs, and keeping the lawn mowed. I remember an attractive young man whose two goals in life were to enter the

---

169 Tillich, Paul. *The Shaking of the Foundations.* (New York: Charles Scribner's Sons, 1948), p. 153–163.

University of North Carolina and to pledge the Sigma Nu Fraternity. He was blackballed by the fraternity. At the age of eighteen, he had failed to achieve half his life's ambition. I wrote my first op-ed article against the blackball process of the fraternity pledge system. I wanted more. Furthermore, I figured that if God could use the weak, flawed, and imperfect people of the biblical witness, that there was a chance that he could use me with all of my flaws and insecurities as well.

At the end of my junior year, I was elected President of the Westminster Fellowship. During the summer, I drove to the nondenominational Pacific School of Religion next to the Berkley, California, campus of the University of California in the San Francisco Bay area. There I attended an eight-week residential program with courses in theology, ethics, and group dynamics with thirty other men and women who were campus religious leaders from across the country. Through that program, I met ethicist John Bennett of Union Theological Seminary with whom I developed a friendship.

In particular, two experiences during my senior year at UNC stand out that broadened my worldview. For a semester, I lived in a cooperative living arrangement with a diverse group of men. These included an Englishman, a Korean, a Jewish American, a German American student who learned to play the drums in all-African American nightclubs in Chicago, my African American roommate, a graduate student from India, and another American keen to introduce me to hangouts that sold white lightning. We shared in the costs, upkeep, and preparation of meals. None of them ever knew of the fat little mouse that I chased out of the pan of meatloaf before cooking it when it was my turn to prepare supper. Everyone raved about the best meatloaf they had ever eaten.

During my senior year, our Westminster Fellowship raised money for a scholarship for an African American student who had graduated fourth in his class from the segregated African American high school in the township of Carrboro, just down the road from Chapel Hill. It was up to me to deliver the news that he had won the scholarship. He lived in the rural countryside down a crisscrossing of dirt roads.

When I finally found him, he was standing in bare feet, wearing only a pair of blue jeans, feeding a group of chickens. After he enrolled at the university, he was tutored by a group of Presbyterian wives of university professors and successfully completed his studies. I am told that by the third year he qualified for a scholarship to study abroad.

Upon graduating from UNC with an undergraduate degree in American history, I was less than well prepared for the world of earning a living. I returned home to Greenwich Village and enrolled in a master's degree program at the NYU School of Education. After six months, I had completed most of the required education and social science coursework. Since NYU would give course credit for actual teaching experience, I joined my fiancée, Janet Sutton, in Orange, Texas, and found a job at the junior high school. I taught English and social studies to seventh and eighth graders for the next two years, using the intervening summer to continue work on my education degree at the University of Texas in Austin.

In 1960, I completed my MA at NYU and entered Union Theological Seminary in Richmond. At Union I was drawn to the person of Jesus of Nazareth, who identified with the poor, the sick, and the outcasts of society, and challenged prejudice and exploitation of the weak. I was moved by the leaders of the social gospel tradition who sought to make a difference in the world by fighting child labor and setting up settlement houses in the most deprived settings. I remember the young man that was the recipient of the university scholarship provided by our Westminster Fellowship. I agreed with the theologians who argued that justice was the expression of love in the social context, and with Paul that the body was not only a metaphor for the church but also for the world, a metaphor in which the health of each part of the body was required for the health and welfare of the whole organism. I have never regretted my theological education because it taught me how to think and how belief systems shape our behavior in all situations. Often there are ways of looking at life that have to be challenged if we are to make progress.

I graduated at the head of my class and received one of three fellowships available for postgraduate study. In the fall of 1963, I attended Yale Divinity School to study social ethics. In 1963, Yale was an exciting place to be. It was the time of the Kennedy presidency and the New Frontier. It was the time of the civil rights movement in America. All things were being questioned and reevaluated. Professor Miller, who taught both at the Divinity School and in the Department of Political Science, would travel to Washington, DC, on the weekends and participate in the think tank sessions of the Kennedy brain trust. We read past Supreme Court decisions, discussed the literature on civil disobedience, and studied the ethical issues behind the proposals to desegregate public establishments. Michael Harrington published *The Other America*,[170] a detailed exposé of a subnation of poverty in the midst of plenty that commanded my attention that year. We were constantly moving our focus between our texts and the daily paper. One could not help but feel that we were to be part of a great historical transformation; there was such hope for the future. That year was also the year of the Kennedy assassination.

By the end of the summer of 1964, I had a wife and two children. I needed a job and I wanted to go back south. In spite of the South's problems, I enjoyed the friendliness and warmth of Southern communities. Big cities were too large. In a smaller area, I could envision having an impact. The Rev. Woody Leach, Presbyterian minister to students at Virginia Tech, helped me get an interview with two Presbyterian churches in Botetourt County, Virginia, that shared a minister: The Presbyterian Church on Main Street in the town of Buchanan and the Virginia Presbyterian Church down the road in an area named Pico, after the Pulaski Iron Company that once mined there. It was in the Pico community that I was introduced to rural poverty with homes whose inhabitants carried water from the creek and used outhouses as toilets. In 1965, I was ordained and installed as pastor of both congregations.

---

170 Harrington, Michael. *The Other America: Poverty in the United States*. (New York: A Touchstone Book published by Simon & Schuster, 1997), p. 230.

I served those two wonderful congregations for the next two years. They were forgiving of my inexperience and understood that we were going through a radical transformation on the matter of race and desegregation. When I held the first African American wedding in an all-white church (for a young woman who had been hired to watch the children while the adult Presbyterians attended church service), I caught hell from some of the community, led by the white Baptists down the street. Little was said by Presbyterians, though they were catching flak as well. When two people were hit by Norfolk and Western trains as they were crossing the tracks that had no warning lights or arms, I led a failed effort to enforce a speed limit on the N&W freight trains until warning lights were installed. The protection devices were finally installed after a Presbyterian elder, Mr. Booze, the owner of the Ford Motor distributorship in town, and his wife were killed late one evening on their way home by an N&W engine coming around the bend.

It was while I was in Buchanan that I heard of business leader Cabell Brand and the forum that he was holding throughout the area on the issue of poverty and the possibility of starting a community action agency. I gave my assistance in helping to organize the meeting in Botetourt County. Little did I know that this would be the beginning of a long friendship and partnership.

In 1965, Total Action Against Poverty was formed in the Roanoke Valley. In 1966, I was asked to head an inner-city ministry of eleven Presbyterian churches in the City of Roanoke. The Presbyterian Inner City Program coordinated with TAP at every juncture. The Presbyterian Center in Southeast Roanoke served as the site for TAP's GED program, community organization effort, and social work assistance program. As a TAP volunteer, I was privy to the initial community organization strategies training of all non-Head Start staff by the University Research Corporation. Under the mentorship of a local African American pastor, the Rev. Thomas Crews, I was asked to visit residents of the Kimball community, one of the communities later demolished under the national Neighborhood Urban Renewal program, and ask them to identify their particular needs. I still recall how terribly dark the homes were in order to save electricity and the sight of infants in walkers in front of a TV that served as a surrogate babysitter. As a result of the organizing effort, I was elected to drive the leaders of these communities to the Justice Department in Washington, DC, so they could present their demands for adequate compensation for their homes, which were being taken by the City of Roanoke under the public right of "eminent domain." As a result, the compensation was increased.

In 1968, I would join the TAP staff as Head Start Director and in the intervening years between 1968 and 1975 serve as Director of Community Organization and Director of Training. From 1975 until January 31, 2015—a span of forty years—I would serve as CEO of the organization. That experience serves as the basis for my thoughts concerning the essential ingredients of a first-class nonprofit business.

Whatever success I might have had that is reflected in this book is a function not just of my connection to my working colleagues but those closest to me, my family. I have been surrounded by five marvelous children, Connie, T.J., Sutton, Maria, Eva, and stepdaughter, Sara. To share in their journeys has been the greatest privilege and joy of my life. There is no greater blessing than to have healthy children and grandchildren and to see them excel, each in their own way. A few years ago when I was hospitalized for a serious undiagnosed ailment, all six adult children made the journey to the hospital and, each in their own way, led to my release from the hospital and my recovery. I am deeply appreciative of their caring and support.

At the head of my support team has been my wife, Liz. We have just celebrated our fourteenth wedding anniversary. Without a doubt, these have been the happiest years of my life. Liz is an extremely intelligent, high-spirited, and deeply caring woman. A woman of striking beauty, she is often mistaken for someone from Greece, Italy, or Israel. She has exemplified a lioness's ferocity in support of her two children and has allowed me to help in raising her youngest, Eva, my adopted daughter, who gave me a new opportunity to be an even better parent. As a former Head Start child, Liz knows firsthand the importance of work with which I have been involved. She has made her own contribution to the Virginia Water Project, where she served as Executive Assistant to the CEO, and to the Southwest Virginia Food Bank, where she simultaneously wore the hats of Development Director, Human Resources Director, and Administrative Assistant before earning her own real estate broker's license and teaching courses in real estate. Late in life, she went back to college and earned a science degree with honors. Together we have created a mutual support system filled with love, laughter, and adventure. Our home is filled with beautiful paintings and carvings from all over the world. In all things she has been my primary encouragement. I am sure that most of my achievements in the last two decades including this book would not have been possible without her support. I am grateful for her close reading of the manuscript and her positive contributions to the final product.

It is my humble wish that this book will serve the reader well in strengthening his or her performance as a first-class nonprofit leader and give rise to the same type of fulfillment that I have enjoyed in my career of service.

APPENDIX

Take-Away Compilation

The Quest to Make a Difference: Launching a Project

- What are the outstanding unmet needs in your community?
- Who are the people most invested in solving that needs in your community?
- What are the current options for solutions to those unmet needs?
- Who will "package" the solution to elicit support from others to create the resources necessary to implement the solution?
- Who are the key people in your community who would constitute a leadership team for moving the project forward?
- What plans have been made for evaluation of the solution?
- Are there factors in the environment that could impact the delivery and sustainability of the solution?
- What is happening in your community that might provide a "surfing" opportunity to provide additional impact?
- What projects have been done elsewhere that could be replicated by your agency or in your community to addresses unmet needs?
- What program success have you had that might yield expanded programming?
- Who are the top leaders in the nonprofit arena that you admire and from whom you could learn if you had increased contact?

Making Things Happen: Scaling Up and Collective Action

- What projects that you have been involved in would be best served if they were scaled up to address a larger geographic area?
- What collaborations are important to produce the desired impact?
- What associations of other nonprofits can be relied on for helping to scale up the project and bring collaborations that result in additional resources and advocacy to better serve the population that your nonprofit is addressing?
- Is there a way to channel the energy of competing organizations into a collaborative structure in which everyone benefits and the clients are better served?

Creating a Vision

- Who have been the past visionaries for your organization?
- Who are the visionaries currently on your board and staff?
- What is your answer to John Rawls' thought experiment? How does it relate to the work of your organization?
- If you were writing an impact analysis on your organization ten or twenty years from now, what would you want it to say?
- If you were writing your own obituary, what would you want it to say about what you have contributed to your organization?
- What is the long-term impact that you want for the organization you serve?
- What visioning activity could you develop that would create a corporate vision for the future?

Executive Leadership

- Does the CEO of the organization: Embrace the characteristics of a Level 5 leader? Have absolute commitment to the mission of the organization? Show a long-term commitment of service to the agency? Display a continual attitude of optimism toward the future of the organization? Boast a proven record of hiring and developing leaders in the organization? Have the ability to adjust to a changing environment?

- Where do you stand on Bristow's core organization principles (The play's the thing, No shoddy performances, No prima donnas, After much input, there can only be one director, Under-management is preferable to over-management if there has to be a choice)?
- What can you do to be more of a Level 5 leader and pave the way for a Level 5 successor?
- Is there a clear division in your organization between the policy role of the board and the executive role in administering that policy, including responsibility for staff?
- Does the personnel policy give the CEO the necessary authority to discipline staff and reorganize staff positions in order to carry out the mission of the organization?
- Does the CEO hire others who, because of their work, become respected leaders in the community?
- Does the CEO create the opportunities for full input on important decisions affecting the organization?

Boards of Directors

- How strong is your board? Beyond the minimum level of activity necessary to fulfill the bylaws, are the members the best that you can find from your community? Do they have the kind of leverage that will garner the required support from other individuals and institutions necessary to fulfill the mission of the organization? Are they strong evangelists for your organization?

- Does the board fully carry out its responsibility for hiring and evaluating the CEO, approving of the strategic plan, budget, and important policies that include bylaws, personnel regulations, financial manuals, and audits?
- Does the board overstep its bounds by involving itself in the hiring, disciplining, and termination of staff?
- How strong is your CEO? When was the last time the CEO was evaluated? Did the evaluation contain benchmarks to be achieved in order to form the baseline for continued evaluation?
- Is your CEO under contract? If you were free to choose the best person to lead your organization, would you choose your present CEO?
- What do you do to ensure board involvement? Have you considered dividing the board up to perform in-depth evaluations of programs?
- When was the last time you did an analysis (SWOT, SOAR, or SCORE) in preparation for a new strategic plan?
- Are there areas of work that might be served more effectively by a board of commissioners that reports to the full board?
- What have you done to develop an alumni association of past board chairs or past board members in order to continue to ensure their support of the organization?
- Have you considered using focus groups to improve board involvement and board training?

Managing for Results

- What are the results or outcomes toward which your organization is working?
- What data are you able to use that documents outcomes? Control group studies? Evidence-based best practices?
- In addition to service outcomes, what are the reform measures for which your organization advocates?

- How would you categorize your organization in terms of the Blake Mouton classification system (1,1; 9,1; 1,9; 5,5; or 9,9) with regard to task and maintenance functions? Where do you need to spend more time, attention, and energy?
- If you were to recast your mission statement in terms of Ken Starr's eight-word formula (a verb, a target population, an outcome that implies something to measure), how would it read?
- On the way to the overall results and goals, what are the key objectives or measurable benchmarks toward which your organization is working?
- What data are you going to collect to measure your success in meeting your benchmarks, and how will you collect it?
- What is your organization's passion? What do you do better than anyone else? What are the economic engines available to your organization? What activities meet all three criteria? Which do not meet all three?
- What can you do to increase your relationship-building leadership?
- In terms of the Johari Window analysis, how would you measure the trust level in your organization? What opportunities do you create for genuine sharing and feedback?
- What is done on a consistent basis to recognize those who contribute to your mission? What can you do to increase the autonomy of those working for you on how to manage their work and the people under them?
- What are the critical teams that make things happen in your organization? What provision is made for annual planning sessions that incorporate sharing, task work, and feedback? What follow-up sessions take place on at least a monthly basis?

Economic Engines and Economic Accountability

- What currently are the major resources that allow your organization to be in business?
- What is it that you do well that you need to keep on doing?
- What additional areas might you add that would help to bring in resources?
- How does your balance sheet read? If you did a "financial snapshot" of your organization, how would it read? What needs to be done to improve the financial condition of your organization?
- What is suggested by your last agency audit?
- What is your organization engaged in that connects with market forces?
- Do you have the right CFO? What further training does your CFO need to meet the needs of the organization?
- In terms of the *Nonprofit Sustainability* criteria, what activities fall into the categories *stop sign, heart, star,* and *money tree?* What does that tell you about where to put your energy and where to stop putting your energy?
- Do you have enough cash reserves to carry three months' worth of salary, including fringe benefits and agency taxes?
- Can you handle your own line of credit through internal reserves or do you have to borrow it?
- What can be done over the next five years to develop an internal line of credit and raise a minimum of $500,000 for an endowment?

The "Right Who"

- What are you doing to ensure that you are the "right who" for your organization?
- Who are the "right whos" in the life of your organization?

- In what circumstances are the "right whos" brought together to work as a team?
- What use have interview panels been in the selection of staff?
- What can be done to enrich supervisory positions by providing more autonomy in the execution of their jobs?
- What can be done to increase the training opportunities for the "right whos"?
- What is being done to celebrate the work of the "right whos" in your organization?
- Have you tried using self-evaluations by staff as part of an annual evaluation process?
- Who are the "wrong whos" that need to leave so as not to block the progress of your organization?
- What kind of evaluation process are you using to help reward the "A" and "B" players on the team, and divest the organization of the "F," "D," and "C" producers who don't improve?
- Are your personnel policies adequate to protect the organization? Do you limit grievances that come to the board to a review of the transcript of the grievance committee hearing?

The Organizational Culture

- How would you describe the culture of the organization that you work for?
- Who is it that defines the culture of your organization?
- How does the culture of your organization differ from the TAP culture as described in this chapter (remember who we work for, never take "no" for an answer, no shoddy performances, real work is when "walls move," whatever it takes, it's all personal, no more organization than necessary, it takes all of us, don't kill the goose)?
- What is it about your organizational meetings, important events in the life of your organization, the space your organization occupies, how offices are connected, the written material that

you produce, your organization chart, the interaction of staff, and the agency's connection with those on the outside that best defines the culture of the organization?

- What plans have you made for attracting discretionary income that can be used to fund important positions or activities and attract other dollars to support your organization?
- What, if anything, would you like to change about your organization's culture? How would you go about making that change?

Networks, Partnerships, Collaborations, and Collective Action

- What are the current strategic partnerships with which your organization is involved?
- Are there organizations with which your agency competes that can be changed into partnerships?
- Are there particular projects you have undertaken that could be scaled up to address similar needs elsewhere and strengthen the resources base for a larger network including your own?
- Which of your partnerships could be turned into collaborations that involve more than one or two partners? And what collaborations can be turned into a network that meet all or many of the criteria that I have suggested for a reform network (an agenda that includes reform as well as service, the involvement of the executive leadership of the membership, a strong planning and financial system that ensures that the mission, goals, objectives, and data gathering will serve the network purpose beyond support for the local members, and training for all of the staff and volunteers who are part of the network agenda)?
- What partnerships and collaborations might be expanded into collective action?

- What issues in your community cry out for new or revitalized partnerships, collaborations, and network development?

Marketing: Getting the Story Out

- What nonprofits in your area are the best at marketing their agency? What makes them so good? What steps can you take to improve your market share of support in your community?
- Is there a board committee in your organization that meets regularly to communicate the importance of the need that your organization addresses, your mission, and accomplishments to the public?
- Have you reviewed the material that you are currently sending out to ensure that there is consistency of style, color, and format, including the agency logo?
- Is it time to reevaluate your agency's name, slogan, and/or logo to ensure that it is connecting with the deepest values of the people whose support you need?
- Who on the staff is in charge of connecting with the media?
- What signature events do you have annually that garner support and further the branding and the work of your organization?

Social Capital

- Describe the present level of social capital for your nonprofit.
- How far is your reach into private businesses, service organizations, government officials, and local decision-makers?
- Does your organization have endorsements by important persons and organizations?
- Who are your champions, evangelists, and super-evangelists?

- Do you have a database of supporters? How well is it maintained?
- What are you doing to communicate with your supporters?
- What events are you holding to create bridges to other potential supporters?
- How strong is your media presence, and what can be done to increase it?
- What can you do to increase hands-on volunteer activities to attract new supporters?
- What are you doing to recognize your supporters?

Keeping it Together: Managing Stress

- What are the steps that you have taken to deal with the daily stress of the job and other areas of life?
- How have you preserved your equilibrium and balance?
- What workout and healthy living practices have you incorporated into your lifestyle to keep you at your best?
- What diversions from the job have you engaged in that help to refresh you on a continuing basis?
- What opportunities have you created for healthy living education for your staff and volunteers?
- What experience do you have with the many "mindfulness" experiences, including yoga, tai chi, qui gong, deep relaxation, and sitting meditation?
- What conferences might you go to that would help you connect with some of these stress-reducing, life-enhancing practices?
- What are the steps you have taken to make these evidence-based approaches to reducing stress available to others?
- What client groups do you serve that could benefit from what you have learned about mindfulness techniques?

Bibliography

Bell, Jeanne, Jan Masaoka, and Steve Zimmerman. *Nonprofit Sustainability: Making Strategic Decisions for Financial Viability*. San Francisco: Jossey-Bass, 2010.

Blake, Robert R., and Jane Srygley Mouton. *The Managerial Grid: Key Orientations for Achieving Production Through People*. Houston, Texas: Gulf Publishing Company, 1964.

Brand, E. Cabell. "America the Strong," *Torch Magazine*, The Journal of the International Association of Torch Clubs, Fall 1987.

Brand, E. Cabell, and Tommy Denton. *If Not Me, Then Who? How You Can Help with Poverty, Economic Opportunity, Education, Healthcare, Environment, Racial Justice and Peace Issues in America*. 2nd ed. Bloomington, IN: iUniverse, 2010.

Brand, Elizabeth. *Community Action At Work: TAP's Thirty-Year War on Poverty*. Blacksburg, Virginia: Total Action Against Poverty in Roanoke Valley in conjunction with Pocahontas Press and R.R. Donnelly, 2000.

Carkhuff, Robert R., and Bernard G. Berenson. *Beyond Counseling and Therapy*. New York: Holt, Rinehart, and Winston, 1967.

Cobb, Edwin. *No Cease Fires: The War on Poverty in Roanoke Valley*. Cabin John, MD: Seven Locks Press, 1984.

Collins, Jim. *Good to Great and the Social Sectors: Why Business Thinking Is Not the Answer: A Monograph to Accompany Good to Great*. Boulder, Colorado: Jim Collins, 2005.

Collins, Jim. *Good to Great: Why Some Companies Make the Leap . . . and Others Don't.* New York: HarperCollins, 2001.

Crutchfield, Leslie R., and Heather McLeod Grant. *Forces for Good: The Six Practices of High-Impact Nonprofits.* San Francisco: Jossey-Bass, 2008.

Edlich, Ted. "Networking: An Overview." *New Spirit Magazine: The Magazine of Human Service,* June 1979.

Goleman, Daniel. "What Makes A Leader?" *Harvard Business Review,* January 2004, vol. 82, no. 1.

Goleman, Daniel. *Emotional Intelligence: Why It Can Matter More Than IQ.* New York: Bantam, 1995.

Hanh, Thich Nhat. *The Heart of the Buddha's Teaching: Transforming Suffering Into Peace, Joy, and Liberation: The Four Noble Truths, the Noble Eightfold Path, and Other Basic Buddhist Teachings.* New York: Broadway, 1999.

Hanson, Rick and Richard Mendius. *Buddha's Brain: The Practical Neuroscience of Happiness, Love & Wisdom.* Oakland, California: New Harbinger Publications, Inc., 2009.

Herzberg, Frederick, Bernard Mausner, and Barbara Bloch Snyderman. *The Motivation to Work.* New Jersey: Transaction Publishers, 1993.

Hsieh, Tony. *Delivering Happiness: A Path to Profits, Passion, and Purpose.* New York: Grand Central Publishing, 2013.

Hunter, David E. K. *Working Hard—and Working Well: A Practical Guide to Performance Management for Leaders Serving Children, Adults, and Families.* Hamden, Connecticut: Hunter Consulting LLC, 2013.

Hyams, Joe. *Zen in the Martial Arts.* New York: Bantam Books, 1982.

Kabat-Zinn, Jon. *Full Catastrophe Living: Using the Wisdom of Your Body and Mind to Face Stress, Pain, and Illness.* New York: Dell, 1990.

Likert, Rensis. *The Human Organization: Its Management and Value.* New York: McGraw-Hill, 1967.

Morino, Mario. *Leap of Reason: Managing to Outcomes in an Era of Scarcity.* Washington, DC: Venture Philanthropy Partners, 2011.

Nonprofit Resource Center of Western Virginia. "The Economic Impact of Nonprofits in the Roanoke Virginia Region," http://www. councilofcommunityservices.com/wp-content/uploads/2010/12/The-Economic-Impact-of-Nonprofits-in-the-Roanoke-Virginia-Region1. pdf (accessed March 4, 2015).

Rawls, John. *A Theory of Justice.* Cambridge, MA: Belknap Press of Harvard University Press, 1999.

Rifkin, Jeremy. *The End of Work: The Decline of the Global Labor Force and the Dawn of the Post Market Era.* New York: G.P. Putnam's Sons, 1996.

Sagawa, Shirley, and Deborah Jospin. *The Charismatic Organization: Eight Ways to Grow a Nonprofit* That Builds Buzz, Delights Donors, and Energizes Employees. San Francisco: Jossey-Bass, 2009.

Selye, Hans. *The Stress of Life,* rev. ed. New York: McGraw-Hill, 1976.

Senge, Peter M. *The Fifth Discipline: The Art and Practice of the Learning Organization.* New York: Doubleday/Currency, 1990.

Sommer, Teresa Eckrich, P. Lindsay Chase-Lansdale, Jeanne Brooks-Gunn, Margo Gardner, Diana Mendley Rauner, and Karen Freel. Abstract. "Early Childhood Education Centers and Mothers' Postsecondary Attainment: A New Conceptual Framework For a Dual-Generation Education Intervention." *Teachers College Record* 114, no. 10 (2012): 1–40, http://www.tcrecord.org/library/abstract. asp?contentid=16678 (accessed March 22, 2015).

Kevin Starr, "The Eight-Word Mission Statement." *Stanford Social Innovation Review,* September 18, 2012, http://www.ssireview.org/ blog/entry/the_eight_word_mission_statement (accessed March 13, 2015).

Tough, Paul. *How Children Succeed: Grit, Curiosity, and the Hidden Power of Character*. Boston: Houghton Mifflin Harcourt, 2012.

Truax, Charles B., and Robert Carkuff. *Toward Effective Counseling and Psychotherapy*. New Brunswick and London: Transaction Publishers, 1967.

Whitaker, Robert C., Tracy Dearth-Wesley, Rachel A. Gooze, Brandon D. Becker, Kathleen C. Gallagher, Bruce S. McEwen. "Adverse Childhood Experiences, Dispositional Mindfulness, and Adult Health." *Preventive Medicine* 67 (October 2014): 147–153. http://www.sciencedaily.com/releases/2014/09/140913141308.htm (accessed April 1, 2015).

Williams, Mark, and Danny Penman. *Mindfulness: An Eight-Week Plan for Finding Peace in a Frantic World*. New York: Rodale Books, 2012.

PERMISSIONS

- Use of the TAP logo and mission statement has been granted by Total Action for Progress, formerly Total Action Against Poverty.

- Permission to use the paragraph from the National Rural Community Assistance Program's website, (htt://www/rccap.org/RCAPhistory), summarizing the achievements of the National Demonstration Water Program has been authorized by that organization.

- The use of the summary paragraph from the Council of Community Services of the Roanoke Valley's study, "The Economic Impact of Nonprofits in the Roanoke Virginia Region," has been granted by the Council of Community Services of the Roanoke Valley.

- Use of Part II: Chapter 8, p. 81, figure 1 "Comparison of satisfiers and dissatisfiers," from *The Motivation to Work* by Frederic Herzberg, Bernard Mausner, Barbara Bloch Snydeman has been authorized by Transaction Publishers.

- The illustration on p. 136, Interlocking Teams, is an adaptation of the link-pin illustration on p.50 of R. Likert's book, The Human Organization, ISBN: 0-07-037815-7, published by McGraw Hill Education which has granted permission for its use. Copyright © 1967 MxcGraw-Hill, Inc. All Rights Reserved,

- The illustration on p. 120 of the "managerial grid" is an adaptation of the Managerial Grid illustration, p. 11, *The Managerial Grid: Key Orientations for Achieving Production Through People* by Robert R. Blake and Jane Srygley Mouton. (Houston, Texas: Gulf Publishing Company, 1965), the use of which has been granted by Gulf Publishing.

- *The Torch* has approved the use of material from Cabell Brand's 1987 Paxton Lecture Competition award winning speech, "America the Strong," in the chapter on Creating a Vision.

- Selections from the copyrighted articles published in the Roanoke Times, the week of June 24, 1975 are reprinted with authorization from the Roanoke Times.

- Wiley Publication has authorized the use of Figure 7.11, "Strategic Imperatives: The adjustments Demanded for Sustainability," and its descriptions in the book, *Nonprofit Sustainability: Making Strategic Decisions for Financial Viability* by Jeanne Bell, Jan Masaoka, and Steve Zimmerman published by Jossey-Boss, a Wiley Imprint. Copyright © 2010 by Jan Masaoka, CompassPoint Nonprofit Services, LLC. All rights reserved.

- Curtis Brown, Ltd. has granted permission to reproduce the illustration of the Hedgehog Concept and short quotes from Jim Collins book, *Good to Great*, in the following chapters of *Navigating the Nonprofit Rapids: Strategies and Tactics for Running a Nonprofit Company: Executive Leadership, Managing for Results, and The Right Who*. Copyright © 2001 Reprinted by permission of Curtis Brown, Ltd.